AN ENGLISH

The Life and Wri
Claude Montefiore

Claude Montefiore 1858–1938

AN ENGLISH JEW
The Life and Writings of Claude Montefiore

Selected, edited and introduced by

EDWARD KESSLER

VALLENTINE, MITCHELL

This edition published in 2002 in Breat Britain by
VALLENTINE MITCHELL
Crown House, 47 Chase Side, Southgate
London N14 5BP

and in the United States of America by
VALLENTINE MITCHELL
c/o ISBS, 5824 N.E. Hassalo Street
Portland, Oregon, 97213-3644

Website: www.frankcass.com

First published in 1989 in Great Britain by Vallentine Mitchell, London
First published in 1989 in the United States by Vallentine Mitchell, c/o Rowman &
Littlefield Publishers, Inc., Savage, MD

British Library Cataloguing in Publication Data

ISBN 0-85303-439-7 (cloth)

ISBN 0-85303-441-9 (paper)

Library of Congress Cataloging-in-Publication Data

A catalog record for this book is available
from the Library of Congress

Typeset by Cambridge Photosetting Services
Printed in Great Britain by MPG Books Ltd, Bodmin, Cornwall

FOR TRISH

Without your patience and love
this book would never have been written

CONTENTS

CONTENTS

LIST OF ILLUSTRATIONS

ACKNOWLEDGEMENTS

I would first like to thank my parents for their support which has been crucial to the success of this work. I wish to thank Rabbi Rayner who initially directed my attention towards Claude Montefiore, and the Liberal Jewish Synagogue who proved most helpful when it came to searching through the synagogue archives. I also wish to thank my brother, James Kessler, and Patricia Oakley who have both read through the entire work and offered valuable advice. I am also grateful to Dr. Lawrence Wills who spent many hours overseeing this work at Harvard Divinity School. I was supported by Justin Stets during the typing of this manuscript. I am indebted to Rabbi Sidney Brichto and the Union of Liberal and Progressive Synagogues who have shown a great deal of interest in this work. Finally, I would like to thank Faber & Faber for permission to quote extracts from *Some Recollections of Claude Goldsmid Montefiore* by Lucy Cohen.

PREFACE TO SECOND EDITION

2002 marks the centenary of the birth of Liberal Judaism in England. It is therefore particularly appropriate that the year is marked by the publication of a second edition of *An English Jew*. Since its publication 12 years ago, colleagues and friends have shared their views with me and many of their comments and suggestions have been incorporated into the revised Introduction.

I would like to thank Frank Cass, who personally encouraged me when the suggestion of a new edition was first mooted. I also particularly appreciate the contributions of my students at the Centre for Jewish–Christian Relations, some of whom have devoted a considerable time to examining the writings of Claude Montefiore.

Finally, I would like to express my heartfelt gratitude to my family for their support and encouragement.

INTRODUCTION

Claude Montefiore was a member of what Chaim Bermant has aptly called 'The Cousinhood' – in other words, the Anglo-Jewish aristocracy. Montefiore was born in 1858, the year in which Lionel Rothschild became the first Jew to take his seat in the House of Commons. Montefiore's father was a nephew of Moses Montefiore and his mother a daughter of Isaac Goldsmid, one of the founders of the non-sectarian University College, London, and also of the West London Reform Synagogue.

Montefiore studied at Balliol College, Oxford, and came under the wing of Benjamin Jowett, who was to be a lasting influence upon him. Jowett encouraged Montefiore to devote himself to Judaism and once wrote:

> I cannot advise you for or against the ministry, but I would certainly advise you to lead an ideal life, by which I mean a life not passed in the ordinary pleasures and pursuits of mankind; but in something higher, the study of your own people and their literature, and the means of elevating them. No life will make you as happy as that.[1]

Upon obtaining a First Class Degree in 1889, he went to the Hochschule in Berlin with the intention of becoming a rabbi. There he was assigned to a young tutor by the name of Solomon Schechter who was already an outstanding biblical and talmudic scholar. Schechter formed quite a contrast to his student – a native of Romania, from a Chassidic family, who received a yeshiva education at a famous Talmudic college at Lemberg (Lwow) in Galacia.

The two greatly respected each other's abilities. Schechter was amazed at the ease with which Montefiore grasped the meaning of difficult texts and the student was so impressed with his tutor that he persuaded Schechter to return to England with him to continue his education. Just a few years later, in 1892, Schechter received the attention he deserved when he was appointed Reader in Rabbinics at Cambridge. His influence upon Montefiore at this period is illustrated in the Hibbert Lectures, which his student delivered in 1892:

> To Schechter I owe more than I can adequately express. My whole conception of the Law and of its place in the Jewish religion and life is largely the fruit of his teaching and inspiration, while most of the rabbinical material on which that conception rests was put before my notice and explained to me by him.[2]

By this time Montefiore was a man of independent means, for he had inherited a large fortune from his father, his brother (who died tragically from rheumatic fever while he was travelling in America in 1879), and from his father-in-law. He was therefore able to devote himself to scholarship, but much of his time was spent on philanthropy. His generosity was as renowned as that of his great-uncle, Moses Montefiore. Lucy Cohen described how:

> A friend of C.M.'s told me how some years previously he required the immediate loan of 1,000 pounds for his business. He wrote three letters including one to his brother and one to Montefiore. His brother wrote: 'Dear old fellow, I am so sorry – don't think me an old Jew, but just now I cannot manage it.' Montefiore's reply was, 'Of course; but would it not be much easier for you to have it as a gift?' The two brothers are excellent friends, but the narrator said that he could not refrain from sending his brother C.M.'s letter with the remark, 'From a Jew; please return it.'[3]

Montefiore's philanthropic work, indeed, his whole life, was focused in four main areas:

1. The Froebel Institute, the board of which he joined in 1882 as honorary secretary, and shortly after became its chairman. It was largely due to his help that the Froebel Institute was able to establish a permanent home at Grove House, Roehampton.
2. Hartley College, which developed into the University of

Southampton. He was president from 1913 to 1934 and made innumerable gifts to the College, such as an 11-acre site which became the centre for its sporting activities.

3. Liberal Judaism. His financial and administrative support was crucial to the survival and development of Liberal Judaism in England. His Liberal Jewish views formed the basis of all his writings.

4. Scholarship. Not only did he write numerous books and articles on fields relating to Judaism and Christianity but his support was essential to journals such as the *Jewish Quarterly Review*, which he founded with Israel Abrahams,[4] and the *Journal of the Jewish Historical Society of England* of which he was president from 1899 to 1900. He was also president of the Anglo-Jewish Association (1895–1921).

Montefiore's involvement with the Jewish Religious Union began in 1899 when he advised Lily Montagu to write her famous article for the *Jewish Quarterly Review*. In a short time the JRU was formed and it arranged public meetings to propagate its cause. He soon became recognised as a leader of Progressive Judaism. Indeed, when the World Union for Progressive Judaism was founded in 1926 he was elected its first president.

Towards the end of his life Montefiore suffered a great deal from asthma and deafness. His last public appearance took place on the first day of Passover 1938 at the Liberal Jewish Synagogue where he mustered enough strength to deliver the final benediction. Two months later he died.

Hebrew Bible

Montefiore's writings examined four distinct topics:

• Hebrew Bible
• Christianity
• Rabbinic Judaism
• Liberal Judaism

He started his first major scholarly exercise when he was invited to deliver the Hibbert Lectures in 1892. He was the first Jewish scholar to receive this honour. The lectures were one of the first Jewish attempts to interpret the history of the Bible in accordance with the conclusions of 'Higher and Lower' criticism. Lower criticism examined the text, comparing and correcting it with ancient manuscripts. Higher criticism inquired into the authorship and dates of different books and weighed their value as historical documents. These lectures attracted enormous attention because Montefiore accepted many of the results of modern scholarship, paid tribute to the teachings of Jesus, and vigorously defended Judaism from Christian criticism concerning the Torah. In the Jewish community the benefit of Montefiore's response to Christian criticism overshadowed any sentiment of alarm, which his opposition to the Mosaic authorship of the Pentateuch and the value of the Synoptic Gospels might have aroused. His work on the Bible was not an attempt by a Jew to add to the criticism but to interpret it.

Montefiore was not concerned with the more primitive aspects of religion in the Hebrew Bible, but with the more sophisticated or higher elements. 'Are you most yourself at your best or your worst?' he often asked. In his view, the Bible is most itself – its true essence is most truly shown – at its best, and not at its worst. His writings on the Bible are based upon the view that its true tendency and issue are displayed, not in Esther but in Jonah.

Following standard Victorian interpretation of Scripture, Montefiore felt free to compare what he saw as more 'primitive' or 'lower' elements with 'higher' aspects. He concluded that the Bible contained the highest truth but that it did not contain all truth. No book could be completely true in word and thought. The Bible was built up during several generations and different sections revealed different degrees of knowledge, faith and culture. This did not diminish the value of the Bible but rather undermined the traditional Jewish understanding of it as perfect and divine. According to Montefiore, the Bible was divine 'because of its religious excellence, because of its righteousness and truth, because of its effects for righteousness and truth.'[5] In other words, the Bible's value did not depend upon its divinity, but its divinity depended upon its value and excellence.

Christianity

Early in his career, Montefiore considered the role of Christianity and, in particular, the New Testament. His views were met with dissent within the Jewish community and provoked a great deal of discussion in Christian circles.

Throughout his writings he expressed the view that it was time for Jews to abandon a negative attitude towards Christianity. At the heart of his approach was the Liberal Jewish understanding of progressive revelation, which viewed revelation as something that did not just exist in the Pentateuch alone but in the Prophets, Writings and Rabbinic literature as well. This was not all. Revelation could also be discovered in other religions. According to Montefiore, Liberal Judaism denied that God had enabled humanity to attain religious truth exclusively through a single channel. This openess allowed Liberal Judaism to select the 'highest' elements of all religions as well as to omit the more crude and primitive elements of Judaism. Consequently, Liberal Judaism became the justification for Montefiore's freedom in criticising both Christianity and Judaism.

Montefiore attacked the tendency of Jewish scholars to denigrate Gospel teaching through cold analysis and dissection. He argued that the atomistic treatment of Christian writings had as its goal the denigration of Christianity. Judaism should approach Christianity with impartiality and its failure to achieve a balance was Judaism's loss, which he wanted to rectify. He made it clear that anti-Christian bias had affected Jewish biblical interpretation to its detriment. He gave as an example the story of the Suffering Servant of Isaiah, which had been neglected by Jewish writers because it had come to be identified with Christianity. The appropriate moment had arrived for a Jewish reappraisal of Christianity and a Christian reappraisal of Judaism. It was time for these two religions to stop judging each other from their defects; instead they should examine their qualities. Montefiore felt that he had an understanding of both points of view and was in a good position to appreciate both religions. He believed that Judaism was on the threshold of a new age and that this age would mark a turning point in Jewish attitudes towards Christianity.

Previously, it had been the norm for Jews to look for defects in Christian works or for parallels in rabbinic writings. 'What was true could not be new and what was new could not be true.' This phrase summarised many Jewish attitudes towards Christianity. Montefiore took a more balanced approach. As far as Christians were concerned he did not have to assume that Jesus was always right; with Jews he did not feel obligated to defend the ancient rabbis. As a result, Christian scholars attacked him for being too Jewish and Jewish scholars for being too Christian. Montefiore attempted to introduce the New Testament to Jews. The New Testament, he argued, was part of Jewish literature. There were no Christian elements; it was entirely a Jewish book. He was in favour of Jews studying the whole work. Its anti-Jewish sentiment and polemic should be understood in its historical context, for early Christians suffered persecution from many quarters including the Synagogue and, consequently, New Testament authors showed little neutrality when writing about Jews.

Montefiore admired enormously the figure of Jesus whose teaching was 'a revival of prophetic Judaism' and in some respects pointed forward to Liberal Judaism.[6] Jesus emphasised precisely those values that Liberal Judaism wanted to bring out. Jesus emphasised inward goodness at the expense of outward forms. He adopted a prophetic attitude towards the Torah. Jesus, Montefiore argued, should be viewed as a great and wise teacher, but in no sense God. Part of the significance of Jesus lay in the fact that 'he started the movement which broke down the old barriers and brought about the translation of Judaism into the Gentile world – the translation of Judaism with many modifications, curtailments, additions both for the better and worse, good and evil.'[7]

Montefiore's writings on Christianity reached their climax in a call for the introduction of a Jewish theology of Christianity. There was a need to look at Christian ideas – were there Jewish equivalents? Were these dropped out of Judaism deliberately because of the existence of similar ideas in Christianity? By too wholesale a rejection of all Christian concepts, Montefiore felt that Judaism might have discarded what was true as well as what was false. It narrowed its own outlook more than was desirable. A theological study of Christianity could lead to the rediscovery of Jewish truths and so to a greater understanding of Judaism. This was the major justification for a Jewish theology of Christianity.

However, there was also another reason. It is likely that Montefiore had in mind the grafting onto Judaism of Christian elements, which had no Jewish parallel. This was nothing short of appropriation:

> We need to find what the great minds of other religions taught and how much is consistent with Judaism and worthy of retention. How much can be translated into Jewish terminology and how much is untranslatable, undesirable and untrue.[8]

It was clear that Montefiore wanted to appropriate some forms of non-Jewish thought whilst remaining within a Jewish context. He argued that there were 'new excellences' in other religions and truths outside of Judaism. It may be helpful to contrast Montefiore's approach with that of Maimonides and especially the latter's tendency to incorporate the Aristotelianism of his day into a Jewish framework. For Maimonides any statement that was true had a divine origin and its source could be found in the Torah. Truths outside of Judaism were incorporated into Judaism and, consequently, not everything outside would be considered untrue. A similar process can be found with Montefiore. Truths outside of Judaism were to be incorporated within and become Jewish. Potentially Judaism possessed all truth but 'the fabric was still to be completed.' It was not by chance that in his call for another meeting between Jewish and Greek thought Montefiore noted that the two had met twice before. The results of these meetings were to be found in the writing of Philo and Maimonides.

As well as attacking Jewish ignorance of Christianity Montefiore also responded to Christian misconceptions about Judaism. His demolition of the ignorant view that the violent and jealous God of the 'Old Testament' could be contrasted with the loving and merciful God of the New Testament is worth quoting in full. In the following passage Montefiore comments on Matthew 25:41: 'Then shall he also say unto them on the left hand, "Depart from me, ye accursed, into the everlasting fire."'

> Such passages as Matt. 25:41 should make theologians excessively careful of drawing beloved contrasts between the Old Testament and the New. We find even a liberal theologian Dr Fosdick saying: 'From Sinai to Calvary – was ever a record of progressive revelation more plain, or more convincing?

The development begins with Jehovah disclosed in a thunderstorm on a desert mountain, and it ends with Christ saying: "God is Spirit: and they that worship Him must worship Him in spirit and truth"; it begins with a war-god leading his partisans to victory, and it ends with men saying, "God is love; and he that abideth in love abideth in God, and God abideth in him"; it begins with a provincial deity loving his tribe and hating its enemies, and it ends with the God of the whole earth worshipped "by a great multitude, which no man could number, out of every nation, and of all the tribes and peoples and tongues"; it begins with a God who commands the slaying of the Amalekites, "both man and woman, infant and suckling", and it ends with a Father whose will it is that not "one of these little ones should perish"; it begins with God's people standing afar off from his lightenings and praying that he might not speak to them lest they die and it ends with men going into their inner chambers, and, having shut the door, praying to their father who is in secret.' [*Christianity and Progress* (1922), p. 209.] Very good. No doubt such a series can be arranged. Let me now arrange a similar series. 'From the Old Testament to the New Testament – was there ever a record of retrogression more plain or more convincing? It begins with, "Have I any pleasure at all in the death of him that dieth?"; it ends with "Begone from me, ye doers of wickedness." It begins with, "The Lord is slow to anger and plenteous in mercy"; it ends with, "Fear Him who is able to destroy both body and soul in Gehenna." It begins with, "I will dwell with him that is of a contrite spirit to revive him"; it ends with, "Narrow is the way which leads to life, and few there be who find it." It begins with, "I will not contend for ever; I will not always be wrath"; it ends with, "Depart, ye cursed, into the everlasting fire." It begins with, "Should I not have pity on Nineveh, that great city?"; it ends with, "It will be more endurable for Sodom on the day of Judgement than for that town." It begins with, "The Lord is good to all who call upon Him"; it ends with, "Whoever speaks against the Holy Spirit, there is no forgiveness whether in this world or the next." It begins with, "The Lord will wipe away tears from off all faces; he will destroy death forever"; it ends with, "They will throw them into the furnace of fire; there is the weeping and the gnashing of teeth."' And the one series would be as misleading as the other.[9]

Throughout his writings on Christianity and the New Testament we find Montefiore influenced by both Jewish and Christian thought. It was the fusion of such thought that led to Montefiore's important position in Jewish–Christian relations and in the Jewish study of Christianity. Israel Zangwill once described Montefiore as a 'queer mixture, half-Jew, half-Christian' [10] and it is this 'queer mixture' that allowed the controversial Jewish scholar to gain the respect, if not the approval, of both Jews and Christians. Montefiore did not inaugurate a new era in Jewish–Christian relations but there is no doubt that his life and work contributed towards a more positive relationship between the two.

Rabbinic Judaism

Naturally, the study of the New Testament led Montefiore to a close investigation of the parallel developments in Judaism itself; he was helped by Herbert Loewe, Reader in Rabbinics at Cambridge, and towards the end of his life the two produced a huge anthology of rabbinic literature. Both wrote separate introductions to *A Rabbinic Anthology*, which remains an excellent example of an Orthodox and Liberal Jew working together although disagreeing in many places. The anthology allowed the rabbis 'to speak for themselves' but Montefiore was keen to stress the differences between rabbinic teachings and those of Liberal Judaism.

Montefiore's tendency to contrast New Testament writings with those in rabbinic literature was paralleled by similar contrast between the Hebrew Bible and the rabbinic literature. He asked how far had the rabbis advanced beyond the Bible. He argued that there was both progression and regression – some of the 'imperfections and crudities of the Hebrew Scriptures were elaborated and hardened by the ancient rabbis',[11] such as the doctrine of merit and reward. The biblical doctrine was simple and unreflective which was preferable to rabbinic elaboration.

There was far too much of an emphasis on merit and reward and this resulted in the 'ugly doctrine that such and such punishments are directly sent by God as the punishments for such and such deeds.'[12]

Montefiore criticised the rabbinic development of some of the 'lower' biblical concepts. The burden of the Bible was the greatest burden the rabbis had to bear for they believed that the whole Bible, and especially the Pentateuch, was divine and true. The rabbis knew the Bible 'almost too painfully well' and to them almost all the statements were equally true. What concerned Montefiore most was that the 'lower' sayings, such as those concerning God's hatred for Edom, became convenient when nationalistic animosities craved biblical sanction; he concluded that rabbinic Judaism was similar to the religion of the Bible – full of inconsistencies and rough edges. Rabbinic Judaism 'lives on the Old Testament and suffers from it.'[13]

Montefiore was especially critical of rabbinic particularism. His criticism is closely linked to his anti-Zionism for anything related to nationalism was an anathema to him. He was unable to distinguish between modern Jewish nationalism and ancient Jewish particularism. Montefiore's criticisms engendered fierce opposition. He was attacked as much for the manner in which he put his criticisms as for the criticisms themselves. For example, he called the anthropomorphisms that are prevalent in Rabbinic writings 'childish'.[14]

However, Montefiore's criticisms did not extend to the condemnation given by the radical reformers. He rejected Samuel Holdheim's extreme position and argued against cutting oneself off from the Jewish community. Violent change was as dangerous as rigid orthodoxy – a new development in the evolving religion of Judaism was the answer, something that had regard for the continuity of Judaism.

Montefiore also extolled the virtues of rabbinic Judaism and argued that the Torah deepened the life of the Jew. It was a specious argument, as some Christians had suggested, that the Torah was an outward taskmaster that demanded fear and not love. No one could understand the rabbinic Judaism with these presuppositions. He agreed with Christian critics that rabbinic Judaism was legalistic but the fundamental reason why the dangers of legalism were so often avoided was because they had succeeded in making the service of God into a passion. God and God's Torah were so loved that the fulfilment of the Torah was carried out for its own sake (*lishmah*) and not merely for the sake of reward.

Montefiore admitted that there were dangers to legalism but emphasised that these dangers were minimised by a love for the Torah and its observance (*simhat shel mitzvoth*). The Torah did not become a burden but a joy. As for the additional restrictions, Montefiore replied that the spinning out of legal distinctions, developments and minutae was as much an intellectual delight to the rabbis as the spinning out of metaphysical and theological distinctions to any of the medieval schoolmen. Another benefit was that the study of the Torah ensured a close association between religion, knowledge and intellect.

Montefiore argued that a Jew might be a legalist, observing every detail of ritual and ceremony, and could still be, and often was, sincere, loving, cheerful and good. Legalism did not necessarily spell formalism, self-righteousness and despair. Strictly observant Jews could be as free as those who believed in the Christian Gospel. In essence, Montefiore showed that the constant antithesis between the outward command to be obeyed (of Jews) and the inward disposition to be acquired (of Christians) was false and unhistorical.

Montefiore was acutely aware of the need to respond to the contemporary Christian polemic, particularly in Germany where anti-Rabbinism – hand in hand with anti-Semitism – had come to the fore of scholarship. For example, Wilheim Bousset was ever keen to stress the antithesis between the teachings of Jesus and rabbinic Judaism. Bousset insisted that Judaism viewed God as no more in the world and the world no more in God. This was a direct consequence of the prophetic exaltation of the uniqueness of God, which had been formalised into abstract transcendent formalism. Bousset's argument typified a general feeling in Christian scholarship that by the end of the biblical period God had become too transcendent and remote and had almost been purified away. For Christians, Jesus filled this 'void' because he caused the transcendent and unique God to become the indwelling and immanent God.

The Montefiore family c.1866

Montefiore participating in laying the foundation for the Liberal Jewish synagogue, 1911

Montefiore responded to this criticism by arguing that the nearness of God was effected partly by the Torah. He showed the extent to which the Torah had been venerated and stressed that it had been a blessing, and not a curse. The rabbis believed that God, in perfect wisdom, had given the Torah to Israel and that Israel, by its faithful obedience, would become wise and holy. The Torah was the will of God and to study it was Israel's supreme joy and brought God near, 'with every kind of nearness.' Montefiore compared the position of the Torah to that of Jesus – both supplied the motive for love and passion; both became mediators between God and the people and the means of bringing God close to the people. In effect, the Torah was the means of maintaining Israel's closeness with God. Montefiore tended to explain rabbinic concepts such as Torah in quasi-Christian terminology. This was partly the result of his position of interpreter of Jews and Judaism to Christians. He was an educator who aim to show the 'true' and 'higher' Jewish values and teachings.

Another Christian criticism of the Judaism of Jesus' day was propagated in the writings of Emil Schurer who argued that the God of first-century Judaism had become isolated and transcendent and was to be obeyed blindly. Consequently, the Torah became a burdensome yoke, which caused suffering among the people. Those who defended it (the Pharisees, and later, the rabbis) were apparently spending their whole time thinking up new restrictions to add to the helplessness and hopelessness of the people: the Torah became merely outward and ceremonial and lost its inward and moral value.

The particular aspect of rabbinic legalism that angered the Christian scholars most was the doctrine of 'merit and reward'. In their view, this doctrine taught that God, as Israel's King and Giver of the Torah, must be obeyed. Those who were disobedient were to be punished and those who were not were to be rewarded. Thus, it was argued, the rabbinic motive for obedience was the fear of punishment and the yearning for the reward: a terror of hell and a longing for the paradise of heaven.

A great deal of Montefiore's writings on rabbinic Judaism centred on the role of the Torah because the New Testament described it as interfering with mercy and loving-kindness, leading to pride and self-righteousness. Yet in the rabbinic writings the Torah became the source of joy and the means of obtaining reconciliation with, and forgiveness from, God. The conflict between Jesus and the rabbis – according to Montefiore – centred on Jesus' interpretation of Torah and the conclusions that he drew from it. For Montefiore the conflict was tragic but inevitable. Both sides were right but Montefiore's sympathies appear to lie more with Jesus than the rabbis. Although the rabbis were 'logically' right the teachings and actions of Jesus were on a 'higher' order. For the rabbis the ceremonial and moral were equal. For Jesus the moral came first.

Liberal Judaism

So far, we have described Montefiore's concern with the development of Judaism in the past. But all the time he was pondering the question: how can Judaism be developed today? Too many Jews were becoming indifferent to their religion and the growing apathy caused great concern.

Although three Reform Synagogues had been established there was no English Reform ideology such as existed in the United States or Germany. This was partly the result of the actions of Moses Montefiore, who was totally opposed to any Reform movement and spent a great deal of his life preventing it from making an impact upon Anglo-Jewry. It is ironic that Moses' great-nephew, Claude, was the leader of the radical Liberal Jewish movement.

Towards the end of the nineteenth century, sporadic attempts were made to provide supplementary religious services; this marked the turning point for the Progressive Jewish movement. In 1890, a Saturday afternoon service was started in order to attract those who found no satisfaction in the existing services: Morris Joseph was accompanied by Claude Montefiore, who was one of a few laymen who delivered occasional sermons. The movement had to face the continued objection of the Chief Rabbi and the services, after making little headway, were soon abandoned. Afterwards a new, more controversial, group under the leadership of Oswald J. Simon sprang up. It was called 'The Sunday Movement' since it offered services on Sunday mornings as well as Sabbath services on Saturdays. Its intent was not only to gain religious interest among Jews but also to propagate Judaism actively among non-Jews. While 60 people showed up at the first service (most of them non-Jewish), there was once again insufficient support for the group to survive.

In 1899 Lily Montagu, on the suggestion of Claude Montefiore, wrote an article for the *Jewish Quarterly Review* on 'The Spiritual Possibilities in Judaism Today'. This evoked a favourable response from several communal leaders, including Orthodox ministers, and showed that there was a significant number of Jews who shared liberal views. Consequently, when a new initiative was being considered, Claude Montefiore was urged to become involved and lead any group that might emerge.

An initial meeting took place in November 1901 when it was proposed that a new religious organisation should be founded under the name of the 'Jewish Religious Union' (JRU) and the first official meeting took place in February of the next year. The leadership committee consisted of ten members including three from the United Synagogue. The ten were: Henrietta Franklin, A.A. Green, Albert Jessel, Morris Joseph, N.S. Joseph, Lily Montagu, Claude Montefiore, Oswald Simon, Simeon Singer and Isadore Spielman. Reforms included:

- A service no longer than 75 minutes in length
- Instrumental music
- One Hebrew hymn and a number of hymns sung in English
- A selection of traditional Jewish prayers (most of which were translated into English and modified to appear more universalistic)
- Men and women sitting together
- Optional head covering

The first service took place on 1 October 1902 led by Simeon Singer; Claude Montefiore gave the address. Between three and four hundred people attended and services continued to attract large numbers. The Chief Rabbi and Orthodox leaders – including Lily Montagu's father, Lord Swaything – bitterly attacked the Union. It was accused of being a 'menace to Judaism' and schismatic in its intent.[15]

The JRU did not view its establishment as a rival Jewish movement, competing with the Orthodox synagogues. It aimed simply at responding to a large number of Jews who were becoming increasingly alienated from the community and who were not

attending services. Its goal was to persuade those who were drifting away that they were wrong, that their drifting was unnecessary, and that they could rightfully call themselves Jews. Learning
perhaps from the experience of previous attempts, the JRU had
no idea of founding a separate synagogue. Although many of the
leading spirits of the movement were 'liberal' in their religious
beliefs, this was not the case as regards the entire number of those
who composed its governing body.

However, this utopian ideal of a broad movement consisting of
different views could not endure. The Orthodox ministers were
pressured into resigning and the Union, without having the base
that a synagogue might provide, began to lose the interest of the
community. In 1909 the majority of the members agreed that the
establishment of a Liberal Jewish congregation was the only hope
for the survival of a 'liberal' view of Judaism.

Shortly afterwards a synagogue was acquired and Claude
Montefiore travelled to America with Charles Singer[16] to find a
rabbi who would lead the congregation. The result was that Israel
Mattuck came to London to lead the community at the Liberal
Jewish Synagogue. The JRU started to develop and expand
into an important force in Anglo-Jewish life. Claude Montefiore
was elected president of the Union and became its spiritual and
academic leader. In 1925 the synagogue moved to a new location
in St John's Wood, London, where it still stands today.

The purpose of Liberal Judaism, according to Montefiore, was
to take up again, on distinctively Jewish lines, the teaching of the
Prophets:

> Much as we reverence the Law, we reverence the Prophets
> more, much as we recognise that the soul of religion needs a
> form or an embodiment, and that doctrine requires a 'cult',
> we yet look upon the 'ceremonial law' with other eyes than
> that of our forefathers. So Liberal Judaism, while preserving
> a true connection with all phases of Judaism, which may have
> preceded it, is yet enormously different from any of them.[17]

Liberal Judaism needed to:

- Take into account biblical criticism
- Be thoroughly universalistic, elevating the Prophets above the
  written Torah

- Expand the concept of progressive revelation and reject the idea of the one perfect revelation
- Develop a theology of other religions and graft onto Judaism suitable elements

Montefiore offended the majority of the Jewish community through his writings on, and leadership of, Liberal Judaism. Perhaps the greatest cause of this offence was his leaning towards Christianity. He was understood by many to be looking forward to a future religion, which would be a fusion of the best of both Judaism and Christianity.

Another controversial aspect of his work was his emphasis on universal Jewish teaching at the expense of nationalism. His universalistic fervour led him to become a vigorous opponent of Zionism because it was diametrically opposed to his concept of universal religion. The Jews did not constitute a nation but the tie, which bonded them, was solely one of religion. The most criticised incident of his career centred on his anti-Zionist activity. In 1917 *The Times* published a manifesto criticising Zionist aspirations, which were then in sight of practical realisation. Montefiore, the chairman of the Anglo-Jewish Association, and D.L. Alexander, president of the Board of Deputies, both signed the manifesto. This unleashed a storm of controversy and Alexander was forced to resign. Montefiore refused to take back anything he wrote and stayed on for four more years. Montefiore was afraid that if a Jewish state did come into existence Jews would no longer be able to freely participate in the social, cultural and political life of their respective countries. It should be added that he was not alone in this fear and that many Jews, Liberal and Orthodox alike, were completely divided in their views on the Jewish State.

When the Balfour declaration was under discussion by the Cabinet the text was privately submitted to six Jewish leaders, of whom Montefiore was one. He particularly objected to one phrase of the suggested version which described Palestine as 'the national home for the Jewish people' and it was his influence that forced a change. The wording in the final draft was altered to 'a national home for the Jewish people.' He believed that a Jewish state in essence would be secular. It would possess inhabitants of all religions and therefore could not be a Jewish state. On the other hand if it became a Jewish theocracy, citizenship would be dependent upon the 'Jewish-ness' of an individual. What would happen, Montefiore asked, if a 'Christian Jew' applied for citizenship? In 1962 that theoretical problem became reality for the Israeli government during the 'Brother Daniel affair' when a Jew who had converted to Christianity applied for, and was refused, citizenship. This case underlined the tensions and inconsistencies in Israeli civil law, which Montefiore had predicted 50 years earlier.

In opposing Zionism Montefiore was also responding to the rise of anti-Semitism. He argued that anti-Semitic hatred had inclined some Jews to despair – hence the growth of Zionism which, at bottom, was 'a surrender to our enemies, and to their contention that the Jews themselves admit that they cannot become, and that they do not want to become, citizens of the countries in which they dwell.'[18] Zionism had 'put the clock back' and had only fuelled the anti-Semitic hatred. He once wrote, that 'Hitlerism is, at least partially, Weizmann's creation.'[19] If there was one point to which his tolerance did not stretch, it was Zionism; he predicted that it would bring great evil upon Jews and his last days were darkened by its growth.

Alongside his scholarly writings, Montefiore's most important contribution to Anglo-Jewry was his leadership of Liberal Judaism. Liberal Judaism was a response to what Montefiore saw as the irreversible decline of Orthodox Judaism. Although Montefiore respected Orthodox Judaism and accepted that for many Jews Orthodoxy was the vehicle through which they drew near to God he felt it was becoming more and more unacceptable to the majority of Jews.

There were two reasons for this decline – the character of observant worship and the nature of its doctrine. Concerning observance he noted that Hebrew was still used in the synagogue although the younger generation hardly understood the language; men and women sat apart and consequently the family was separated. Some Jews had little choice but to work for a living on Saturdays and little effort was made to offer services at different times. Sabbath restrictions such as driving made service-going more difficult. The dietary laws hindered social intercourse between Jew and Christian.

Doctrinally there were other factors. If Jews really believed that

God ordered Jews never to eat oysters, or to keep men and women apart during services, surely every Jew would make the necessary sacrifices. Yet how could Jews believe this to be so? How could Jews believe that the Pentateuch was wholly inspired and divine? Was the command 'you shall love your neighbour as yourself' no more authoritative than the command 'a garment of two kinds of stuff mingled together shall not come upon you', which immediately succeeds it? Montefiore felt that most Jews could not follow the practices of Orthodox Judaism because they did not believe in them or in the perfection and authority of the Pentateuch. This unbelief helped the unobservance and the unobservance was rooted in unbelief. This vicious circle was the fundamental reason why Montefiore was certain of the decline in Orthodox Judaism, be it in his lifetime or in the future.

If Orthodox Judaism was not satisfying those Jews who went to synagogue or those Jews who did not, what could take its place? The answer, quite obviously, was Liberal Judaism. He believed Liberal Judaism would attempt to save all that was true and valuable in Orthodox Judaism and release all that was moribund and obsolete. There were six aspects of Liberal Judaism that gave it the ability to face the future with optimism:

1. Liberal Judaism was free as regards the results of criticism and history. It did not have to worry whether there was one, two or three Isaiahs. It was almost lifted above historical scholarship. It had to concentrate less on authorship and more on meaning and significance.
2. Liberal Judaism had the capacity to expand and absorb. Montefiore had no objections to the appropriation of some aspects of Christian thought, for example, as long as they were not inconsistent with Jewish fundamentals. A living religion was never too old to learn. Judaism could learn from its daughter religions as well as those of India. The critical factor, as we saw earlier, was what Montefiore understood by Jewish fundamentals.
3. Liberal Judaism was still a historical religion. It was the heir to many ancestors, including the rabbis, and although it was separated from them in some points, it was united with them in the deeper issues.

4. Liberal Judaism was a matter of faith. It was a faith in Judaism and a belief in God. Faith illumined the past, sanctified the present and guaranteed the future. Israel had been charged with a certain mission and this charge had never been cancelled.

5. Liberal Judaism had the capacity to universalise and spiritualise what was national and particularist. Liberal Jews no longer saw Israel as a race but a religious community, the borders of which were not limited by ties of kinship or blood.

6. Liberal Judaism was a crucial phase in the development of Judaism. It offered hope for the future and maintained a link with the past. In Montefiore's mind, Liberal Judaism appeared to be the most dynamic form of Judaism. Only Liberal Judaism could ensure Judaism's long-term survival and health. There were many aspects to Judaism at the time but there was only one that could make the Jewish religion a significant force among the religions of the world.

Epilogue

Claude Montefiore died in 1938. In some ways one feels a distance from him of many more than 60 years. Was Montefiore the last representative of the pre-Holocaust generation of Jewish scholarship and theology?

If we turn to Montefiore's hostility to Zionism the answer for most people will be an emphatic 'yes'. The successful establishment of the State of Israel has rendered the earlier controversies between Zionists and anti-Zionsts matters of historical interest. Montefiore's criticisms read strangely, although we should remember that Zionism was only of a peripheral interest to him.

If we turn to other aspects of his writings we see that many of his teachings have undoubtedly taken root. His positive attitude towards Christianity will not shock you as it did his contemporaries. His writings in this area deserve serious thought and are still of interest and value today. Yet, his true concern was Jewish theology. In many ways, his views strike the modern mind as fundamentally unsound: can human intellect determine which aspects of religion are 'higher' or 'lower'? Can mankind achieve a progressive improvement from the depths of biblical primitiveness to the ideals of Liberalism? Montefiore was an optimistic man, born out of era of optimism. He never lived to witness the horrors of Auschwitz and Treblinka.

Today, Anglo-Judaism as a whole, and Progressive Judaism in particular, is beginning to emerge from the trauma of the *Shoah*. Perhaps Progressive Jews are beginning to face the Jewish and non-Jewish world with more confidence and more optimism. Montefiore has been judged harshly over the years partly because of his controversial views but also because of his optimism in the future of modern Judaism. Should we continue do so? We might suggest that at the same time as searching for our position in society and promoting our views within Judaism, Progressive Jews would do well to rediscover Montefiore, re-absorb his optimism and consider the principles behind his teachings.

CHAPTER ONE

THE HEBREW BIBLE

INTRODUCTION

The study of the Bible in the nineteenth century was marked by the growth of the 'critical method'. Its principal founders were Jean Astruc, who was the first to use the criteria of different Hebrew names for the deity in Genesis in order to separate sources,[1] and Johann Eichorn, who suggested that the sources were different in style and vocabulary as well as in divine names.[2] Based upon such studies German scholars, in particular, began to examine in detail the variety of documents in the Pentateuch and to come to some shocking conclusions.

One man dominated the scholarship in such a way that Biblical criticism was to be forevermore associated with his name. Julius Wellhausen, the symbol of all that the critical study of the Bible stood for, produced a brilliant synthesis of all previous work and based upon it a comprehensive view of the history of Ancient Israel.[3] Others beside him were also influential such as W. Vatke, who recognised the lateness of the Grundschaft,[4] and Martin de Wette who isolated Deuteronomy as a separate source and connected it with the reformation under Josiah in the seventh century (II Kings 22).

German scholars uncovered four basic layers of the Pentateuch and concluded that these layers, or documents, were written at different periods of time, all of which were dated many centuries after the life of Moses.[5] This conclusion, known as the 'Documentary Hypothesis', was diametrically opposed to the traditional view that the Pentateuch was written by Moses. It also questioned the traditional attitude to the Prophetical literature. If the Pentateuch did not have Moses as its author but was written centuries after his lifetime – in fact, after the lifetimes of the eighth and seventh century prophets – should it not be dated later than the Prophetical literature? This, indeed, was the position of German Biblical scholarship, and the Prophets were interpreted to have lived long before the writing of the Pentateuch.

These two major conclusions help explain the negative response in England to German Biblical scholarship. At first, and for much of the nineteenth century, the dominant concern of English Christians was either to ignore the works and writings of German scholars, or to ensure, by identifying them with unbelief and with the undermining of Christianity, that they never affected academic or religious life.[6]

These attempts, however, were unsuccessful, partly because law suits against the supporters of Biblical criticism, such as Bishop Colenso and Robertson Smith, in the second half of the century, kept the subject controversial and topical in the public mind and academic world. Colenso attracted attention when he published the first part of a series entitled 'The Pentateuch and Book of Joshua critically examined'. Five additional parts followed in rapid succession and they sparked bitter debates, notably concerning his position as Bishop of Natal. Robertson Smith came to notice in 1875 when he wrote the article 'Bible' in the new edition of the Encyclopaedia Britannica. *He asserted the composite nature of the Pentateuch and accepted the conclusions of German scholarship. He argued that evangelical Christianity should embrace Biblical criticism and make it part of its own study of, and approach to, the Bible. The 'Robertson Smith Affair' continued for many years, and eventually, in 1872, he was ejected from his professorship at the Free Presbyterian College in Aberdeen.[7]*

A sign of the readiness of some Christians to accept Biblical scholarship was also indicated by the publication of two major compilations of writings. We have already referred to the publication of Essays and Reviews, *and 30 years later another important collection of writings was published by a variety of well-known Anglo-Catholic scholars under the editorship of Charles Gore (1889). The authors of this work,* Lex Mundi, *'wanted the Church, while standing firm in the truth given, to enter into the apprehension of the new social and intellectual movements of each age, and give its place to the new knowledge'.[8]*

The spread and ultimate success of Biblical criticism in England was signalled by the appointment of S.R. Driver to the chair of the Regius Professorship of Hebrew at Oxford in 1883. In contrast to his predecessor, E.B. Pusey, who was not an avid supporter of German scholarship,[9] Driver closely followed the critical method and his work marked its complete victory in England.[10] Thus, we find that discussions on Biblical scholarship in academic circles were widespread in the later part of the nineteenth century. This is a decisive factor for understanding the work of Claude Montefiore, since he was initially concerned with the study of the Bible. With an intimate knowledge of German from his youth, Montefiore was immediately able to learn about and struggle with the conclusions of Biblical criticism. His career at

Oxford during the late 1870s and early 1880s was devoted to academic work and his liberal Jewish views were challenged and stimulated by the controversy surrounding the study of the Bible.

The Jewish response to Biblical criticism varied enormously. Although there had been a long history of Jewish study of the Bible the modern critical method went outside the boundaries of what was acceptable to Orthodox Judaism.

It has been argued, however, that the founders of Biblical criticism were not Christian scholars but Jews.[11] The first who openly challenged the traditional view of the authorship of the Pentateuch was a Persian Jew of the ninth century, Hiwi Al-Bakhi. More famous was the commentator and grammarian, Ibn Ezra, who apparently believed that there were post-Mosaic additions to the Pentateuch. However, this view has been hotly disputed and, at best, the writings of Ibn Ezra only offer veiled hints as to what were his real views. What we can be more sure of is that his work influenced Baruch Spinoza and that the latter understood Ibn Ezra to have suggested that the Pentateuch was composite in nature.[12] We may conclude that modern Christian Biblical scholarship, perhaps unknown to the scholars, was influenced by, and to some extent relied upon, early Jewish Biblical scholarship.

Jewish Orthodoxy, however, was not willing to accept the conclusions of Biblical scholarship. Jewish scholars who had questioned the authorship of the Pentateuch were denounced (Spinoza) or their views were interpreted in such a way as to appear in harmony with the tradition (Ibn Ezra). Orthodox Judaism staunchly upheld the divinity and unity of the Pentateuch and wholeheartedly rejected Biblical criticism.[13] Would not Judaism crumble if the notion of divine legislation to Moses was rejected in favour of ideas of historical growth and the composite nature of the Bible? Samson Raphael Hirsch, a major exponent of Orthodoxy in the nineteenth century, argued that the text of the Bible which was read in synagogue was identical in every significant detail with the original scroll of the Torah written by Moses. David Hoffmann was also an Orthodox Jew who dismissed Biblical criticism. He rejected the critical position by reason of his faith and then went on to attack the views of the critics with their own methods and principles.[14]

One reason for the Jewish opposition was the subtle (and not so subtle) anti-Semitism which often accompanied Biblical criticism. Christian scholars tended to illustrate the superiority of Christianity by means of *their criticism of the Hebrew Bible.[15] This was certainly one factor behind the Chief Rabbi of Britain's polemics against Biblical criticism. Dr Hertz was a fervent upholder of the Mosaic authorship of the Pentateuch. He called for a 'holy war on behalf of the Torah'[16] and argued that 'criticism of the Pentateuch associated with the name of Wellhausen is a perversion of history and a desecration of religion'.[17] Isadore Epstein was another English Orthodox Jewish scholar who attempted to dismiss entirely the claims of Biblical criticism: ' "Higher Criticism" can no longer be considered as an exact science, and there is nothing in its so-called "assured results" to upset the traditional acceptance of the unity and Mosaic authorship of the Pentateuch.'[18]*

Other Jewish scholars were aware of the anti-Semitism which existed side by side with Biblical criticism, but nevertheless did not reject the theory behind it . Solomon Schechter stated that he was 'in no way opposed to criticism' but argued against its abuse and joked that 'if tradition is not infallible neither are any of its critics'.[19] Schechter pointed to the history of Jewish Biblical scholarship in general and to modern Jewish Biblical scholars such as Krochmal, Rapoport and Zunz in particular. 'It is not merely coincidence that the first representatives of the historical school were also the first Jewish scholars who proved themselves more or less ready to join the modern school of Bible criticism.'[20]

A more positive attitude was held by most liberal Jews, who accepted the conclusions of Biblical criticism and, although hesitant about the anti-Semitic tendencies of some of its supporters, found it relatively easy to incorporate into their Weltanschauung. Morris Joseph exemplified the positive liberal Jewish views when he wrote that the 'Critical Theory has been carried to undue length. . . . But the soundness of the theory itself is unaffected by the improper uses to which it has sometimes been put.'[21]

THE VALUE OF THE HEBREW BIBLE

The Old Testament

The Old Testament, even if we weld its highest conceptions together, and attempt to make of them a consistent and rounded whole, would nevertheless present a religion with many difficulties, some inadequacies and ragged edges. The difficulties we must solve, or leave unsolved, as best we can; the inadequacies we must supply, the ragged edges we must smooth, from other sources. But, even so, it is striking how many fundamental religious conceptions ... we gain and draw from the Hebrew Bible. There is, for instance, first and foremost the union of religion and morality. People speak, and rightly, of the ethical monotheism of the Prophets. It is that ethical monotheism, with all its difficulties, which is our monotheism today. We cannot learn from the Old Testament what is the origin or explanation of evil. We cannot learn how to combine God's goodness with His omnipotence. The great puzzles are unexplained. But whether in wise or foolish faith, whether as children or as philosophers, whether as saints, or (for the huge majority of us) as very ordinary, average and erring people, who strive to believe in the supremity of righteousness, we all can draw from the Old Testament our hold upon the divine goodness. That God is good; that goodness, righteousness and love are more inexplicable without Him than with Him, that He is the source of goodness and its cause – these doctrines constitute the kernel of the monotheism today, as they constituted the monotheism of the author of the fifty-first psalm or the fortieth chapter of Isaiah. Then, again, that we stand in a certain relation to God; that He is our Father and King, our Master and Saviour; this, too, we find in 'Old Testament' religion and this, too, constitutes a large portion of our own. We are His servants and children ordered to obey, but also glad to obey. In obedience is our wisdom and our happiness. And obedience means just that we must try to be 'good', to execute justice, to love compassion, to walk humbly; to aim at holiness, to 'imitate' the Inimitable, and to love Him. We all admit that such a religion has many difficulties . . . [but] in spite of the difficulties, this religion satisfies our reason, our wills and our hearts more than its denial, and more than other religions of which we happen to know.[22]

The lack of deficiencies

Does the Old Testament at its very highest, leave any religious gaps and deficiencies? Are there, in other words, any rough edges in the Old Testament to the smoothing of which the Old Testament itself makes of itself no contribution whatever? I think the answer must be that there are remarkably few. It may be that the higher doctrine and the complementary conception is only very occasionally taught; it may be that we can only cite as examples one or two brief passages, incidental and disconnected. Nevertheless, an indication, a suggestion, often, indeed, a definite, if isolated statement, are there. That is why, I suppose, Jews are usually so emphatic that, possessing the Old Testament, they have nothing to learn from the New. It is not merely prejudice. It is not merely a wilful shutting of the eyes. It is also something more and better. It is that they are so familiar with these incidental and occasional utterances of the Old Testament that they regard them as its dominant and prevailing view. They get everything they can get out of the few sentences which teach the doctrine they desire and cherish; they squeeze out of them all that can possibly be extracted, and perhaps a little more! They ignore the many, or the prevailing, passages which could be quoted on the other side. As an estimate of the Old Testament as a whole this Jewish attitude towards it is unscientific and inaccurate. Nevertheless these occasional and exceptional passages are in the book; they do form part of it. If attention is concentrated upon them, if what is in conflict with them is neglected (or explained away), then it is not unreasonable, and it is certainly not surprising, that men should repudiate the view that for the source, or for an exposition, of the doctrines which these passages contain, it is necessary to go beyond the pages of the Old Testament. And it is true that there is much more filling out to be found in the New Testament than actual or entire novelty. The rough edges of the Old Testament are smoothed, its gaps and deficiencies are, for the most part, filled up, by the Old

Testament itself. It is its own correction and supplement. What the New Testament does is to correct and supplement afresh, sometimes more fully, sometimes more brilliantly, sometimes with fresh illumination and from a novel point of view. Or again, as we have seen, it develops a doctrine and pushes it towards its logical end. But it does not, for the most part, contain what we, from our Liberal Jewish point of view, can regard as completely new doctrine which is also true doctrine. And of those few Old Testament edges which are rough, and which the Old Testament itself makes no incidental and occasional attempt at smoothing, the New Testament smooths by no means all. Some it leaves untouched, no less rough than it found them.[23]

The traditional view of the Old Testament

It may at once be conceded that the old Jewish view, according to which the Old Testament, and more especially the Pentateuch, enshrined religious and moral perfection has gone for ever. No doubt many orthodox Jews still naively believe it, but they could not obtain any hearing from those outside their own ranks. He who would make a claim for the religious greatness of the Old Testament can only do so today if he frankly recognises its imperfections and its limitations. If he attempts too much, he must inevitably lose all. For him the half, or perhaps a smaller fraction still, must be much larger than the whole. The fact is that one great argument for the greatness of the Old Testament is precisely to be found in those very imperfections and crudities which are now so often brought up to its discredit. It does contain these: it starts with them, and by no means sheds them all. The latest portions of the Old Testament have crudities and imperfections of their own, and some crudities and imperfections which are comparatively naive and harmless in the earliest, are much more definite, offensive, and elaborate in the latest, portions of the 'book'. All this must be frankly conceded. But these crudities and imperfections are not the only things in the Old Testament, and they make the other things the more remarkable. An achievement, some of which, in a sense, goes against the grain, is all the greater an achievement. What is the soul of a book, a person, a spiritual creation? What is its tendency, its essence? Is it the evil, the dross, the crude, the common, the ordinary? Surely not. Is it not rather the good, the special, the peculiar? And is this not the case with the Old Testament? What is it straining to produce? The worst bits of Joshua and Esther, or the finest things in Deuteronomy and Isaiah? The imprecations and particularism of the Psalter, or its spirituality and universalism? I think the latter. Do you say: 'This argument, put more clearly, merely declares that the few fine things in the Old Testament prepare the way for the noon-day splendour of the New'? I am not going to accept or deny the inference, but I would add to it this: that the Old Testament also prepares the way for the Judaism, and especially for the Liberal Judaism, of today. It may be that the Old Testament could fulfil itself in many ways. And in any case, the genius, the inspiration, the higher nature of a book reside surely in its qualities, and not in its defects, in its special greatness, and not in its common weaknesses and ugliness.[24]

Higher and lower elements (i)

Suppose . . . we take a glance at Yahweh in his least satisfactory aspect, and where he is most open to easy criticism and attack. He starts his career in the closest possible association with Israel, and with the least possible concern for the rest of humanity. Moreover, every enemy of Israel is ipso facto an enemy of Yahweh. But how great is the religious achievement, which not only changes Yahweh from being one national God out of many into the Sole Divine Power in heaven and earth, not only produces the Book of Jonah besides Judges and Esther, but also creates the conception that the defeat and overthrow of guilty Israel is the work of Yahweh and the vindication of justice, and the still profounder conception that the very purpose of Israel's election by Yahweh is to publish the knowledge of the true God to all the nations of the world. From the Song of Deborah to the 49th and 53rd chapters of Isaiah: what a tremendous development! It may be admitted that the development is not merely chronological. You can make up a very disagreeable picture of Yahweh and of Israel from passages which are very late as well as from passages which are very early. The dross and slag continue to the end. But the point is that the higher is actually present in the Old Testament as well as the lower, and that it is the higher which counts, which manifests the Spirit of God, which truly differentiates. There is nothing specific, original, or essential about Esther. No struggle was needed to produce it. It did not go against the grain. It was not thrown up by the victory of the Higher against the Lower; of the Spirit of Righteousness, Universalism and Purity warring against National Prejudice and Hatred and the Desire for Revenge. But the conception of the Suffering Servant is profoundly original, and seems to represent the genius of the Old Testament at its height. And even though Esther-like passages be more numerous in bulk than parallels to Isaiah 49 and 53, yet, nevertheless, it is, I repeat, the great and original things which constitute the real essence of the Old Testament, and not the common and cheap things.[25]

Higher and lower elements (ii)

It must be frankly allowed that the supposed relation of God to the enemies of its authors is the weak spot in the Psalter. We do not know enough of the internal history of the Jews from Ezra to the Maccabees to enable us to fully explain the attitude of virulent hostility between the party of the Psalmists and the party of the wicked. But whatever could be pleaded in extenuation, the attitude is of no moral or religious value to us today. It is human, but painful; it is customary, but regrettable. There are few greater ethical or religious dangers than to identify one's own party with the cause of God. Such an identification produces almost inevitable narrowness, cruelty and pride. And yet – I speak in all reserve and humility – there was a measure of truth in the Psalmists' identification. Go forward to the dark days of the Maccabean revolt. The cause of true religion, of ethical monotheism, of the spiritual foundations of our European culture, was bound up with the triumph of the true Israel; its enemies were apostate Jews and the armies of Antiochus Epiphanes. There was, therefore, some real justification for those who believed that their defeat was the defeat of God, and their triumph His victory. It is one of the greatest of the Psalmists who breaks into the passionate exclamation 'Do I not hate them, O Lord, that hate Thee?' It is he whose deepest wish is, 'O that Thou wouldest slay the wicked.' Was it not right, he would have argued, to hate and to curse those who were the foes of God, the enemies of His revealed will, the would-be destroyers of his glory, which was so inextricably bound up with the glory of the True Israel.

Truth and falsehood were strangely knitted together in such beliefs. The glory of God upon earth may be said to consist in the diffusion of goodness and of pure religion among mankind, and the chances of such a diffusion were, so far as we can judge, in direct proportion to the triumph of the 'true' Israel. And yet we refuse to believe that God has enemies, we refuse to believe that the goal of any human soul is mere annihilation, we refuse to rejoice in the destruction of sinners on earth, we refuse to believe in their destruction beyond it. Like Beruria, the wife of R. Meir, we would fain pray that sin, rather than sinners, may be consumed out of the earth, and that in this sense only the wicked may be no more. God's perfect hatred is reserved for evil, His punishments are disciplinal, infinite pity is the complement of infinite wisdom, divine justice is inseparable from divine love, and before that pity, wisdom, justice, love, before that unity in perfection or that perfection in unity, all difference of race and creed and party fade utterly away.

These convictions, to us so natural, are wanting in the Psalter. For the wicked enemy there is no hope or desire of amendment and reconciliation; just as there is no doubt of his hostility to God, so there is no doubt of God's hostility to him. He is morally incurable, beyond the limits of the working of the divine pity. Yet it is our convictions which are the legitimate outcome of the Psalter. God's supposed attitude of pure hostility to sinners outside the pale is in flagrant contradiction to the most constant beliefs of the Psalmists themselves. It is only one more instance of the way in which our own interests and injuries, our wrongs and troubles and prejudices, can blind us to inevitable inferences and obvious truths.

> The Lord is gracious, and full of compassion;
> Slow to anger, and of great mercy,
> The Lord is good to all;
> And his tender mercies are over
> all His works.

There is no better authority with which to convict and overthrow the limitations of the Psalter than the Psalter itself. [26]

Sin

Original Sin, in the sense of a punishment inflicted by God upon the whole human race because of the first man's disobedience, is unknown. It is unknown, too, in the sense of a sort of transmitted poison, curse, or guilt, which passes with divinely appointed inevitability, from generation to generation. It is only original in the sense that it is native to the race, that the make and constitution of man render it inevitable. It is true that in one remarkable verse in the greatest, or one of the greatest of the Psalms, we find the utterance; 'Behold I was brought forth in iniquity and in sin did my mother conceive me,' but the passage is isolated and the meaning uncertain . . .

As to the nature of sin the writers of the OT again show their simplicity. We find no speculation or theory. But even the quotations already made are enough to show that sin, while expressing itself in sinful deeds, and more specifically in the violation of God's commands, is yet recognised to proceed from man's inmost constitution, from his self, from his heart. The sin may be the deed, but the sinfulness of the sin, so to speak, is the wicked self, the wicked heart, the evil desire. Only God can fully know the heart in its complexity and in its sinfulness. 'The heart of man' says Jeremiah, 'is deceitful and woefully sick: who can know it? Only God, therefore, who searches (and does know) the heart can render unto every man according to his ways' . . .

The general attitude of the OT may be summed up by saying: (1) Every man is sure to sin, (2) yet man is responsible for his sins, (3) he ought not to sin, or he ought to get the better of his sin; he need not sin unless he chooses. How far, then, it may be asked, is such an attitude or view of use to us today? Is it shallow, hopeless, inadequate, and contradictory? For if every man were bound to sin, how can it be true that no man need sin unless he chooses? Or if man is bound to sin, is not God, his maker, rather than himself, responsible for so unsatisfactory a result? . . .

It cannot be truly affirmed that all these questions were fully present to the minds of any OT thinkers. Most of the troubles which the questions raise did not harass them because the questions themselves had scarcely occurred to them. Nor can it be said that they were fully grasped by subsequent Jewish thinkers of the Rabbinic period. Some of them came acutely to the mind of Paul, but the reply which he gave to them raises fresh difficulties in its turn, greater even, according to our Jewish ideas, than those which he sought or thought to solve.

If the problems raised are, in their fullness and entirety, insoluble then the fact that they are not realised by the OT writers may not be so very harmful. The simplicity of the OT attitude may turn out to be a merit; for solutions which are unacceptable or inaccurate are worse than no solutions at all. Better that the puzzles should not be recognised than that replies should be given which are false or which do not fit the facts. And this is what seems to be the case. Sin is a part of the problem of evil, and that problem is confessedly insoluble. It does not appear to be eradicable to the human race. Yet that does not prevent the propriety of the feeling of obligation to resist and diminish it. Man can never become sinless, partly because the better he becomes, the higher is the demand made upon him by his own conscience. With greater power the ideal rises. The various sides of the antinomy must be consciously accepted. In spite of our 'frailty' we are to regard sin with horror. In spite of our frailty, we are to ever strive to conquer our sinfulness and to get the better of our sins. In spite of our frailty, we are to hold ourselves responsible for our sins. This is the doctrine of Judaism, and upon the whole, we may say that it is the doctrine of the deepest OT thinkers and saints. Nevertheless, it would be an inadequate doctrine, liable to lead to despair or perfunctoriness, if it were not supplemented by others. These are the doctrines of repentance and forgiveness, the doctrine of 'grace', the doctrine of the Messianic Age, and the doctrine of future life. About almost all of these doctrines the OT has at least something to say, and about some of them it has a good deal. The later literature developed them all and we have to develop them further. For even in their Rabbinic form they are not wholly acceptable to us today. Meanwhile, the feeling of despair because of the inevitability of sin is lessened more especially by the conviction that moral progress is possible both in the individual and the race; by the realisation that through all 'sin', there are yet tremendous differences between man and man, between 'sinner' and 'saint', and by the faith that with God's help and grace even the sinful heart can be made comparatively pure. And this conviction, realisation, faith are all based upon OT doctrines or utterances, even if they may not go beyond them in explicitness and depth.[27]

THE ETHICAL TEACHINGS OF THE BIBLE

The ethics of the Old Testament

We can see the inadequacies of the OT ethics quite as clearly as our Christian neighbours. But it is not of importance and urgency for us to dwell upon these inadequacies as it is of importance for them. We do not want to make contrasts. We want to show developments. It is, as we saw, of great importance and satisfaction to some Christian writers to emphasise the limitation in the command, 'Thou shalt love the "Ger" as thyself.' If Ger meant foreigner, the result would be too terrible for words! It is of immense importance for some Christian critics to dwell with glowing satisfaction upon the fact (and it is a fact) that the command 'Thou shalt love thy neighbour as thyself' only refers to fellow countrymen (though most of them in the fervour of their satisfaction, forget the resident alien of 20 verses later).[28] But as for us while we do not unscientifically forget or deny these limitations, we need not gloat over them or constantly dwell upon them. We stand above our documents, but we stand above them all, not merely above one or two. They are all stages in a process in which we ourselves form a part. And the beginning of this process has a value for us which is peculiarly its own.

Thus – another example – the 10 Commandments are to us valuable for what they contain in their most literal sense. Nor are they any less valuable because their contents may have been known to, and represented in, the ethical literature or injunctions of other races at an earlier date than they were known to, or written down by, Israelites. The 6 ethical commands of the Decalogue do, with much tact, single out 6 of the great ethical pillars upon which society rests. We honour and value them for their literal meaning. And even if the 10th word only means 'defraud not'; if it be 'directed against a desire associated with an act', we still may value, and still may honour it. Desires so end. ("'Tis one thing to be tempted, Escalus; another thing to fall.' Shakespeare was not so wrong.) But beyond the literal meaning of the 10 Words, they stand in our minds and hearts for what they have been made to include, for what men have read into them or distilled out of them. Jesus and the Rabbis made murder include anger; Jesus and the Rabbis made adultery include lustful desire. And we, in their footsteps, can make stealing include much at which our ancestors would perhaps, stare. But it is the 10 Words which began the process, and what is much more, it is the continuous existence, recollection and pressure of the 10 Words which have sustained and stimulated us in the development.

Again the 10 Commandments mean for the Jews that the most sacred portion of the Law emphatically associates together religion and morality. Except for the 4th word, which in Deuteronomy has an ethical foundation, there is no ritual included in them. The 5th and 7th words sanctify the family. The 6th, 8th and 9th imply for us the demand, elsewhere definitely expressed, for justice and truthfulness, while the 10th, however interpreted, forbids envy. When we combine together Exodus 20 and Leviticus 21, and read them in the spirit as well as in the letter, read them in the light of their developments (including in those developments both the NT and the Rabbinical literature) we are filled with gratitude, honour, admiration. Here for our own present ethical ideals – the ethical ideals of modern Judaism – is the 'rock' whence they have been 'hewn', and the 'hole of the pit' whence they have been 'digged'.[29]

Ethical teachings

The moral principles which we hold highest are the very principles which underlie, or are exemplified by, the best Old Testament injunctions, maxims, and aspirations. In some respects there has been a certain reversion to Old Testament ideals in quite modern times. For in one important point the Old Testament needs supplementing by the doctrine which grew up between the Old Testament and the New – the doctrine which is as important to the Rabbis as it is to the authors of the Epistles and the Gospels – I mean the doctrine of the resurrection and the future life. But all the more keen, therefore, is the Old Testament on a good and holy earth, an earthly society of justice and compassion and love. And is not the best temper of our own time determined that, whatever may be in store for men after their deaths, we will seek to make this earth a better dwelling place for them during their lives? The Kingdom of God is to be realised upon earth as well as in Heaven. It is worthwhile, it is right, it is desirable, to renovate and transform earth, as well as to expect and look forward to heaven. But this renovation or transforming of earth is an Old Testament ideal.

And how is it to be achieved? Should we not, too, say by the two or three virtues of justice, compassion and lovingkindness? Are not these virtues the moving forces of the best Old Testament morality? Think how they possessed the prophets. How they informed the prophetic religion. Justice, mercy, lovingkindness: these are the prophetic ideals. Social justice and social loving-kindness: the prophets set in motion a passion for these excellences, which found expression in the Law, the Psalter and the Wisdom literature, and, later on, in the Rabbinic teachings as well. The best spirits in Israel showed, I think, a genius for social morality, they set going a passion for righteousness, which was so finely expressed by Amos when he said, 'Let justice roll down as waters and righteousness as a perpetual stream.' [30]

Justice and compassion meet and mingle in, and are gathered up by, lovingkindness and love. The desire for justice and compassion spring from, and stimulate, a certain spirit of fraternity, of humanity. Do we then find fraternity and humanity in the best utterances of the Old Testament? Yes, certainly; not, indeed, perfectly expressed, but on the road, and even far along it. I do not mean humanity as a mere synonym of compassion, but I mean humanity even in the broader sense of respect for man as man. It is not yet perfect; it meets with difficulties; it is confronted with prejudices, 'defects of qualities', old established institutions, and inherited hatreds. But yet it grows, and the ideas and injunctions which it generates are easily capable of enlargement and purification. Think, first of all, of the respect demanded for the old, the deaf and the blind. Think of the charity inculcated to be shown to the widow and the orphan; think of the tremendous sympathy exhibited by the Prophets, and reflected in the Law and in the Proverbs, for the oppressed and poor. No castes. 'The rich and poor meet together: the Lord is the maker of them all.'[31]

The Prophets

It was the prophets, men few in number, but great in power, who

40

gave to the religion of Israel its specific character and direction. The seed was sown by Moses, the Founder; the ground was watered by Samuel, by Nathan and Gad, by Elijah and Micah; but the harvest was gathered, or rather it was ripened, by the prophets of the eighth century. It was they who definitely connected the worship of Yahweh with the practice of morality, and conceived the idea of a holy nation, divinely chosen and divinely trained. They were the first to show how the triumph of a nation's God – his veritable 'day' of glory – might be signalised by his people's punishment and defeat. It was the prophets who purified the conception of Yahweh as a God of righteousness and naught besides, and began the transformation of the only God of a single nation into the only God of the entire world. And, lastly, it was the prophets of the eighth century who began to teach the doctrine – so strange to antiquity – that a single God of one people might become the One God of all. Thus the prophets point forward on the one hand to the Law, which sought by definite enactment and discipline to help on the schooling of the holy nation, living apart and consecrated to God, and on the other hand to the Apostle of Tarsus, who carried the universalist idea to its final and practical conclusion.

It was inevitable that the prophets should leave some room for future development. Their teaching contained the seeds of many subsequent antinomies. Their attitude towards the outward embodiment of religion was left vague and undefined. They had attacked the cultus, but they had suggested nothing in its place; they had inveighed against forms, but they had not given the people any vehicle of ceremonial expression for religious life: they had only said, 'Seek God, seek goodness', counsels too elevated or too abstract for their generation to apply. Moreover, in spite of their denunciation of present abuses, they had been all too optimistic as to the not too-distant future. They had threatened a sinful society with summary punishment; but anticipating a speedy recovery from disaster, they had predicted a renovated community, chastened by suffering and purged of guilt. They contracted the progressive drama of history into a single scene.

All kinds of puzzling problems arose out of their teaching. The punishment and the deliverance came, but the Messianic age did not follow. Was sin still uneradicated, or were the children suffering for the iniquities of their fathers? Again, the prophetical unit was the nation and not the individual, and national well-being was characterised in outward and material terms. Sin brought adversity, but reform and penitence would bring welfare and content. Prosperity was the test of goodness and its reward. Even for nations this doctrine has its dangers; apply it, as later teachers did, to the individual, and you find yourself hopelessly at variance with fact. And lastly, although the prophets began to emancipate the religion of Israel from its tribalism – to turn Yahweh into God – they helped at the same time to produce a particularism narrower and more fatal than that which they had destroyed. For Yahweh, though the only God, remained the God of Israel, and the nations were not solely regarded as independent creations of the One Creator – ends in themselves, as we should now say – but also, and sometimes mainly, as instruments to promote God's purposes in the training of his chosen people. For as Wellhausen has finely said, 'the present which was passing before the prophets became to them, as it were, the plot of a divine drama which they watched with an intelligence that anticipated the denouement. Everywhere the same goal of development, everywhere the same laws. The nations are the dramatis personae, Israel the hero, Yahweh the author of the tragedy.' But in this tragedy, of which Israel is the hero, the nations only too readily assumed the villain's part. The eighth century prophets did not yet so characterise the players, and the universalism of Isaiah enabled him to change Assyria, the rod of Yahweh's anger, into Assyria, the work of Yahweh's hands. But already in Ezekiel the nations are naturally and essentially the wicked enemies of Israel and God, and the same identification was repeated again and again, though not without excuse, by subsequent writers after the captivity in Babylon. This, as we shall see, was the problem which the Judaism of Ezra and his successors, in spite of a never forgotten and never renounced idea of universalism, failed to solve. Only Modern Judaism, upon the moral side at least, has effected a solution.[32]

LAW IN THE BIBLE

The Prophets and the Law

The backbone of Judaism is made up of the two doctrines of the one and only God, who rules the world in love, righteousness and wisdom, and of the service of this God, the true worship of Him – in other words, religion on its active side – consisting in social rectitude, justice and compassion. Love, righteousness and wisdom are the supreme attributes of God, and love, righteousness and wisdom, manifested and exercised towards and for the benefit of his fellow-men, are the watchwords and methods of the human service of God. That is religion as the best Hebrew Prophets conceived it in their highest moments. In all this, it will be observed, there is nothing of an immaculate and divine code . . .

The twin doctrines of the absolute goodness of the divine character, and of the service of God by man being rightly manifested by goodness and by goodness alone, are in their purity and fullness the creation of the eighth century prophets. Amos and Hosea and Isaiah knew nothing of a perfect law, half moral and half ritual, given by God to Moses; and the reason why they knew nothing about it seems to be that such a law, claiming such an authority did not exist. There were laws, and collections of laws, both moral and ritual, so far as one can make out, but there was as yet no Pentateuch, no one 'perfect' and universally acknowledged Mosaic code. The Prophets of the eighth century and of the seventh century are quite independent of the Law. They speak on their own authority. They never appeal to it or to its Mosaic authorship. Even to Moses himself, the Prophet and Founder, they hardly ever allude.[33]

The legalism of the Old Testament

There would seem to have been a legal element in Judaism from the beginning, just as there was from the beginning, and always, something more than legalism – other elements besides the legal element. Tradition makes Moses both prophet and lawgiver. It did not seem absurd to the tradition to think of him as combining

43

functions which we are wont to think of as distinct, or even as antagonistic. It could even think of him as Priest, a function which we, I think, combine more easily with the Lawgiver than with the Prophet. It is also noteworthy that Biblical Hebrew has no word which exactly translates our word Law. The Ten Commandments are called the Ten Words, or Sayings. 'Remember the Torah of Moses my Servant', and Torah is not quite rightly translated by Law. Teaching of which ordinances form a part, and from which ordinances and rules of conduct and practice may be deduced seems to be the meaning of the word which soon predominated. The Rabbis declared that the Prophets were Torah, the Psalms were Torah; indeed the whole Bible was Torah.

Yet, though there were Laws and ordinances from the days of the Founder onwards – many of which, it may be presumed, have perished – the gradual writing of them down, the gradual general acknowledgement of them as the ordinances of God, the gradual attribution of them all to the Founder, and the gradual acceptance of that strange, unhistoric attribution, till it became a fixed and fundamental dogma of the Faith – all this, together with the welding together of those various codes and accretions to codes into one 'book', the text of which was long before fixed and unalterable, whether for addition or diminution, constituted events of enormous importance and influence in the history and development of Judaism: Judaism created the Pentateuch, but it is, nevertheless, largely true to say that, in the form which Judaism assumed for some two thousand years, the Pentateuch created Judaism.

The legalism of Judaism must, therefore, be acknowledged. It must neither be emphasised too little nor too much. The Pentateuch became the most important portion of the O.T., and perhaps the unsystematic nature of Judaism, its varying tones, its manifold aspects, may be due to the fact that the sacred writings on which it rests are not the 'five books of Moses', but the strange medley of documents which form the O.T.

To the men who formed the Judaism that has continued from their day to this – I mean the Rabbis and Teachers of the couple of centuries, shall we say, before Christ and of a couple of centuries after him – it was no inconsistency to use the Prophets to back up the Pentateuch, and the Pentateuch to back up the Prophets. The

Rabbis of the Talmudic ages, at all events, seem to have known the whole O.T. by heart, and they freely quote from every part of it. Hence their legalism (as Jewish scholars have often pointed out) is not precisely the legalism which the non-Jewish community supposes it to be. It has, indeed, the characteristics of the conventional legalism, of the conventional legal religion, and is liable to some of the faults usually attributed to that legalism. To that extent, the Pentateuch, and the O.T. as containing the Pentateuch, are responsible for the existence of these faults. But the odd thing is that the O.T. is also responsible (by reason of its variety) for the excellences of Jewish legalism, for its peculiar character which made it so different from the legalism of modern convention, which made it, as it were, include the corrections to its own weaknesses. To every Christian generation since Paul legalism has something of the evils and the weaknesses which this singular genius found in the religion he abandoned. But every Jewish generation since Paul (though some more than others) found in it the road to God instead of the road to sin, the means of overcoming temptation instead of the cause of it, the source of joy and freedom instead of the source of anguish and slavery. So strange is that Jewish legalism which the O.T. contributed to produce.[34]

The Book of Leviticus

The book of Leviticus is supposed to consist of nothing but laws about sacrifices and other obsolete ordinances. Yet in the 19th chapter of that book are found some moral laws of the most vital significance. These laws may be said to culminate in the famous command: 'Thou shalt love thy neighbour as thyself.' It does not in any way (in my opinion) detract from the value or the greatness of this command that 'neighbour', to the writer of the law, meant 'fellow countryman'. For one thing, few persons have any opportunity of loving anybody beside their fellow countrymen. For another, it can be safely assumed that if a man were really possessed by a passionate love of all his fellow countrymen, whatever their status and class, whatever their 'party' or their creed, such a one would not hesitate to extend his 'love' to those who were not fellow countrymen, but were only fellow children of God. And for a third thing, it is open for any of us, if we are

adequately sure of ourselves, so to extend the meaning of neighbour as to make it co-terminous with humanity. I say 'if we are
adequately sure of ourselves', for I would much prefer an active,
helpful love of neighbour in the limited sense to a vague, sloppy
and verbal love of mankind, which never practically showed and
practised love to anybody in particular. From the smaller circle to
the larger circle. There are some people who are pleasant abroad,
but disagreeable at home. For them it might be better if the, or, at
least a command ran: 'thou shalt love the members of thy family
as thyself.' But as a matter of fact the law does extend the radius of
the demanded love. In a command which follows the bidding to
love the 'neighbour' we are enjoined to love a class of men who
were, it would appear, not uncommon in the Israel of the writer's
day. These were people who, while dwelling in the land, were not
an integral part of the people among whom they dwelt. As we,
using a modern term, might say, they were not naturalised.
Such people, who were very liable to be oppressed, or looked
down upon, or uncared for, the Pentateuchal writers call *Gerim*
(singular '*ger*'). The Authorised and Revised versions translate
ger by 'stranger' but the more accurate and illuminative translation is 'resident alien'. So the law runs: 'And if an alien is
resident with you in your land, ye shall not oppress him. The
resident who resides with you shall be as one born among you,
and thou shalt love him as thyself, for ye were resident aliens in
the land of Egypt. I am the Lord thy God.' Of this ordinance, with
questionable propriety of diction, but with, perhaps, justified
enthusiasm, I wrote, 'This is the greatest commandment of the
Law. Great as Leviticus 19:18 is, verse 34 beats it hollow'[35] (*The
Old Testament and After*, p.83). The book from which these words
are taken was published in 1923. Thirteen years have passed. Do
not recent events throw a lurid light upon them and justify them
more and more?[36]

Goodness and the Law

Goodness tended to be looked at as a series of actions, and,
moreover, as a series of specified actions: the good man was
not he who possessed a good heart, whose will was good and
set on goodness, but rather he who avoided certain specified
prohibitions (both ceremonial and moral) and performed certain

specified injunctions.[37] Such a view of goodness tends to lower it in various directions. (1) It confounds the moral and ceremonial together: both are ingredients of the Law; they tend to become equal in value. Indeed, the stress tends to be placed upon the ceremonial rather than upon the moral enactments, for they are easier, and more distinctive of the particular 'church', 'denomination', or 'party'. (2) It lowers the ideal, for it is comparatively easy to fulfil,in a more or less outward manner, any series of laws. (3) It tends to make goodness negative, for it is easier to abstain from violating prohibitions than it is to fulfil injunctions. (4) It tends to self-righteousness, for the cool, strict legalist will be proud of his easy outward conformity, especially in all ceremonial matters, and in the prohibitions and negative precepts of the code. (5) It makes goodness and wickedness a mere matter of more or less. If the code contains 743 injunctions, including both ceremonial and moral, positive and negative enactments, the man who fulfils 372 is more good than bad, whereas the man who fulfils 371 is more bad than good. The very inaccurate and outward nature of such a conception is now obvious to us all. (It is another question: How has it become so obvious to us all?) A man, as God sees things, even as clumsy man sees things, who does little and often fails, may yet be morally worth much more than he who does much and fails seldom. And so on. The passion for righteousness is chilled and even extinguished. Ideal and performance are both degraded . . .

Another danger in the Law was connected with the conception of God as the giver of punishments and rewards. Such a conception always contains within it a certain danger. Live so as to avoid the punishment and to obtain the reward. When to this conception of God and life a complicated code is added, which maps the whole of duty in laws, ceremonial as well as moral, the danger of looking at all life as a field for the reaping of reward and the avoidance of punishment is vastly increased. The wise man is he who orders his life to the best profit. He fulfils more laws than he will transgress, and will reap, upon the balance, a sure reward. His whole view of life receives a false and selfish orientation. Legalism stimulates the passion and lust for reward, for fear of, and the worry about, punishment. From this point of view, too, it degrades goodness and cheapens it.

There is a third danger of legalism, and that is its intellectual element. There was a pre-legal strain in Judaism which tended to increase this danger. For, apart from the Law, there was a certain line of thought (of which we see the product in the book of Proverbs) which tended to confound wisdom and goodness. The Law strengthened this tendency. One had to know the Law in order to fulfil it . . . Here, then, was another opening for pride, exclusiveness, formalism, and a false and narrow intellectualism.[38]

CHAPTER TWO

CHRISTIANITY AND THE
NEW TESTAMENT

INTRODUCTION

Jewish attitudes towards Christianity have been determined by social and religious factors. Christianity was deemed by many to be idolatrous. Maimonides, for example, was concerned with whether Christianity was in violation of the principle of monotheism. In an Epistle to the Jews of Yemen he argued that Christianity and Islam were demonic attempts to undermine God's covenant with Israel. However, a contrary and more well known view is to be found in the Mishneh Torah, in the uncensored version of Hilkhot Melakhim. He stated that although Christianity claimed to supersede Judaism it was, nevertheless, God's instrument for universal messianic salvation. Its activity would help make possible the eventual triumph of Judaism.

The fact that for many centuries Jewish philosophy was influenced mainly by Islamic thought only strengthened this view. It was argued that in contrast to Christianity Judaism shared with Islam a more monotheistic view of God. Judah Ha-Levi, the Spanish philosopher and poet, was one of many Jewish thinkers who was influenced by Islamic thought. His major work, **Sefer Kuzari,** *described a king's search for the true religion. As a polemical work it was directed against Aristotelian philosophy as well as against Christianity and Islam. Based upon the conversion of the King of the Khazars to Judaism, it attempted to prove the superiority of Judaism to other religions and philosophies. Occasionally, however, Jewish thinkers suggested that Christianity, with its recognition of the divine character of the Bible, should not be placed in the same category as that of classical paganism. This development occurred towards the end of the Middle Ages and is epitomised by the views of Menahem Ha-Me'iri. He felt that Christians and Muslims should be excluded from the category of the idolatrous.[1]*

Although Ha-Me'iri provides an example of a more positive, or rather a less negative attitude towards Christianity, there was still little that had been written about Christianity in an objective or sympathetic light. Rabbi Solomon ben Isaac (Rashi) maintained this anti-Christian tradition, for he did not distinguish between Christianity and 'the nations of the world' of whom the Bible and Talmud had spoken. Thus Christianity was not excluded from the category of the idolatrous.[2]

51

David Kimhi, the grammarian and exegete, was another important Jewish commentator. Although he allowed for the possibility of the prophethood of a Gentile, he was involved in polemical activity against Christianity.[3]

Until the eighteenth century little change could be perceived but with the Haskalah (Enlightenment) there began to develop new Jewish approaches to Christianity. The pioneer in this effort was Moses Mendelssohn, known as the 'first modern Jew'. His life marked the start of a serious dialogue between some Jews and Christians which has continued to the present day. Forced into a public debate with Johann Lavater in order to defend Judaism, his call for tolerance to be shown by both religions and his eloquent philosophical defence of Judaism made a great impact upon German Christian society.

Jewish interest in Christianity reflected the altered condition of the Jews in the Western world. Modern society loomed not so much as a threat but as a temptation. Most Jews wanted to enter wholeheartedly into Christian society and conversion seemed to guarantee economic and social success in areas closed to them. As a result there was a tremendous increase in the assimilation and conversion rates (paralleled by a growing Christian missionary activity).[4] *Thus, Judaism maintained a defensive posture towards Christianity. Jews were still fighting to gain equality and for some Judaism had to appear equal, if not superior to Christianity. This effort was directed at both the Christian community and the half assimilated Jew, who needed proof of the value of Judaism.*[5]

Finally, Jewish interest in Christianity must in part be understood as a response to the general Christian ignorance of Judaism, and especially Rabbinic Judaism. Beginning with Abraham Geiger, Jewish scholars laboured to correct misconceptions and various forms of scholarly Christian anti-Semitism.[6] *Scholars such as F. Weber, E. Schurer and W. Bousset drew a negative picture of the Judaism in New Testament times. Although quite aware of the Jewish origin of Jesus and his followers, they were convinced that what had been a religion of strength and vitality had deteriorated into one of stagnation and decay. Legalism was the sum and substance of Judaism while the Jewish God had become quite inaccessible. It was during this sad retrogression that Jesus had appeared to stand in absolute contrast to a rigid and intolerable system often described as 'barren formalism'. His opponents became the symbol for hypocrisy and foolishness on account of their rejection of his universal and humane teachings. Christianity, on the other hand, was diametrically opposed to Judaism – a religion in communion with God who was ever ready to come to its aid.*[7]

There was a direct Jewish response to Liberal Christian interpretations of Jesus. Jewish Liberals such as Abraham Geiger and Joseph Salvador argued that Jesus uttered no new thought nor did he break through the boundaries of nationalism.[8] Claude Montefiore and a few others also spoke out against this portrayal of Rabbinic Judaism.[9] The Jewish response was generally limited to discussions about the Pharisees, Rabbinic Judaism and their description in the New Testament.

Montefiore, however, made this the foundation of his work and went on to discuss not only the characters of Jesus and Paul but also what should be the right relation between Jews and the New Testament and Judaism and Christianity. He dealt with Christian bias but also with what he saw as partisan Jewish scholarship. Montefiore hoped that his work would be the catalyst which would bring the two traditions closer together in a relationship of mutual acceptance, if not one of supplementation.

The Jewish community looked on with great suspicion. Some were hesitant because they remembered the unpleasant consequences of the Medieval public debates between Christians and Jews, while others considered the study of Christianity to be outside the scope of legitimate scholarly effort. Defending Judaism was one thing; a sympathetic treatment of Christianity was another. This somewhat explains the vigorous criticism Montefiore received.[10]

Montefiore felt that Jews should understand Christianity not in national terms (J. Klausner)[11] nor with a historical perspective (S. Sandmel).[12] Rather, Christianity was a concern for Jewish theology.

JUDAISM AND THE NEW TESTAMENT

Jews and the New Testament

It might be asked: what is, or what should be, the Jewish interest in the New Testament, in the Synoptic Gospels, or in the life and character of Jesus? . . . The origin of a great religion, which filled so immense a place in the history of the world, must surely be of interest to every cultivated person. To know something about a Book and a Person that have been of such huge and amazing importance, and that are of such great importance still, is a right and reasonable thing – a desirable part of knowledge. But the European Jew lives in a Christian environment, a Christian civilisation. He has absorbed much of this civilisation himself; he breathes in it; it is part of him. He reads the history of the country of which he is the citizen. This civilisation and this country are unintelligible without Christianity. They rest upon the New Testament and the Gospels. The book which has had the greatest influence upon European history and European civilisation is the Bible. The Jew does not mind saying and repeating this. But he too often forgets that the Bible that has had this influence is not merely the Old Testament. It is the Old Testament and the New Testament combined. And of the two, it is the New Testament which has undoubtedly had the greater influence and has been of greater importance. It is the Gospels and the life of Christ which have most markedly determined European history and has most influenced for good or evil many millions of lives. If it is an improper ignorance not to have read some portions of Shakespeare or Milton, it is, I am inclined to think, a much more improper ignorance not to have read the Gospels.

The curiosity of the Jew as regards these writings might also be legitimately aroused when he reflects that the Gospel hero was a Jew, and that the books of the New Testament were mainly written by Jews. Jewish ignorance of the New Testament is indeed not unnatural. It has many causes which I will not here enumerate. It needs, even today perhaps, some detachment of mind to say: 'I will read and study the book upon which is based the religion which has inflicted upon my ancestors such incalculable cruelty and wrong. I will read and study the book from which comes the religion which vaunts itself to be a religion of love, but which, so far as my race is concerned, has usually been a religion of hate. I will read and study the book from which proceeds a monotheism, less pure and lofty than my own, a monotheism, if it can be called such, which has deified a man and invented the Trinity. I will read and study the book from which was evolved the religion which pretends to have superseded and to be superior to my own – to be purer and better than my religion, of which the cardinal doctrines are contained in such words as: "Hear, O Israel, The Lord thy God, the Lord is One. Thou shalt love thy neighbour as thyself. What does the Lord require of thee, but to do justly, and to love mercy, and to walk humbly with thy God?'

Yet this detachment of mind must now be demanded. Judaism, and therefore the Jews or some Jews, must answer the questions, and answer them better and more impartially than they have yet been faced and answered: what is the right Jewish attitude towards the New Testament? What are we to think about the Gospels and the Gospels' hero? I cannot believe that the best and final answers will be purely negative. They will not be formed along the familiar lines that what is new in the Gospels is not true, and what is true is not new.[13]

The Synoptic Gospels

Till recent times it was scarcely possible for Jews to disassociate the Christian claim that Jesus lived an exceptional life, and that his teaching was uniquely great and original, from the further Christian claim that he was divine, or indeed that he was God. It was the divinity of Jesus that was for Jews the true stumbling block to any scientific estimate of his teaching. If all Christians had been Unitarians from the first, a drawing together and a good understanding between Jew and Christian as regards the place of Jesus in the history of Judaism and of religion would have been far easier. The objections to Jesus as a heretic, or an iconoclast, or as a critic of the Law, would not have been so insuperably difficult. Moreover, for many centuries, to say publicly that Jesus was a good man and a fine teacher, but not divine, was exceedingly dangerous. It meant the stake or the sword. Hence to keep silence was much easier, and this negative attitude gradually became extremely general. And when the danger of speech was removed, the old objections and stumbling blocks were still in force.

Yet in England the time has come when it is right and possible for a Jew to look at the Gospels in a more historical, comprehensive, and impartial spirit. This at all events is my aim, and though I am very deficient in learning, the circumstances of my education, environment and life, perhaps too the 'cross-bench' cast of mind with which I chanced to be born, have given me some advantages for its partial attainment.

I do not wish to depreciate the Rabbis or their teaching, but I have no desire to unduly exalt them. And at the same time I do not wish to depreciate Jesus or unduly exalt him. It may be sometimes necessary to indicate parallels or contrasts, but the object which I have set before myself is not to find either the one or the other. So far as I can, I am anxious to get at the facts, and to let them speak for themselves; to look at things as they really are.

Yet I know that one cannot get rid of one's upbringing, one's origin, and one's own particular point of view. I have no doubt that a Buddhist or Mohammedan critic would be able to detect in my book many a prepossession or prejudice. Yet that I shall seem to Jewish critics too Christian, and to Christian critics too Jewish is, I trust, likely, and is to me a source of hope that now and then I may have said the truth.[14]

A Jewish study of Jesus

For Jews – so long as they are and remain Jews (i.e. members of the Jewish faith) – the great interest or value of the Synoptic Gospels lies in the teaching of Jesus rather than in his personality or the life. We persist in separating the one from the other, whereas to Christians they form a unity, a whole. From his childhood upwards the Jew's highest conceptions of goodness and God have never been associated with Jesus. These conceptions may have been due to an idealisation of O.T. teaching or Rabbinic teaching or both. Some might argue (whether wrongly or rightly) that they are partly due to a conscious absorption and adoption of Christian and Gospel teaching. But, consciously and deliberately, his highest conceptions of goodness and God have been ever presented to the Jew, whether the orthodox or liberal Jew, as wholly, and characteristically Jewish. Moreover, he has it ingrained into him that there need and can be nothing – no mediator, no divine man – between himself and God. The position of Jesus, the place he fills, even in Unitarian Christianity, is impossible for the Jew, for two reasons which, at first sight, may seem somewhat irreconcilable with each other. God is too 'far'; God is too 'near'. To make Jesus as 'divine' as Christians make him seems to the Jew presumptuous and out of the question. Man is man, he says; God is God. The best man is infinitely removed from the perfect goodness of God, and the fullness of the divine righteousness can be revealed in no man's life. On the other hand, God is so near that there is no room, as well as no need, for a tertium quid between man and God. The Jew, so long as he is and remains a Jew, simply cannot believe that any man was ever endowed with the fullness of every conceivable moral excellence – that any man was ever wholly sinless, and conscious of his sinlessness, the more perfect because of this consciousness, the acme and cream of goodness and love. The Jew simply cannot believe in such a being, on the one hand, and he has no room or place for him on the other. Jesus has not introduced the Jews to God in their childhood; they do not require him in order to get to God in their manhood.

But the teaching of Jesus abides. The unprejudiced Jew, even remaining a Jew, can find bits of his teaching which go beyond O.T. teaching, or which at any rate, bring out occasional utterances and teachings of the O.T. more clearly and fully. Jesus links on to the Prophets, and sometimes seems to go beyond them. Let us imagine that the writings of a new Hebrew Prophet, a contemporary of, say, Isaiah or Jeremiah, were brought to light. The Jewish position would not be changed but the Jews would be delighted to obtain some fresh teachings and sayings of beauty and value, and even of originality, to add to those which they already possess. So it is, or so it can be, as regards Jesus and the gospel. But the Christian, even the Unitarian Christian, has received the highest conceptions of God and righteousness through Jesus. To the Christian, alike in his teaching and in his personality and life, Jesus reveals God. To the Christian, even to the Unitarian Christian, the N.T. is the book which tells him most truly and fully about goodness and God, and within the N.T. it is the Gospels which tell him best of all. He fits in Jesus with his purest thoughts of God; Jesus brings God near to him. Whereas to the Jews, Jesus – or any man – would be in their way in their relations with, and in their approaches to, God, to the Christian, even to the Unitarian Christian Jesus smooths the way to God and shortens it. He is the way. Without Jesus – if that fatality could for a moment be conceived – God, even to the Unitarian Christian would be more distant and more dim; without Jesus, God to the Jew, would be no less near and no less bright.[15]

JESUS

Jesus the prophet

Jesus is often described (especially in Luke) as a prophet. And it is from the prophetic point of view that his teaching, with the conflicts that it brought about, must primarily be regarded. This does not mean that Jesus was specially a foreteller of future events. It means that Jesus seems in many respects to take up the role, and continue the teaching, of the eighth and seventh century prophets, of Amos, Isaiah, Jeremiah and Ezekiel.

Like the prophets he announces a doom – a doom upon the unrepentant, upon sinners. It is true that the Judgement, the denouement, the crisis, which is imminent will affect the Gentile as well as the Jew. But Jesus – so far at least as we may gather from the fragments of his teaching which have been preserved to us – was mainly concerned to emphasise the doctrine that Israel, just because of its 'sonship' would not be exempt from punishment. There are many sinners in Israel; sinners in high places as well as low. And many who proudly think themselves secure will, unless their hearts are changed, be swept away in the coming storm. We may conceive that Jesus would have heartily concurred in the most famous words of Amos: 'You only have I known of all the families of the earth; therefore will I visit upon you all my iniquities.'[16] It is not improbable, therefore, that Jesus may have predicted the fall of the Temple, even as we find it stated in Mark (12:1,2).

But Jesus was not merely the prophet of collective or general doom. He is much more the teacher of the individual than was Amos or Isaiah. By his time religion was individualised: the process which had begun with Ezekiel was continued, or, shall we say, completed, by him. Jesus, like Ezekiel, is the watchman; he is to warn the wicked and turn him from his evil way.

He is sent, as he himself says, to the lost sheep, to the sinner. But to them, as we have seen and shall abundantly see, his message is not merely one of denouncement. He goes among them and eats with them. He will touch their heart in a number of different ways: he will touch it by arousing admiration, hope, and love, by encouragement and consolation, by the powerful suggestion that the bonds of sin can be, or have been, broken, and that a new life can be, or has been begun. Like the God of whom Ezekiel teaches, Jesus has 'no pleasure in the death of the wicked', he is desirous 'that the wicked turn from his evil way and live'; and so he goes about intentionally and directly 'to seek that which was lost and to bring again that which was driven away' (perhaps driven away by the false severity, or pride, or carelessness of man). He will 'bind up that which is broken and strengthen that which is sick.' . . .

In the next place Jesus's teaching was prophetic because he announced the coming of the Kingdom of God. The Judgement is to culminate in the Kingdom. Indeed the real importance, so to speak, of the Judgement is that it must herald and usher in a new order. The Kingdom of God seems to have been the central feature in the teaching of Jesus, and to his conception of it attention must constantly be directed. To enable as many to enter the Kingdom as the conditions would allow, and to enunciate and explain what these conditions are, occupied much of his time and care. Many who thought that they would infallibly enter it, would, he held, be excluded. Many whom others thought would be excluded he, Jesus, would cause to enter. So far as it was supposed that, if the Kingdom was soon to come, all Jews would enter from the mere fact of their birth, Jesus, we may be sure, like the true prophet that he was, combated a confidence so erroneous and irreligious; whether, however, he went further, and, building upon and developing certain well-known prophetical utterances, declared that the inmates of the Kingdom would be rather Gentiles than Jews, is a point upon which opinion is still divided. Two things, at any rate, seem clear. First, that Jesus himself never dreamed of preaching outside Israel (either directly or by his disciples). Secondly, that no universalist element in his teaching constituted any part of his conflict between himself and the Jewish authorities, whether Sadducean or Pharisaic . . .

What were the conditions of entry into the divine Kingdom? Like Ezekiel Jesus represents the entry both as grace and as a guerdon.[17] 'God will give you a new heart: make you a new heart' says Ezekiel. And Jesus says: 'God will choose those who are to enter the kingdom, God will bring them in; strive to enter the Kingdom, and this is how you should set about it.' The demands of the prophets are the demands of Jesus. Justice, charity and pity towards man, humility and love towards God; the prophets had inculcated these, and Jesus inculcated them again.[18]

Jesus: the successor to the eighth-century prophets

He [Jesus] is in the genuine succession to Amos and Isaiah. It is not just that the title of prophet is, in Luke, repeatedly ascribed to him. Not that the differences between him and Jeremiah or Isaiah are not marked. Not that, whether it is to be regarded as an advance or a retrogression, Jesus does not lay much greater stress upon his mission, authority, and person than was laid by the prophets upon theirs. But, nevertheless, marked as are the differences, no less marked are their likenesses. And as Liberal Judaism derives so greatly from the prophets, is it not wonderful that it should rightly find much to admire and use in the prophet of Nazareth. The two great points and poles of the prophetic teachings were, first, the exclusive worship and recognition of the One God; secondly, that the service and demands of this God consisted not in ceremonial or sacrifices, but in justice, righteousness, mercy, and lovingkindness . . .

Jesus, as the prophet of inwardness, can never cease to appeal, and in spite of their legalism there are many parallels to his teaching in the sayings of the Rabbis. For the Rabbis, too, had often their prophetic flashes and visions. The teaching of Jesus about prayer and fasting, or about adultery and almsgiving, in the Sermon on the Mount, links itself on to the true prophetic tradition. No less prophetic is the summing up of the Law in the love of God and the love of neighbour, or the appreciation of the widow's 'mite'. It is only true prophetic teaching developed when Jesus bids us love our enemies. None of these prophetic utterances, however, gave rise to conflict. They would not have been denied by the Rabbis, nor are they really antagonistic to the spirit of the Rabbinic teaching at its best. Where the prophet in Jesus was likely to come into antagonism with practice and life was in relation to the Sabbath, the dietary laws, and the laws of clean and unclean. And according to the records it was just here that the issue was joined between the new teacher and existing authorities. The great saying that the Sabbath was made for man, and not man for the Sabbath, was also uttered by a Rabbi, but only Jesus properly appreciated it, and ventured to make a proper application of it. He applied to the sabbath law a sort of inspired common sense; he preserved the spirit in violating the letter. He saw, moreover, that a deed of love must take precedence over a ritual command, and it is significant that he actually quotes the sublime words of Hosea, 'I desire love and not sacrifice.' We can still learn from here. Still more important, however, was his pronouncement as to inward and outward purity. It does not matter for us whether he was theoretically consistent; whether, that is to say, in his deprecation of outward uncleanliness, he was not in unconscious conflict with his unabandoned belief in the full divinity and obligatory character of the Law. In a way, it is all the more splendid that in crises and in moments of struggle, he was able to free himself from consistency.[19]

The originality of Jesus

What strikes the impartial outsider as new and formative and original, are a certain tone and temper, a certain fire and enthusiasm that breathe through the whole. Sometimes the high value of what is taught may be said to lie not in the substance, but in the manner, the expression. A pedestrian parallel may be quoted in vain: it does not and cannot derogate from the value and the greatness of the Gospel utterance. It is with some of the sayings and parables of Jesus as with poetry. The wording is seven-eighths of the battle. But the wording is not the mere wording: in it is contained the poetical sense; the sense which the poet intended. No paraphrase can really give the sense . . .

But if we attempt to characterise this spirit or tone more precisely, I think it might fairly be said that there are four points about it which are noteworthy and novel. They fuse and fade into one another, but may be kept separate for purposes of analysis or description. These four points are partly conditioned by the circumstances of the time, by a certain belief common to Jesus and to his surroundings, and by his particular relations to the population around him, but they are not entirely so conditioned. They are at least as much the product of his own genius, his own native way of looking at things, his own faith. These four points are: (1) The teaching is heroic. It is an ethic of extreme demands, of passionate idealism. (2) It is an ethic of activity; it is forthgoing. Man is not to wait on circumstances: he is to set out and act. (3) The teaching is a remarkable blend of what might be called the higher selfishness and the highest unselfishness; it is altruistic and self-regarding in one. (4) The teaching contains the germ of a double ethic; a lower demand for some, a higher demand for others. In the first three points it may be argued that, in most matters concerning which they come into play, they emphasise and carry forward Old Testament teaching. As regards the fourth point, however, this is not so. A new principle appears to be here introduced, of which the ethical and religious validity is at least disputable and the ethical and religious results are still more so.[20]

The ethical demands of Jesus

The heroic and passionate nature of the ethical teaching of Jesus is illustrated not merely by the general demand of unlimited sacrifice, but also by certain definite and particular demands all framed on the same lines, and all exemplifying that quotation of Browning to which I have often alluded: 'A man's reach must exceed his grasp'. The ethical ideal must be one to which a saint here and there seems to attain, but to which we ourselves never attain. So far from its being a reproach against an ethical teaching or ideal that is suited for saints and angels, and not for the average working-men and women, it is, on the contrary, a right and necessary quality. Every ideal must be beyond fulfilment: every lofty ethical teaching must be beyond the powers or the will of the average person. What good would an ideal be, what beckoning, stringent, demanding power would it have, if ordinary people could fulfil it? Just because we can never do enough, just because we cannot fulfil it, therefore we are enabled to do a little more than otherwise we should be able or inclined to do. A low ideal is no ideal. Who loves God with his whole heart and with all his soul? What value would the demand possess, what force or driving power, if it said, 'You must love God a good deal; not much, if at all, less than you love your brother or your mother or your wife?' It is the unqualified love which stimulates.[21]

Jesus, the Rabbis and prophecy

An essential feature of the prophet is the sense of commission and vocation. He is called by God to deliver a message, and thus stands towards God in a certain special relation. What he speaks he speaks in God's name, and he believes that it is the divine spirit which impels him to his work and directs his words. Jesus does not preface his speeches with 'thus saith the Lord', but in the conviction of inspiration, in the assurance that he too was called and chosen by God to do a certain work, he entirely resembles Amos, Isaiah and Ezekiel . . . We do, I think, know enough about the Rabbis of the first century A.D. to say that, however fine and noble their teaching may have been or was, it cannot properly be called prophetic. They were not called prophets, and they could not have properly been called so. However much they may have recognised that, at bottom, the Pentateuchal laws of morality were greater than its laws about Sacrifice or clean and unclean, they could not, they did not, deal with the subject in the same way and spirit as Jesus. Hillel was ever the servant of the Law, and never its Judge. In a sense he was more consistent than Jesus; but for that very reason he was less prophetic. Sabbath conflicts, such as happened to Jesus, could not have happened to him. That is why, or that is 'one' why, the production of parallels from the teaching of Hillel with the teaching of Jesus is mostly futile. The spirit is different. The prophetic touch is present in one case and absent in the other, and it is the prophetic touch which makes the difference.[22]

New teachings of Jesus

If we ask wherein his hearers found the teachings of Jesus new, inspired, prophetic . . . it is not quite easy to reply. For, except as regards the Law, one can probably discover parallels in the Rabbinic literature to every portion of his teaching. But the words 'new, inspired, prophetic' are nevertheless not rashly nor falsely chosen. It is the spirit of the teaching, its unity, its fervour, its intensity, its enthusiasm, which were new, inspired, prophetic, rather than any one particular part of it. Pity, faith, love, trust – contemporary Rabbis spoke of all these things, but they did not, perhaps, speak of them with the same intensity and genius. They did not, perhaps, quite in the same way, demand all for the Highest. They did not preach the same impassioned doctrine of sacrifices. They did not show the same yearning to save the sinner from the fastnesses and morasses of sin or from the physical or mental evils which in those days were so closely associated with sin. It was in these more indefinable and subtler ways that the teaching, like the bearing, of Jesus was new, inspired, prophetic, rather than in any novelty of doctrine in any one definite particular. The important points in which the teaching of Jesus was opposed to the Rabbis are all connected with the Law. His teaching about divorce, about the Sabbath, about clean and unclean, was in the spirit of the prophets, but not in strict accordance with the letter of the Law. His conflict with Rabbis did not come because he went beyond their teaching about loving one's enemies, or about the deep value of inward purity in itself, or of every sort of inwardness itself; the conflict came because Jesus drew certain practical conclusions in respect to Inwardness and these conclusions led logically to a transgression of the Law. The doctrine of the divine Law put both ceremonial and moral injunctions on an equal footing, and never contemplated any conflict between them. It gave no clear guide for action should such a conflict ever arise. This doctrine of the divine law, with divinity extending to the ceremonial as well as to the moral, placed both Jesus and the Rabbis in a very difficult position. For Jesus, too, though less fervently than his Rabbinical opponents, professed to believe, and did actually believe, in the divineness of the Law. But his impassioned prophetic attitude drove him on to action and teaching which were in violation of the Law, while the Rabbis, in their profound veneration and adoration of the God-given and perfect Law, could not look at the relation of morality to ceremonial, of the Inward to the Outward, from a purely prophetic point of view. The conflict between Jesus and the Rabbis was thus inevitable and had all the elements of tragedy. It was 'tragic' and produced a tragedy.[23]

The dietary laws

There is nothing outside a man, which entering him can make

him unclean; but the things which come out of a man, these are what make him unclean. (Mark 7:15)

Here Jesus enunciates a doctrine which appears not only to be new and emancipating, but which seems to constitute one of the two chief justifications or reasons for the way in which Liberal Judaism looks at the old ceremonial law. For first of all came the old prophets of the eighth and seventh centuries B.C. They said: the true service of God is not ceremonial, but moral; God desires love and not sacrifices, the knowledge of Him rather than burnt offerings. Or again, as the Psalmist, upon the basis of this prophetic teaching, declared: 'Thou desirest not sacrifice else I would give it; thou takest no pleasure in burnt offerings. The sacrifices of God are a broken spirit; a broken and contrite heart, thou O Lord, does not despise. This teaching is resuscitated by Jesus; we have already met with it, and we shall meet with it again. But here he says something which is akin to the prophetic theme, but is yet novel. There were two aspects of the old ritual and ceremonial practices, two sides to them. Some of them were supposed to affect God and some of them were supposed to affect man. The prophets dealt mainly with those which were supposed to affect, please, or propitiate God, and they tell us that God does not care for them: it is not so that He is propitiated or pleased. In this section Jesus deals with those which were supposed to affect man, and these were mainly rules and customs about clean and unclean, which again depended upon conceptions – very old, widespread conceptions – about clean and unclean. Just as the prophets upset the old ideas about the service of God, so here Jesus upsets old ideas about clean and unclean. As the prophets moralized and inwardized men's ideas about the service of God, so Jesus moralises and inwardizes men's ideas about clean and unclean; nothing else. Only man can make himself clean or unclean; outside things cannot make him clean or unclean. The conception of ritual or Levitical purity and impurity is overthrown and abolished . . .

The world is profoundly indebted to Jesus for his liberating and clarifying words.[24] They are spoken in the very spirit of Amos and Hosea. The true province of religion needs to be defined. It was the greater and the purer by being limited to the realms of spirit and personality. Moreover, the dietary laws and the laws of clean and unclean have doubtless occasionally led, as they led in the days of Jesus, to formalism, hypocrisy, self-righteousness. Outward 'cleanliness' can occasionally mask inward corruption.

Yet, although this can all be so, it was impossible for the Jews to accept the saying, nor can we safely say that Jesus was consistent in asserting it. For though the occasion which (as Mark tells the story) drew it forth was a Rabbinical law, though it was only a Rabbinical law which the disciples transgressed, yet the great principle laid down by Jesus runs, as we have seen, directly counter to the laws of the Pentateuch.

Now the Pentateuch makes no difference between some laws and other laws. It does not say that the moral laws are divine and eternal, the ritual are human and temporary; it ascribes the same divinity and immutability to them all.

From the Pentateuchal and Rabbinic point of view, the dietary laws, the laws about women, the laws about corpses and ablutions, were as much given by the wise and righteous God as were the laws about honouring our parents or loving our neighbours. If the one set of laws is divine, so is the other set. It was illogical for Jesus on one occasion to appeal to the 'Law of God', violated by Rabbinical enactment, and to enunciate a principle antagonistic to that Law on another. It is true that Jesus is not recorded to have said, and he would probably not have dreamed of saying, that the Pentateuch was not in all its parts the Law of God. It is more than doubtful whether he would have urged his followers to partake of rabbits and hares. Nevertheless, his great *logion* (whatever occasioned its utterance) flies in the face of the dietary laws which are ordered in the Pentateuch by God. But if the wise and perfect God has ordered them, they too are wise and perfect. If the wise and perfect God has said that what enters into man's mouth can and does defile him, then he must be right and Jesus must be wrong.

How far Jesus was conscious of his own inconsistency is doubtful. How far in his mind he separated the moral from the ritual law, and thought that God had ordered the one, but had not ordered the other, we do not know. But we do know that he never enunciated the principle of such a separation and the difference of origin. Moreover, there are a few indications that he himself obeyed and urged others to obey, the ritual laws of the Pentateuch. But all the same he promulgated a principle which invalidates them all. If, however, Jesus was unaware of his own inconsistency, the Rabbis must have perceived it well enough, and they were quite justified in denying his principle and the authority of him who uttered it . . .

The principle of 7:15 . . . is not a question of an observance of the Law being in conflict with a prophetic principle, as one might argue that the observance of the Sabbath law conflicts with the prophetic principle of loving-kindness, if, being able to heal a man on Saturday, you ask him to wait until Sunday. For here no question of loving-kindness comes in. There is no conflict. The principle of 7:15 does not say that ritual is secondary; it sets up a counter principle which really cuts the ground from under the whole set of Pentateuchal enactments. That is its new greatness. Dr. Bartlett says that for Jesus 'the Law (even in its details, so Matt: 5:18[25] seems to imply) had for him abiding value until the end of this age or dispensation of God's providence, i.e. until the Kingdom of God was actually come (cp Matt. 11:13–15; Luke 16:16).'[26] But the logical deduction from 7:15, though Jesus did not realise it, is that the principle upon which a big section of the Law depends (that material things can make men and women religiously unclean) is a mistaken principle. We can see that; we know the origin of these laws. Jesus did not. You cannot have it both ways. It is true that the Rabbis did bravely attempt to get rid of the superstitious element in many Pentateuchal laws by turning them into arbitrary ukases[27] of the perfectly wise and good God. 'It is not water which purifies: it is God's law, which, because He is perfect in goodness and wisdom, it is your duty to obey, even as He has bidden you'. That is also, in its way, a bold and sublime utterance, but it leaves the problem of outward cleanliness and physical defilement unsolved. Yet I cannot see that the Rabbis were wrong in their opposition to 7:15. If the Law is throughout Mosaic, perfect and divine, then it must be obeyed throughout; but a saying like 7:15 would imply that God made a mistake. In ordering Moses to bid the children of Israel observe for ever certain laws about food, etc., God apparently meant that there was such a thing as outward defilement. He meant that some things that go into the mouth or which touch the body, or some bodily positions or impurities, do or can, as a matter of fact, religiously defile and make religiously unclean. And so believing, He ordered Moses to proclaim the observance of certain laws which depend upon that feeling. Jesus in 7:15 practically declares that the divine opinion is wrong. And yet the Law as a whole was divine, divine throughout (he never said to the contrary), and to be observed 'in its details'. Is not this inconsistent? The inconsistency does not, indeed, matter for us. The splendour of 7:15 remains as before. But I do not see how it can be contended that there is no inconsistency, and, if so, from their point of view, not only were the Rabbis justified in protesting against and rejecting the new doctrines of 7:15, but they could also observe the laws of outward cleanliness, and yet be also keen on inward purity as well. The two things can go together. The two purities can be, and often were, and often are, combined. If one is sufficiently detached, one can appraise the truth and splendour of 7:15 at their right level, and yet perceive that no hypocrisy and no blame of any kind attach to the Rabbis. In fact, one can be just to, and one can admire both Jesus and the Rabbis. Jesus attacked the Rabbis; the Rabbis attacked Jesus. Both (I am not dealing here with the bad Rabbis) were blameless. But the inconsistency of Jesus was grander than the consistency of the Rabbis. It was more prophetic. It has moreover been proved more true.[28]

The seeking out of sinners

The teachers of the Old Testament constantly call the sinner to repentance, and if he repents, if he turns from his evil way, they assure him of divine forgiveness. But till he repents, there is little to be said or done for him. He can repent; he should repent. Till he begins to do so, he is threatened with punishment and woe. Jesus goes further. Most sinners are conceived by him not as outcasts from the divine favour, not as objects of the divine judgement, but as sheep who have strayed from the fold, or as the sick who need a spiritual physician. For his mission is, not to destroy, but to save. Here, too, he builds upon and carries forward Old Testament ideas. We have seen how Ezekiel had urged that God does not delight in the 'death' of the wicked. He desires their repentance. If they cannot make them a new heart, he will give them a new heart. If they cannot wash their stains of sin from them, he will himself sprinkle clean water upon them that they may be clean. Gracious are His words of promise (for Ezekiel is not merely the stern 'legalist', but he is also the 'evangelical' prophet): 'I will seek that which is lost, and will bind up that which is broken, and strengthen that which is sick.'[29] Upon these divine principles and promises Jesus – it was a new and great departure – fashioned his methods and shaped his path. He conceived his mission not as directed to the whole, but to the sick, and not merely to call them to repentance, as at first he said, but to seek for them, to win them back to goodness and to God. He calls them to repentance, not merely by preaching, and still less by threats, but by going among them, by showing them compassion, by winning their hearts, by showing them love. We do not hear of any such methods having been practised by any Israelite before him.[30]

The rejection of the Pharisees

I would not cavil with the view that Jesus is to be regarded as the first great Jewish teacher to frame such a sentence as: 'Love your enemies, do good to them who hate you, bless them that curse you, and pray for them who ill-treat you (Luke 6: 27–28).[31] Yet how much more telling his injunction would have been if we had a single story about his doing good to, and praying for, a Rabbi or Pharisee! One grain of practice is worth a pound of theory. (Luke 23:34 is of doubtful range and doubtful authenticity.)[32] We have at all events from the Rabbis one or two tales of kindness shown to the Romans in their hour of need . . . I repeat that one would have wished to find in the life-story of Jesus one single incident in which Jesus actually performed a loving deed to one of his Rabbinical antagonists or enemies. That would have been worth all the injunctions of the Sermon on the Mount about the love of enemies put together. Even if such a deed were only reported, and it were of dubious authenticity, how valuable it would be. 'Father forgive them' is of dubious authenticity, but it is little the less beautiful and inspiring. Even though it refers only to the Roman soldiers and not to the Jews, it is, nevertheless, of high ethical import. 'The deed! The deed!' as the poet has it. But no such deed is ascribed to Jesus in the Gospels. Towards his enemies, towards those who did not believe in him, whether individuals, groups, or cities (Matt. 11:20–24),[33] only denunciation and bitter words! The injunctions are beautiful, but how much more beautiful would have been a fulfilment of those injunctions by Jesus himself.[34]

Did Jesus seek the salvation of his enemies?

To seek and save the lost was doubtless one of the objects which, as he believed and truly believed, God had commissioned him to discharge. And of how much goodness and self-sacrifice through the ages has not the imitation of Christ in this regard been the source! It has been the motive for innumerable deeds of patient heroism, and has redeemed much sinfulness, and restored many wanderers from virtue and goodness to God. But how strange it is that Jesus himself did not realise that if this was the Son of Man's mission, it should have been applied, and it was applicable, to the Scribe and the Pharisee as well as to the outcast and the tax-collector. Had not the Scribe and Pharisee souls to save? And if they opposed the new teacher, was it not his business, on his own principles, to return the soft answer which removes wrath? But so it was and so it is. To follow the ideal when it is personally distasteful is ever the hardest thing for a mortal man. And so strange is the human heart in its casuistry, that Jesus probably had no idea that he was violating his own principles. Though he taught that it was the Pharisees and Scribes who were really lost, he made no genuine effort to win them over or to save them. By his denunciations – assuming them to be genuine – he only deepened their antagonism, and from his point of view made the lost souls still more certainly lost. If he saved some, he destroyed others, or at least permitted, and foretold, their assured destruction. And the Church has followed in the footsteps of their Master. She too has both reclaimed and rejected, saved and destroyed. She has indeed sought out the lost when they were willing to agree with her dogmas, but directly they did not see eye to eye with her in all things, she has scattered ruin and ban, fulminated and destroyed. She has persecuted the heretic on earth, and proclaimed his eternal damnation in hell.[35]

The death of Jesus

Those who believe in a God of righteousness can only bow their heads in awed and yet truthful submission at the strangely mixed means which He takes for the progress of mankind, at the painful and involved interconnection of good and evil. In spite of the endless misery which was to come upon the Jews because of the death of Jesus; in spite of the false theology and the persecutions and sore evils (apart wholly from the Jewish misery); in spite of the wrongs which were done to liberty, to enlightenment, and to toleration by the Christian Church – one yet sees that the death of Jesus, even as his life, was of immense benefit to the world. Christianity, as we know it, and as Paul made it, was due to his death as much as, if not more than, to his life. Some fundamental truths of Judaism (though not all of them) have been taught to a large part of the world by Christianity; and while in some directions it has obscured those truths, in others it has expanded them. That this might be done, the 'chosen people' has had to suffer. For the law of election seems to go even further than Amos realised, though what he said was sufficiently startling and revolutionary. For Amos said: 'You only have I known of all the inhabitants of the earth; therefore I will visit upon you your iniquities.'[36] But even this is not enough. Nineteen centuries of suffering compel us to realise that for some august reason or purpose we must say, 'You have I called: therefore you shall suffer undeservedly.'

The precise proportion of responsibility which belongs to any section of the Jews of Jerusalem for the death of Jesus must always remain doubtful and uncertain. But the probability, as we have seen, is that the Sadducean priesthood, perhaps backed up by some leading Rabbis, were responsible, together with the Romans, for his death. Yet what matters this, so far as God is concerned? We are disposed to find a difficulty in the 'third or fourth generation' of the second commandment. Yet if the death of Jesus had been unanimously voted by the entire Jewish people, with the votes taken in a plebiscite or referendum, what difference would it make? Third or fourth generation! Why, there have been fifty generations! And the roll is not yet ended, and there seems no prospect of its close. For in substitution of the Master's command, 'You shall love your enemies', there has been forged another: 'Ye shall hate your enemies to the fiftieth or sixtieth generation.'

But this is the will of God in His scheme for the progress of the world. We do not understand why. But the Jews have ever to realise that they have received the consecration of supremest suffering, and that they still in many lands remain the hunted, hated, wounded, but deathless witnesses of God.[37]

The significance of Jesus

To Jesus we owe the diffusion of Judaism – with modifications of good and evil – throughout the world. He brought about this diffusion not only because he was great and good, an enthusiastic lover of God and man, but because he showed a certain indifference to the political status and national glory of his people, because he rebuked the pride of race, displayed now and again friendliness to gentiles, and on occasion predicted the inclusion of many of them in the Kingdom of God, and lastly because under different and difficult circumstances, he spoke depreciatingly, like one of the older prophets, though without a theory and without theoretic consistency, about this and that detail and ordinance of the ceremonial law. Herein I find his special significance, but I find it also in the new note of authority, in his peculiar and messianic self-consciousness, which, while leading on to his worship and deification, was also in itself one of the very reasons which caused the survival and diffusion of his teaching. For it was not merely the teaching of a passing prophet: it was the teaching of a beloved and commanding personality. There was, indeed, as the generations passed, a shifting emphasis, but this very shifting is, in the last resort, due to Jesus himself. The centre of the teaching of the historic Jesus is God: the centre of the teaching of the Church is he. And yet the centre is in a sense brought back again to where it was before. For the Son becomes at last to the Christian believer of one substance and co-eternal with the Father.[38]

PAUL

How to understand Paul

One can best explain the Epistles [of Paul] by assuming, first, that Paul's pre-Christian religion was poorer, colder, less satisfying and more pessimistic than Rabbinic Judaism; secondly, that a special feature of that poorer religion was its more developed and less 'human' conception of the Messiah; thirdly, that Paul was already anxious and worried as to the fate of the gentile world and the great mass of gentile sinners; fourthly, that his pessimistic outlook drove him to gloomy views about the power of the 'evil inclination' and the impossibility of overcoming it; fifthly, that his knowledge of the mystery religions made him ready and eager to discover a universal method of salvation, suited and pre-destined for all men, whether gentile or Jew. His profoundly religious nature had not been given the nurture it required. The near Rabbinic God who longs to forgive His erring children at the first sign of repentance, was unknown to him ... then there came the vision at Damascus, and the way for which he yearned was revealed and made clear to him for ever. Lastly, with the duty imposed upon him by God to preach to all the world the Gospel of the Divine Son, he was met with Jewish antagonism and hostility. The new truth becomes not merely the complement of the old religion and its fulfilment, but in one important sense its direct antithesis and contrary. The Law is the strength of sin. Christianity is not the Law plus Jesus Christ. It is Jesus Christ alone: it is the end of the Law and of its bondage. It is the advent of the Spirit and of liberty. The letter, which is the Law, kills and leads to death: the Spirit, which is the Lord, gives life and leads Godward. Thus Judaism and Christianity become utterly severed and sundered from each other. The saints of either religion refuse to believe in the possibility of sainthood in the other. In Abraham's bosom each one would be surprised to meet the other. But God, who is above and beyond these human limitations, is not surprised at all.[39]

THE OLD AND NEW TESTAMENTS

The position of the New Testament

In the greatest gifts of God to struggling humanity there seems to be a double strand. Even in the Hebrew Bible, for example, we found doctrines which we could not regard as good and true, and we found them mixed up and blended with, and even sustaining and assisting, doctrines which seemed to us wholly right and pure. The world seems to be carried forward by new good which is not yet wholly good, or which yet contains within it seeds of evil. It is taught and helped by fresh truths which contain within them germs of falsehood. Great and noble results are often achieved through illusion and error: few recognise the illusion till the results are secured. . . .

To my mind, and to the mind of most Jews, this mixture of truth and falsehood is curiously illustrated by the religious teaching of the 'New Testament'. There is much in that book which is great and noble, much which is sublime and tender, much which is good and true. Of this 'much', the greater consists in a fresh presentment of some of the best and highest teaching in the 'Old Testament', in a vivid reformulation of it, in an admirable picking and choosing, an excellent bringing together. But a part consists of a further development, or in a clear or more emphatic expression of certain truths which previously were only implicit or not fully drawn out. Thus of its excellence part may in this sense be called old, and part in this sense may be called new. But in close and curious combination with what is good there are some things which are erroneous and harmful, and there are others which are liable to dangerous perversion, or which hold within them germs of evil and have borne evil fruit . . .

For good and for evil – and the two have been strangely interwoven together – the New Testament has been of enormous influence in the moral and religious history of the world. For that reason alone all Jews who, like other civilised persons, want to know about that history must read the New Testament, and read it, if they can, with impartial minds, ready to receive the good and

75

to reject the evil. But it cannot be admitted into a Jewish Bible for Home Reading. Not only that the critical study of it is unsuited for the young. There is more than this involved. For if it be said that within the Hebrew Bible too we have found higher and lower teaching, doctrine to reject as well as doctrine to receive, this argument would not suffice for the inclusion of the New Testament into the Bible of the Jews. It is one thing to observe, with growing thought and developing conceptions of religion and morality, deficiencies and unevenness in the sacred scriptures which have been your community's sacred scriptures for 2,000 years; it is quite another thing to add on to those scriptures other writings in which evils and errors, some of them which I have mentioned above, are known and recognised to exist. Moreover, the grave errors which we Jews think that we can detect in the New Testament are very closely connected with, even if they do not actually constitute, its most essential teachings. These errors are in fact among the very points which the great mass of Christians regard as its most peculiar characteristics and its most vital truths. Some of them, at any rate, seem to us to contradict the teaching of the Old Testament just where that teaching is at its truest, its purest and its best. For these reasons, even if there were no others, the Bible of the Jews must remain limited to the books which now compose it.[40]

Advances in the New Testament

There is a certain advantage and even progress gained by the New Testament combination of the two Hebrew words Chesed and Ahabah into the single word Agape. By that amalgamation we get the emergence of love (Agape), as both the highest attribute of God – His true essence – and as the highest quality of man. In the Old Testament, especially in Deuteronomy, man is urged to love God, and the word used is Ahob. Sometimes the love of God for Israel is also alluded to by the verb Ahob and the noun Ahabah. Again, a good deal is said of the divine Chesed, or loving-kindness, and sometimes this same quality of God is put forward as a human ideal as well. 'I desire Chesed and not sacrifice', where the Chesed which God desires is a quality to be shown by man to man. But there is no clear combination of Ahabah and Chesed, no final emergence of love, as the one great supreme link between man and God, as at once the essence of the divine nature and the ideal of all human action.[41]

The New and Old contrasted

To develop seems easier than to lay the broad foundations. We will not minimise the greatness of the New Testament, or cheapen the originality whether of Jesus or Paul. But when we compare the achievement of the Old Testament with that of the New, we realise how much greater is our obligation to the Old. When you have won through to your monotheism, and to the doctrine of the One Good God, when you have got your prophets with their weaving together of religion and morality, when you have got your commands and ideals to love God with all your heart, and the neighbour and resident alien as yourself, when you have reached the ideals of justice and compassion, of the clean hands and the pure heart – why, then, it was, in a sense, comparatively easy to supplement, to bring together, to purify, to universalise. Only comparatively easy, of course! The achievements of Jesus and Paul (in spite of some sad retrogressions) are great achievements. But what we owe to them seems but little in comparison with what we owe to their Old Testament predecessors. The bulk of our religion and the bulk of our morality seem due neither to Jesus nor to Paul, neither to Plato nor to Epictetus, but to the Sacred Scripture of the Jews. For Liberal Jews and Liberal Judaism, the Old Testament remains primary and fundamental, the New Testament secondary and supplemental . . . the supplementary and complementary teachings in the New Testament we will also make use of and frankly admire, but the Old Testament, both in regard to what it says and to what it does not say, to what it contains and what it omits, abides as the basis of our faith, as our stronghold and our charter.[42]

A comment on Matt 25:41: 'Then shall he also say unto them on the left hand, Depart from me, ye accursed, into the everlasting fire.'

Such passages as Matt. 25:41 should make theologians excessively careful of drawing beloved contrasts between the Old Testament and the New. We find even a liberal theologian Dr. Fosdick saying:

From Sinai to Calvary – was ever a record of progressive

revelation more plain or more convincing? The development begins with Jehovah disclosed in a thunderstorm on a desert mountain, and it ends with Christ saying: 'God is Spirit: and they that worship Him must worship Him in spirit and truth'; it begins with a war-god leading his partisans to victory, and it ends with men saying, 'God is love; and he that abideth in love abideth in God, and God abideth in him'; it begins with a provincial deity loving his tribe and hating its enemies, and it ends with the God of the whole earth worshipped 'by a great multitude, which no man could number, out of every nation, and of all the tribes and peoples and tongues'; it begins with a God who commands the slaying of the Amalekites, 'both man and woman, infant and suckling', and it ends with a Father whose will it is that not 'one of these little ones should perish'; it begins with God's people standing afar off from his lightenings and praying that he might not speak to them lest they die and it ends with men going into their inner chambers, and, having shut the door, praying to their father who is in secret.

(*Christianity and Progress*, 1922, p.209.)

Very good. No doubt such a series can be arranged. Let me now arrange a similar series.

From the Old Testament to the New Testament – was there ever a record of retrogression more plain or more convincing? It begins with, 'Have I any pleasure at all in the death of him that dieth?'; it ends with 'Begone from me, ye doers of wickedness.' It begins with, 'The Lord is slow to anger and plenteous in mercy'; it ends with, 'Fear Him who is able to destroy both body and soul in Gehenna.' It begins with, 'I will dwell with him that is of a contrite spirit to revive him'; it ends with, 'Narrow is the way which leads to life, and few there be who find it.' It begins with, 'I will not contend for ever; I will not always be wrath;' it ends with, 'Depart, ye cursed, into the everlasting fire.' It begins with, 'Should I not have pity on Nineveh, that great city?'; it ends with, 'It will be more endurable for Sodom on the day of Judgement than for that town.' It begins with,' The Lord is good to all who call upon Him'; it ends with, 'Whoever speaks against the Holy Spirit, there is no forgiveness whether in this world or the next.' It begins with, 'The Lord will wipe away tears from off all faces; he will destroy death forever'; it ends with, 'They will throw them into the furnace of fire; there is the weeping and the gnashing of teeth.'

And the one series would be as misleading as the other.[43]

CHRISTIAN ANTI-JUDAISM

Ezra, his successors and Biblical Scholarship

The long interval between Ezra and Judas the Maccabee was full of religious fervour and vitality. The spirit of religion expressed itself in a variety of ways. What manifold thought and activity there must have been in an age which edited the Law and expanded the Prophets, which produced the Psalter and the Proverbs, the books of Job and Ecclesiastes, Joel on the one hand, Jonah on the other, Chronicles and Ruth! What fresh inspiration and true religious zeal in an age which created the synagogue and its early ritual to serve as a complement to, and afterwards to take the place of, temple and sacrifice! And this, be it remembered, in an age when ancient prophecy had ceased, when the letter of the law had succeeded the free spirit which mocks at forms. How many the prejudices which should be corrected in this newer, more critical and more truthful view of the post-exilic age! We used to be told that the rule of the law, which began with Ezra, inaugurated a period of gradual sterilisation and decay. More and more the legal yoke was supposed to crush out inspiration and originality; a mediocre and depressing uniformity was believed to take the place of the fresh and breezy variety of pre-exilic days, when, amid much wild disorder and many strange aberrations, there was yet room and opportunity for an Amos and a Jeremiah; instead of prophecy, there is the letter which kills; a chilling external legality causes the level of true religion to sink lower and lower, till the measure of its worthlessness becomes full, and the time for a new teaching is at hand.

It is now no longer possible to represent the post-exilic period in such a light as this. But prejudices die hard; and the antagonism to the Law and to its religion, which still reigns supreme in the greater number of Christian theologians, is trying to find a way out of its obvious difficulty. The imperfections of post-exilic literature and religion are explained as direct results of the Law; its excellences are a dying protest against its stifling dominion. Thus the Psalter, albeit it has been the beloved possession of

Judaism ever since the days of the Maccabees, is yet a reaction of old Israelite piety against Judaism, a proof that the religious genius of Israel could not be quenched even by Ezra and the Pharisees! That old Israelite piety, which was expressed erewhile in superstition and idolatry, is awakened once more, and lo! its outcome is the Psalter . . .

The religious fervour which marks much of the literature of the pre-Maccabean period was no less, but even more, a characteristic of the Judaism which succeeded it. Religion has never been a purer joy and a deeper satisfaction. God has never been more truly loved and more nobly served, than among those who followed the full-blown particularism of the Rabbis. Under the influence of Hellenism and in the waning of the national religious idea, God, to the author of Ecclesiastes, had become distant. It was the Law and the national idea which brought God near. In orthodox Judaism the Law supplied the place of the person of Christ in orthodox Christianity. It was the almost living link between the human and divine.[44]

Christianity and the Law

Beyond the New Testament there is no clear evidence that outside the observers of the Law stood what one great American scholar likes to call the 'disinherited masses'. On the contrary, the masses were the champions of the Law, and the Law was their inheritance; while sprung from the masses, their friends and spokesmen, were the great majority of the Rabbis. Nor again is there good and clear evidence, beyond the New Testament, that the Law, either to those who observed it, or who sought to observe it, was regarded, not as a distinction and a privilege, but as a grievance, an oppression and a burden. When the early Christian community contrasted the Law of Christ with the Law of Moses, and found freedom in the one and servitude in the other, the ease and comfort and repose of the New Law was unfavourably compared with the burden and anxiety of the Old. But we remember the rule that those who are outside a religion know not its intimacies, and those who have left it forget them. To those within there was no bondage, but freedom . . .

The worst of a wrong polemical theory is that it tends to make those who oppose it exaggerate in their turn. We must not forget two things – one general and one particular. The particular thing is that, both in Judea and Galilee, there must have been many religious and moral evils in A.D. 30 – a great deal, that is, for a reformer and a prophet to denounce and to lament. What society has ever been without them? And the general thing is that there is no religion which has not the defects of its qualities. There is none which has not its own peculiar dangers. Jewish legalism is no exception to the rule. First of all comes the obvious danger of putting the ceremonial above the moral. It is easy to be strict about food and drink and cooking, and washing one's hands; it is harder to be humble and loving and sweet-tempered. Again, there is the danger of self-righteousness and formalism; many laws are negative; it is comparatively easy to keep them. A man may have observed many laws, and in his pride may think that he has observed the whole Law; it may be but a poor, negative, formal, limited, and outward sort of morality and religion to which he has attained, and yet he may thank God for his own excellence and that he is not as other men. The picture of the Pharisee in Luke's parable -a ludicrous caricature of the average Pharisee, a monstrous caricature of the Pharisaic ideal – may yet be true enough of one particular perversion of the Pharisaic religion. And why should there not have been several living examples of such a perversion in the age of Jesus? All that I beg of you to remember is that you can have (and still do have in many Jewish circles) a combination of the purest and most saintly piety with the most careful and minute observance of every detail of the ceremonial.[45]

Christianity and Jewish legalism

Under the influence of Paul, and of Luther and of other teachers of the Reformation period, there is no doctrine against which many Protestant theologians fulminate more violently than the doctrine of reward. They do not mind punishment; they could hardly mind it, when the extended use of the Gehenna and Hell from the Gospel onwards right down to Luther and Calvin and up to modern times, is borne in mind, but they hate what they call eudaemonism – so much good action paid for by so much reward – and they assert that reward is the sheet anchor of Judaism, and especially of the Rabbis. Man earns his reward in Judaism:

the grace of God gives undeserved and unearned beatitude in Christianity. The result is, in one sense, the same: both Judaism and Christianity assume that the good and believing will enjoy bliss, but what is earned reward to the one is a free gift to the other. Legalism, the hated red rag and unclean thing to Lutheran theologians, involves reward. Legalism and eudaemonism go together. It was necessary to smash legalism to get rid of the bribery and degradation of reward ...

There is an exaggeration in all this tilting against reward. It has been shown by Schechter and Abrahams and others that there is not only less 'eudaemonism' in Rabbinic theology than its antagonists would allow, but also that its eudaemonism is tempered by several other and very different strains. It has also been shown that the assurance and even the delineation of reward do not necessarily mean that good acts were performed for the sake of the reward, or that pure and disinterested piety was not as prized and familiar to the Rabbi as to the Christian. The familiar doctrine of Lishmah ['for its own sake'] which ninety-nine out of a hundred German Protestant theologians ignore, or have never heard of, is the best proof that the motive of reward was regarded as the lower and less desirable motive, 'for its own sake' or 'for love' as the higher and more desirable motive. Again, Jesus, who was happily ignorant of these antagonisms and oppositions, was quite ready, every now and then, to use the doctrine of reward, and to enunciate it, as here, in the very strongest and simplest terms. The Protestant theologians try hard to show that he does not really mean what he says, or that somehow his doctrine of reward is wholly different from the Rabbis' doctrine of reward; his is pure, theirs is impure; his is a mere use of popular language, theirs is seriously meant; his is an exquisite statement of the gracious goodness of God, theirs is calculation and bribery - and so on. But for those who stand above the facts these differences are largely the creation of the theologians.[46]

The telling silence of Christian scholarship

With very few honourable exceptions the Christian scholar, and more especially the German Protestant scholar, simply ignores what Jewish scholars have to say. If he would argue the point, if he would discuss, if he would deign to notice us, there would be some pleasure and interest. But what on earth is the good of returning to the charge when no enemy appears? Is it possible that what the Jewish scholars say is so silly, so contemptibly prejudiced, so utterly erroneous, that it is really too much to expect that any Christian scholar can notice it? But, after all, are we necessarily so much more prejudiced on our side than the Christian scholars are on theirs? If we write on the New Testament or speak about Jesus and Paul, do we ignore the great Christian divines? . . .

The policy of silence would be less conspicuous and less significant if Christian scholars never noticed what Jewish scholars had to say about anything whatever. But this is far from being the case. On any other subject than Rabbinic religion and theology, the Jewish scholars are at once sure of a respectful and intelligent attention. . . . But theology is taboo. Nothing escapes the marvellous ingenuity of a German scholar like Schurer. If a Jewish writer makes some foolish suggestion as to the size and population of a Palestinian city in the Maccabean era Schurer will at all events do that writer the honour of alluding in a footnote to his suggestion as 'völlig unannehmbar' or 'haltungslos'. But let the greatest Rabbinical scholar of the age write a series of epoch-making studies on Rabbinic theology Schurer will not even deign to mention or contradict him.

Far less important matters than Rabbinic theology are worried about persistently. However there are special reasons why this particular matter must not be allowed to rest; why Jewish writers must continue to plead for discussion and fair consideration of what they have to say.

After all, Rabbinic theology has some relation to the early history of Christianity, and it does make some difference whether the Rabbinic religion was good or bad. Is that the real reason why the Christian scholars refuse to listen when so unique a scholar as Schechter addresses? . . .

It is easy to see that great confusion would be caused in current opinions if the commonplaces of the theologians were wrong. For suppose, after all, that the Law was not a burden, that the Sabbath was a day of delight, that ceremonies and spirituality, letter and spirit, could, did and do go together, how very awkward the result might be. Then, though Christianity might be a far greater religion than Judaism, there would be two good religions instead of one, two ways of approaching and finding God instead of one. Then though Paul's doctrine might be great and noble, it would not be the only way to salvation, then one could be spiritual and commune with God through the Law as well as through the Gospel, then true prayer, self sacrifice and disinterested religion might be the possession of Judaism and Christianity, of living orthodox Jews as well as living orthodox Christians. And surely this would never do. Schechter's articles are highly dangerous: leave them alone! . . .

Schechter has shown that the God of the Rabbis was not 'remote', that their righteousness was not 'hollow', that they knew the highest meaning of prayer, of holiness, of disinterested love of God. These things he, the foremost scholar of his age, has to my thinking shown. But even if he has not shown them, he has produced material so new and large, so interesting, so counter to current conceptions and popular verdicts, that it surely demands consideration. Let it be refuted, if possible, by all means, but do not let it be ignored.[47]

Common uses of the words 'Jewish' and 'Christian'

The primary meaning of the two adjectives is purely neutral. If I speak of the Jewish religion or the Christian religion, I pronounce no verdict as to their goodness or badness any more than if I speak of the Buddhist or the Mahommedan religion . . .

But if, in addition to its obvious neutral sense, 'Christian' means something very excellent and mature, what must 'Jewish' mean? Clearly something poor, immature or even bad, for the two adjectives almost inevitably tended to be used as opposites. A parallel was at hand in the common contrast between the Old Testament and the New. For instead of what I venture to think is the proper and historic way of looking at these two collections – namely that each has its own excellences, and has its own defects, the usual line is taken to find a series of contrasts . . .

To use the word Jewish to mean something religiously and morally imperfect and bad, and to use the word Christian to mean something religiously and morally perfect and good, seems to me to measure two living religions with unequal weights. What would be thought of a Jew who, writing a history of Christianity, spoke of cruelty, persecution and intolerance as specifically Christian? And yet, what endless examples he could find and give of ardent Christians who in deed and writing were cruel, persecuting and intolerant: 'In the tortures of the auto-de-fé's of the Inquisition, in the blood bath which accompanied the capture of Jerusalem by the Crusaders, in the fires of Smithfield, in the doctrine of everlasting hell fire, in the deaths of Bruno and Servetus, the true character of Christianity is conspicuously revealed.' What a shocking sentence.

But something of the same sort can be said about Judaism, and it would hardly be noticed . . . There is a good deal of glass in both our houses. We had better not throw stones at each other . . . Nevertheless, the ideal remains. Christians have every right to quote with pride the sayings of Jesus about the love of enemies. And Jews have no less right to quote with pride the Rabbinic sayings that he who is not merciful and kind cannot be of the true seed of Israel, or that he who is reviled and does not revile, returning good for evil, is like the sun when he sets forth his might. For the adjectives Jewish and Christian, if used in a non-neutral sense, can and should mean only that which is good and tender and pure.[48]

CHAPTER THREE

TORAH AND RABBINIC JUDAISM

INTRODUCTION

In the traditional Jewish understanding, Torah is divided into two parts. The first is the Written Torah which consists of the Five Books of Moses. The Written Torah is understood as a record of the revelation which took place on Mount Sinai and, in addition, is the ultimate authority on matters of Halakhah.[1] The second is the Oral Torah, which consists not only of interpretations and explanations of the Written Torah but is also an ongoing exposition of Jewish life through the experience of the Jewish people. The Oral Torah, according to Tradition, is believed to have been delivered to Moses simultaneously with the written Torah but was not committed to writing until the Rabbinic period. The Mishnah, Talmud and Codes are all products of the Oral Torah and represent Jewish thought and values at different periods of time. Once written down, they became the 'new' ultimate authority for the development of Halakhah. New books, intended to to interpret these works, were written and the tradition grew and the number of 'sacred' texts increased. The traditional Jewish view, based upon Rabbinic teaching, asserts that these texts are merely practical expressions of the further unfolding of the revelation at Sinai. All interpretations of the Written and Oral Torah, and all elaborations of Halakhah, are held to be 're-discoveries', as though they had already been received by Moses on Sinai.

The Rabbinical literature is composed of Aggadah and Halakhah. Aggadah has a broad meaning and refers to literature which is not of legal character, for example, legends, stories, folk tales, homilies, sermons etc. It is not considered to be as authoritative as Halakhah, which has the same authority as the Written Torah. The Midrash is another feature of Rabbinic literature. It consists of Rabbinic interpretation and exposition of Biblical texts. It contains both Aggadic and Halakhic teaching.

From an historical point of view we find that for about two thousand years, from the Pharisees until the Emancipation, the Torah constituted the pivot around which all Jewish life revolved. It was the authority in Jewish affairs. It might appear that such a system was inflexible and rigid. Indeed, as we have seen, this criticism of Rabbinical Judaism had existed for many years. However, it was not realised by the critics that there was room for development and change through re-interpretation. The Oral Torah, by definition, is an ongoing process, an unfinished tradition. The Rabbis were successful in responding to new and different situations. In countless ways they shaped and moulded their Jewish heritage and the Halakhah so that Rabbinical Judaism maintained its diversity, flexibility and creativity.[2] On the other hand new interpretation could allow only so much room for change . . . and no more. A Biblical law, whether Jews lived by it or not, could not be explicitly dismissed. As the Rabbis said, 'a Scriptural verse never loses altogether its plain sense' (Shabbat 63a). In addition, there was no legislature, no Sanhedrin, which could make new rulings and reject outdated ones. How could there be outdated laws if they were received from God? These laws were part of a divine and therefore perfect constitution. As a result Rabbinic flexibility diminished from age to age as every generation of Rabbis tended to defer to its predecessors[3] and, over time, the system solidified. It became harder and harder to maintain flexibility and avoid the negative consequences of an ever powerful built-in rigidification factor.

Judaism entered a new phase of its development with the rise of the Emancipation which transformed Jewish life economically, politically, socially and culturally. As long as Jews had constituted a world apart, the Talmud and its interpreters, the Rabbis, could rule Jewish life. However, when Jews no longer lived solely amongst Jews, Halakhah no longer solely governed their life. As Solomon Freehof wrote, 'When modernity broke the walls of the Jewish community and Jews began to be integrated into the larger European community, the walls of the Jewish legal structure and of Jewish practices began to crack.'[4] There were three major consequences of the Emancipation which drastically changed Jewish life. They represented a new challenge to Judaism, and in particular to the central position of Torah and Halakhah.

(1) Jews in vast numbers began to break away from what seemed to them to be the dead hand of the past without pausing to wait for Rabbinic sanction. A cleavage grew between Halakhah and modern life which resulted in non-observance. Traditional religious life was threatened and appeared less than appealing when compared to the bright lights of Western society and the picture of security painted by secular life.

(2) There was a change in the way Jews viewed the world. The modern outlook challenged the assumption that the Torah was perfect and contained the truth, the whole truth and nothing but the truth.

Questions were directed towards the divine sanction of Rabbinic teachings and, consequently, to the basis of Rabbinic authority.

(3) There was a successful attempt to respond to the newly found freedom on the one hand and to the new thought processes on the other – Reform. The pioneers of reform modified the modes of religious expression and tackled the problem of authority in Judaism. They called for changes in ritual and in religious practice and their reform affected almost every aspect of Jewish life.

All three factors, but perhaps the third most of all, led to a growing hostility and resistance among the traditional authorities. Not only did the early Orthodox responsa of 1819 (Eleh ha-Divre ha-berit) denounce the Reformers; their general approach was that it was utterly forbidden to make any changes in the traditional ritual, even to use the vernacular in services.[5] Their intransigence and hostile stance contributed to the attractiveness and effectiveness of the approach of the radical reformers in their more extreme calls for change. The radicals argued that the only way to reform was through revolution and a complete rejection of traditional Jewish authority. Since no reform could take place without challenging the Orthodox Rabbinate, this anti-Rabbinical stance resulted in many reformers taking a negative attitude to the whole corpus of Rabbinic literature. Little attempt was made to distinguish between traditional texts or to select Rabbinical material which might justify and support new developments. The total rejection of the reform position by Orthodoxy strengthened the hand of the radical reformers.[6]

The radical position is marked by the life and thought of Samuel Holdheim. His views evolved from an orthodox position to one of radical reform. Holdheim received a traditional Jewish education and was known as an excellent scholar of the Talmud, but he reacted violently against his upbringing and argued that the Rabbinic interpretation was 'nothing else but a product of the religious point of view of their [the rabbis'] time'.[7] It was thus but a small step for Holdheim to argue that his views (as well as those of his fellow reformers) were the contemporary authority for his time; the importance and significance of the authority of Rabbinical teaching was undermined. Holdheim's radical views spread to America where they took a firmer hold on Reform Judaism than in Europe.

There can be little doubt that American Reform, under the influence of Holdheim and others such as David Einhorn, was antinomian in *its formative period. Its emphasis upon ethical idealism resulted in a weakening, and even rejection, of the legal disciplines. Positive views held towards Halakhah were limited solely to the Bible with an almost total rejection of the validity and authority of the Halakhic Rabbinic literature. The Reformers saw the Bible as idealistic and empowering while the Rabbinical literature was merely a form of barren legalism.[8] The opposition to radicalism within the Reform camp was led by Isaac Wise but his views, in the early years, represented a minority position. He argued that there was great danger in eliminating the Talmudic and Rabbinical phases of Jewish development and limiting nearly all authority to the Bible – this would make Reform Judaism a mere pale form of Karaism.[9]*

It is interesting to note that the tendency towards Karaism was exemplified by the position of the West London Synagogue. An emphasis was placed on fulfilling Biblical law first and Rabbinical law second. It was not that Rabbinical law was rejected, but that Biblical law was understood as authoritative while Rabbinical law was considered merely as a guide.[10] This ambiguous attitude to the Halakhic literature must have been an influence on Claude Montefiore, for not only did he receive his Jewish education under the guidance of David Marks, minister of West London Synagogue, but he also remained a member of that synagogue for the whole of his life. We must also remember that when Montefiore and the Liberal Movement were searching for its first rabbi, they turned to the United States where the radical reform was dominant and not to Europe where a more conservative trend was apparent. We might suggest that the anti-Rabbinical stance in American Reform made it more attractive than the European movements to English Liberal Jews.

German Reform, and European Reform in general, made a greater effort than their fellow reformers in America to maintain a close relationship with the traditional Jewish sources and Halakhah. Abraham Geiger, for example, emphasised the independent attitude of Reform in contrast to Orthodoxy, but not at the expense of a rejection of the Halakhic tradition. 'Not in violent and reckless amputation of all that has been transmitted to us from the past lies our salvation, but in the careful investigation into its deeper message and in striving, even now that we have become organs of history, to continue to develop historically that which has grown up historically . . .'[11] Geiger's view represented the dominant position in European Reform and radical opinions, such as those of the Friends of Reform in Frankfurt, were rejected.

It is important to note that Montefiore must not only have been aware of the European Reform position but could even have been influenced by it while living and studying at the Hochschule in Berlin. It is not insignificant that his tutor, Solomon Schechter, was a renowned Rabbinical scholar who brought the Rabbis 'alive' for his students.[12] However, in time, Montefiore's views became more radical and he appeared to take a path similar to, but not so dramatic as, that of Samuel Holdheim. Montefiore became more and more hostile to the dominant aspect of Rabbinic literature – Halakhah. It is no coincidence that almost all of Montefiore's writings on the Rabbinic period are devoted to Aggadah and not Halakhah.[13]

There is one further factor which we must discuss – the Christian attitude to the Rabbinical literature. Montefiore was ever an interpreter of Judaism to Christians, and the fact that Christian interest in Jewish literature was polemical rather than historical pained him. The anti-Rabbinical tendency in Christian writings of this period was pervasive. For example, Emil Schurer, in The Jewish people in the time of Jesus Christ, *identified Judaism with 'legalism', and 'legalism' was his most cherished antipathy. Jewish life, in his opinion, became a service of the letter of the Law for the letter's sake ie., the outward correctness of the action was crucial and not the inward end or motive.[14]*

A perverse caricature of Rabbinic Judaism was often the consequence of Christian studies. In addition, Christian theologians were normally ignorant of the literature they tended to decry and Jewish scholars such as Montefiore were forced to defend the Rabbinic literature from accusations. Other Jewish scholars who became involved in this battle included Israel Abrahams and Solomon Schechter. Some Christian scholars such as Travers Herford also made an enormous effort to correct this false position.

What makes Montefiore's work on the Rabbis so fascinating is that he was caught in a dilemma – on the one hand he had little feeling, and even a distaste, for the Rabbinic writings, especially Halakhah; on the other he realised that the Christian understanding of the Rabbis (and their predecessors, the Pharisees) was unfair at best, and needed to be rectified. There were also the conflicting influences of Solomon Schechter and the West London Synagogue. As a result of this tension Montefiore struggled throughout his life to offer a comprehensive and consistent view of Torah and Rabbinic Judaism.

THE RABBIS AND THE BIBLE

The Rabbinic contribution

How far have the Rabbis advanced beyond the Old Testament? Such a question, so reasonable to us, would to them have seemed a blasphemy. As to them, roughly speaking, everything in the Sacred Scriptures was on one level of supreme excellence, so all their religion was for them contained in those Scriptures, and they never expressed any view, or enunciated any doctrine, which they did not seek to justify or substantiate by some biblical passage or utterance. They merely drew out what was already there. To us it would be very doleful to think that there was no religious progress in Judaism for, say, 500 years, and, as a matter of fact, there was a good deal. Not only were several quite new conceptions put forward – an advance direct and clear-cut – but some implicit things in the Scriptures were made explicit, some occasional teachings of value became more frequent, and some indefinite or casually advanced ideas, became definite and dogmatic.

I have already indicated that the drawing out of every biblical idea ran a danger of cutting both ways. For one can obviously draw out the 'low' as well as the 'high', the bad as well as the good. The Rabbis did not entirely escape this danger. Some, at any rate, of the imperfections and crudities of the Hebrew Scriptures were elaborated and hardened by the Rabbis, as for example the divine partiality for Israel, and the doctrine of tit for tat. This is unfortunate. For when the Old Testament is what we now call 'particularist', it is so usually in a simple, primitive, unreflecting, and 'natural' way, and this is less upsetting to us than when the Rabbis utter their particularism with reflection, when they make a theory of it or for it, justifying the, to us, unjustifiable. Again, although the Old Testament is for them the word of God, and all is Torah, yet the Pentateuch is pre-eminently the word of God and pre-eminently Torah. The legalism and ceremonialism of the Rabbis are in some respects far better than the legalism and ceremonialism of the Pentateuch; they are less priestly, less

94

primitive, freer from superstitions; but they are also more pronounced, theoretic, elaborate, and pervasive. Things are said, for
example, about circumcision which are positively painful to the
modern mind, so that we feel inclined to say: better than this
advance is the primitiveness of the Pentateuch. Reflected or
justified imperfections are worse than naive and spontaneous
ones. What is said about hell in the Gospels is bad enough; what
is said about hell by St Augustine is much worse. The anthropomorphisms of the Hebrew Bible are often crude and glaring;
but they are usually naive and sometimes grand. Some of the
anthropomorphisms of the Rabbis jar upon us more. The things
which God is made to say and do and think and feel are sometimes so completely on the human level that we are repelled and
troubled. Sometimes, too, in doctrine we prefer the primitive
spontaneity of the Hebrew Bible. Thus we prefer the simple
unreflective tit for tat teachings of the Old Testament to the
elaborations of the Rabbis, to the silly idea of such and such
divine punishments for such and such sins, of which a shocking
and odious instance has found its way from the Mishnah into the
orthodox Prayer Book, from which no orthodox authorities have
had the manliness or the decency to remove it (cf. Prayer Book
p. 121).[15]

In some ways, therefore, the Hebrew Bible is nearer to us than
are the Rabbis. It is also nearer because it is more familiar.
Moreover, it contains writers and passages much greater than
any writers or passages in the Rabbinical literature. There is
nothing from the Rabbis to compare with the Prophets or with
Job or with the nobler Psalms. What is splendidly original and
full of genius appeals to us more closely. Because the Old Testament is more creative and original than are the Rabbis, we are
more drawn to it.

Yet in some respects we are nearer to the Rabbis than the
writers of the Bible. And so far as advance and retrogression
are concerned, when all is said, the good outweighs the evil.
The advance is more conspicuous than the retrogression: the
elaboration, the development, the refinement, of the good are
larger than those of the 'evil'. Moreover – and this is very pleasing
– there are not many instances to be found of the elaborations of
the 'evil', where we do not also find some flashes of a vivid sense

of the inadequacy or questionableness of the 'evil', and some suddenly interjected sayings in the direction of the good. A 'low' doctrine is flatly contradicted by a 'high' utterance, even though the 'low' teaching is not formally renounced or rejected by the man from whom the 'high' utterance proceeds. Such a formal rejection would be impossible for those who, like the Rabbis, fervently believed in the perfection and inerrancy of the Sacred Scriptures. It is only the modernist who is free. We cannot expect the Rabbis to be modernists . . .[16]

Progression (i): Advances of no value today

It was the Law which, in the eyes of the Rabbis, gave Israel its worth in the eyes of God. Their love of God is inseparable from their love of His perfect Law. How far is there anything in their conception of the Law, and in their attitude towards the Law, which, with our profoundly different ideas, is yet of value to us today? Here we have to distinguish. There may be much in the Rabbinic doctrine about the Law which is an advance upon the Old Testament, and yet, though it be an advance, we are unable to make use of it. For instance, the Rabbinic view that such ritual commands of the Law as the ordinance of the red cow, or of the waters of purification, are just arbitrary commands of God which must be obeyed, because He, for some unknown reason, in His perfect wisdom and goodness, ordained them, completely removes from such injunctions any kind of superstition. Not the water purifies, but God. This is an advance upon the Old Testament. But for us it is of no use because we no longer accept the premise. We no longer regard these laws as derived directly from the will and the mouth of God. The Rabbinic love of the Law, the joy in its observance; the delight in its study; all this must be freely acknowledged. That the Law was to the Rabbis, and to thousands and millions whom they influenced, not a burden but a delight, that it led to God and righteousness, and not away from them is assured. But all this advance, for advance it was, is no longer available for us.[17]

Progression (ii): Lishmah

The commands of the Law may at first be a purification, but the ideal is that they should be a joy. He who serves in joy serves in love, and he who serves in love serves *lishmah*, for the sake of the Law itself, or for the sake of God. Single-minded must be God's service, for it is rendered to Him who is 'single'. Every command must be fulfilled to please God, and this, again, means that it must be fulfilled just because it is a command and with no ulterior motive. As for him who does not fulfil the Law for its own sake, it were better he had never been born. Over and over again we find the same idea, so that if there is a strong naive desire for reward, as a sign of God's grace and of the victory of righteousness and of Israel and Israel's cause, there is no less strong an assertion that all 'good' actions are only good if they are done for God's sake or for their own sake. These assertions are undoubtedly a great advance upon anything we find in the Old Testament. It is quite characteristic of the odd mixture of the Rabbinic religion that if, on the one hand, an Old Testament weakness is emphasised by the Rabbis, it is also overcome.[18]

Progression (iii): Imitation and Sanctification of the Name

The Imitation of God ideal depends upon such O.T. verses, or bits of verses, as 'Holy shalt thou be, for I the Lord your God am holy'. Or again, 'What does the Lord require of thee, but to cleave unto Him and to walk in His ways?' But the Rabbis taught more deliberately the imitation of God. How could man walk in His ways? By imitating His ethical qualities. As God is just, so be thou just. As God is merciful, so be thou merciful; as God is loving, so be thou loving ... I do not pretend that towards the enemies of Israel, towards idolators, persecutors, heretics and apostates, this level or aspect of the Imitation was always maintained. But we have to remember that the ordinary life of the ordinary member of any religious community has much more to do with the fellow members of his own community and, as far as enemies are concerned, with his own personal enemies within the community, than it has to do with any individuals outside. Parallel to the idea of becoming like unto God is the idea of becoming a partner with God. And so we find: 'Whoever hears himself cursed and is silent, though he had the power to stop the cursing by destroying his enemy, becomes a partner with God, who hears the blasphemies of the heathen and is silent' ...

Still more important, perhaps, than the imitation ideal was the ideal of Sanctification. The term Kiddush ha-Shem, the Hallowing of the Name, with its opposite Chillul ha-Shem, the Profanation of the Name, became and remained two of the most popular and widely known religious terms throughout every generation from the days of the early Rabbis till the present time. As with all the other Rabbinic conceptions and ideals, so this one too is based upon the Old Testament, but goes far beyond it in ethical power. The profanation and hallowing of God's Name in the Pentateuch are especially associated with correct ceremonial and outward purity: the fundamental passage occurs in Lev. 22:31–2, where, after a long series of ordinances about the purity of the priests and about sacrifices, it says: 'therefore ye shall keep my commandments and do them: I am the Lord. And ye shall not profane my holy name: but I will be hallowed among the children of Israel: I am the Lord who hallows you.' Thus God by His ordinances hallows Israel: that is, Israel, if it keeps God's ordinances, is hallowed: and, on the other hand, this very hallowing of Israel causes the hallowing of God . . . God is certainly pleased by Israel's obedience, but the great point of the hallowing of His name is the effect of it outside Israel upon the nations of the world. And this hallowing, just as the profanation, is effected by ethical purity or ethical defilement – by uprightness and probity and every kind of virtue, and finally, in the highest degree, by martyrdom. In martyrdom the hallowing is wrought no longer merely by ethical actions, but by what we may fitly call a religious action, yet it is not a ceremonial action; it is outward, but, in the highest degree, inward as well.

The Kiddush ha-Shem or Name-hallowing motive became deeply ingrained in the popular Jewish consciousness. It must have had an immense influence for good throughout the ages. It made virtue more necessary and more virtuous: while its opposite, Name-profanation, made sin more atrocious and more sinful. Sin is always sin, whether committed in private or in public: yet it is worse to commit a sin in public, or in such a way that it becomes known to others, than to commit it in private, because directly your sin is known to others you profane the Name, and if the others are non-Jews, you profane most of all. It is highly curious to notice the effect that this point of view had upon Rabbinic and Jewish ethical theory, and most assuredly also upon Jewish ethical practice. The religion and ethics of the Rabbis grew up and were developed under conditions in which the Jews were practically always a subject people, and, far more often than not, an oppressed, despised and persecuted people as well. In these circumstances it was inevitable that there should have grown up the usual relations and feelings of the hunted animal towards the hunter: in other words, a tendency to argue or to feel that the same lofty morality which was right towards the fellow Jew was not incumbent upon the Jew in his dealings with the gentile. The Rabbis were patriots, though they cared for the Law much more than political dependence: they were also human, and liable to human passions and emotions. Therefore, you can undoubtedly find in the Rabbinical literature some ethical pronouncements in connection with the dealings of the Jew with the gentile which are unsatisfactory, particularistic and low. But these comparatively few pronouncements are crossed by others of a precisely opposite tendency on account of the Sanctification or Profanation of the Name. And these opposite pronouncements are, I think, both more numerous and more authoritative. To wrong a gentile obviously causes the gentile to say, 'What a wretched religion Judaism must be, what a miserable God must the Jewish Deity be, when His worshippers act so.' But when the Jew acts honourably, or, still more, with any special honesty, towards the gentile, then the gentile will be inclined to say, 'What a fine religion Judaism must be, what a noble and true God must the Jewish Deity be, when the Jew acts towards me in such a manner.' Supposing the gentile had oppressed the Jew, and the Jew, when he could have cheated the gentile, acts with uprightness towards him, the God of the Jews is hallowed all the more. Hence we find it stated in many plain and simple words in the Rabbinic code: 'To rob or cheat a gentile is a heavier sin than to rob or cheat a Jew, because of the Profanation of the Name.'[19]

Regression (i): Reward and punishment

While the doctrine of life after death, whether immediately in heaven or in hell, or after the resurrection, greatly relieved biblical difficulties, there was, on the whole, a persistency of biblical conceptions, and in many ways a hardening and systemisation. Here we have, surely for the good, moved away from the Rabbis. They seem to be constantly thinking about rewards and punishments, whether in this life or another. And they do not hesitate to develop the ugly doctrine that such and such punishments, are directly sent by God as the punishments of such and such sins....there are many other illustrations which could be given of the extraordinary emphasis laid by the Rabbis upon punishment and reward, as for example, the constantly repeated remark (in which they seem as far from us moderns as it is possible for men of the same religion to be) that the righteous are punished on earth for the few and trivial sins which they may commit here, in order that they may be the more fully and uninterruptedly rewarded beyond the grave, while the wicked are rewarded here for their few righteous deeds in order that they may be more uninterruptedly and thoroughly punished after their death.[20]

Regression (ii): Fundamentalism of the Rabbis

The horrible story of Phinehas and the Midianite woman and the plague and the slaughter (Num. 25:1–18)[21] were to them [the Rabbis] as fully inspired and as true and as commendable as those passages in the Bible which breathe a very different spirit. They could make no distinctions. Sometimes, even as they deepen, and enlarge upon, the good things of Scripture, so they, in a wrong sense, improve upon the bad things, as when, for example, they say in this very section,[22] 'He who sheds the blood of the wicked is as he who brings a sacrifice.'[23] So, too, when they even condemn David because he showed kindness to Hanun the Ammonite, which they regard as against the spirit of Deut. 23:3–6,[24] and they quote Eccles. 7:16, 'Be not righteous over much', and say, 'A man should not seek to go beyond, or to be more virtuous than, the Law'; David sought to do a kindness to an Ammonite, whereas God had said, 'Thou shalt not seek their peace and their prosperity for ever.' Such was the burden of fundamentalism...[25]

The burden of the Old Testament

The real trouble with the Rabbis, the real check upon religious advance, was the burden of the Old Testament, the burden of the Book. For in spite of some efforts . . . to explain away, to reconcile the lower with the higher at the expense at the lower, it remains broadly true that to the Rabbis, the whole Old Testament, and especially the Pentateuch, was true and good and divine: the crudest statements about God were somehow not less true than the noblest; the taboo survivals – the red cow, the waters of impurity, the dietary regulations – were hardly less good, and were certainly no less divine, than 'Thou shalt bear no grudge, and shalt love thy neighbour as thyself'. . . . Moreover, the burden of the Book acted in another evil direction as well. It stimulated the passions and hatreds and prejudices of the natural man. There was only too much reason why the Rabbis should be intolerant, particularist, and narrow where the gentile and the 'nations' were concerned. Now the Old Testament, instead of checking these tendencies, did, upon the whole, stimulate and intensify them. It gave them the sanctity of religion. It threw over them the veneer of holiness. It gave them divine authority. Thus God is not made usually less partial in Rabbinic literature than He is in the Old Testament. He is usually more partial. He hates the enemies of Israel with an even deeper hatred. And, sometimes, painfully ingenious reasons are given for this partiality which makes it all the worse. The crude anthropomorphisms of the Old Testament are often imitated by the Rabbis. It is true that they do not seem to believe in these anthropomorphisms; but they were dangerous to use, and in Rabbinical literature they are often used in an unseemly and childish manner, which could not have effects for the good. It is even difficult to say how far all the Rabbis were perfectly aware that the anthropomorphisms were anthropomorphisms. They became entangled by them, and the burden of the Book often impaired the purity of their conceptions both of the divine nature and of the divine character. You cannot use crude and childish metaphors too long and too frequently without danger.[26]

THE RABBIS AND THE LAW

The Law: outward manifestation of inward spirituality

The Law does in a way present a compromise between primaries and secondaries. It has incorporated much of the prophetic teaching, but it has also watered it down. Or, perhaps, we should rather say that it has mingled primaries with secondaries for the very preservation of the primaries. Is it not the case that gold and silver coins need a certain amount of alloy in order to make them hard and durable? Human nature could not have accepted the pure teaching of the Prophets without any admixture. 'Seek me and live' was not enough, or it was too much. 'Let righteousness flow down as an everlasting stream' was not enough, or it was too much. Religion requires outward forms, visible signs, ceremonies, festivals. Moreover, religion is more than doing pious deeds. There is a service of God, there is a communion with God, there is an adoration of God, which is over and above the deeds of righteousness and love, and which, like them, takes time. Now this communion with God can be effected without any forms, and without any material help. A man can pray quietly in his heart, anywhere and at any time. But here again human nature needs, or shall we say more simply and truly, the vast majority of men and women need, the help of the outward, the visible, the formal. By the aid of the visible they find their way to the invisible.[27]

The study of the Law

The Rabbinic study of the Law seems to us today both strange and undesirable. Much of it was casuistic; much of it narrowing; much of it trifling; much of it an appalling waste of time and brain. Some of the Rabbinic laudations of various ritualistic prescriptions of the Law are to us positively distasteful, and when these laudations are even ascribed to God, they make unpleasant impressions. Such, for instance, are the many passages about circumcision. It is said, Some sections of the Law may seem ugly for public recitation, such as those about menstruation, or nightly pollution or issues, but God says they are pleasant to Me. Stress is laid upon the great importance of the sections about the sacrifices . . . But, nevertheless, the study of the Law has its good side. It kept the intellect alive; it was a form of idealism; it associated knowledge with religion. To bless God as the gracious giver of knowledge is a fine characteristic of Judaism. I am astonished, said one teacher, that the prayer for understanding is not used on Saturdays, for without understanding how can one pray? We have to translate this association of study and knowledge with religion into modern terms and apply it to modern needs. And this modern Rabbinic study of Law, however wrong-headed, however casuistic, however trivial, had one other great and noble distinction. It was disinterested and democratic. Jewish aristocracy became an aristocracy of learning, and this learning was free to all. Birth and wealth were nothing compared with knowledge. Let a proselyte become learned in the Law, and he was acknowledged superior to the most blue-blooded, native born Jew. Before the Law rich and poor were wholly equal. None must use the 'crown' of the Law for his own advantage . . . 'Happy is the man who delights in God's commandments,' says the Psalmist. Yes, remarks R. Eleazar, in the commandments, not in the reward of the commandments. And it is important to note, with all their insistence and glorification of the study of the Law, the Rabbis realised and proclaimed that the final object of study was practice. If study is said to be greater than practice, that is only because study leads to practice.[28]

The consequences of the Law

The Rabbinic literature shows us the Law as an ideal – as the source of joy and happiness and freedom; as the fountain of humility and justice and lovingkindness, as the means for obtaining the victory over sin, and for obtaining reconciliation with, and forgiveness from, God.

How, it may be fitly asked, did these good results come about? The answer, I think, may be found in two strangely held beliefs. First, that the Law was the gracious gift of the perfect God, the God who was supreme in lovingkindness and in justice and in wisdom. As His gift it shared His perfection . . . The second belief was that this wonderful creation of God had been delivered and

entrusted to Israel, and that it was Israel's privilege and preroga-
tive, its delight and its happiness, its glory and its honour, as well
as its duty and obligation, to observe its commands. This second
belief sank deeper and deeper into the hearts of the whole community. It caused a certain amount of objectionable particularism, of pride relative to the gentile, but as it gradually became the
belief of the whole community, it did away with the pride of one
section of the community over against any other section. For all
Israelites tended to become lovers of the Law, all tended to
become its humble followers within the limits of their power and
to the limits of their frailties. And it was especially the ceremonial
portions of the Law which seemed, and were believed, to be the
glory and distinction of Israel. The commands against murder,
robbery, incest, had been, so it was held, given to all the descen-
dents of Noah, but the ceremonial laws, from the Sabbath down,
shall we say, to the fringes on the borders of the garments had
been given only to Israel. Why had they been given? All sorts of
replies were offered, and the main replies sank deep into the
Jewish consciousness. It was held that the ceremonies were to be
a test of ready obedience to the inscrutable and not-to-be-
criticised will of the Father in heaven. Or, again, that they were
intended to connect every part of life – even the most seemingly
secular and ordinary parts – with the thought of God. Or that they
were meant to beautify life, to add to it adornment and joy, or
again to sanctify it, so that through them many passions and
instincts might be restrained and hallowed. Or, again, they were
meant to discipline and purify men; they were to be – as I must
mention again – the counter attraction and retort to the solicitations and temptations of the Yetzer ha-Ra, the evil impulse, the
source and instigator of iniquity and sin. Nevertheless, it is only
fair to say that the distinction between the ceremonial and moral
was not lost sight of, and the higher importance, though not
the superior beauty, of the moral laws was, upon the whole,
effectively maintained. And this happened for several reasons.
First, the enactments of the ceremonial law became more and
more obeyed by all sections of the community: the class of
persons who deliberately disobeyed them, or found them too
difficult to observe, became fewer and fewer. Secondly, the
Prophets taught Torah as well as the Law, and the teaching of the

Prophets was by no means ignored, even though it never entered the heads of the uncritical Rabbis that there was any opposition between the Prophets and the Law. Thirdly, most of the Rabbis were gifted with a strong dose of common sense. However delightful it was to kindle the Sabbath lights, or to observe the dietary laws, the Rabbis knew well enough that justice and mercy were more fundamental commands, more imperative for the well-being of society. Fourthly, another Rabbinic ideal – the imitation of God – tended in the same direction. 'As God is merciful, so you be merciful,' they said: but never, 'As God observes the Sabbath – for He does observe the Sabbath – so do you.' And the imitation ideal was tremendously strong.[29]

Holiness and the Law

In spite of Christian theologians (who are ignorant of the true effects of the Law and of the inner spiritual life of the orthodox Jewish congregations of the past and the present) the Law did produce holiness; it did sanctify life. In every generation it did produce a large number of saintly and holy persons – persons whom the purest and most spiritual and moral would declare to have been holy. It is true that, mixed up with that holiness, there were conceptions and practices which to us seem to have nothing to do with holiness; and it is true that these conceptions and practices have had evil effects: the ceremonial has sometimes triumphed over or submerged the moral. The legalism, which could and can be a noble and spiritual type of religion, became sometimes cheap, outward and mechanical. But it is also true that these very conceptions and practices which seem to us so distant and so strange were (and are) by the better and more religious minds in each generation wrought into the very texture of holiness itself; instead of spoiling the result, they formed part of its excellence; the outward was transfigured and became also inward. The mechanical forms were shot through with the purest spirituality; they were woven into the very warp and woof of the saintly life.[30]

Intellectualism and the Law

On the whole the good sense of the Rabbis enabled them to see that great as might be the study of the law, practical goodness was better still. 'He whose works exceed his wisdom, his wisdom shall endure.' That is the dominant teaching ... Unlike the priests, the Rabbis made no profit from their calling as teachers, and indeed repudiated the sinful idea that the law, as they expressed it, should be made a spade wherewith to dig. They were thus compelled to turn for their subsistence to ordinary occupations and handicrafts. But though doubtless the ideal was 'to have little business and be buried in Torah,' Rabban Gamaliel, son of Judah the prince, was wont to say: 'Excellent is the study of the law combined with some worldly occupation, for the labour demanded by them both makes sin to be forgotten. All study of the Torah without work must in the end be futile and become the cause of sin.'[31]

Nevertheless, a strong dash of intellectualism is a prominent feature of the Rabbinic religion. Its highest satisfaction is as much the study as the fulfilment of the law. The learned Rabbi has ever been the subject of the deepest veneration. To this day, among the orthodox communities in the east of Europe, there is no reputation so glorious as that given by knowledge of the law, and every family in all ranks of society is proud to possess some member who is learned in the Torah. To the Jew, the law with its study has ever been the great spiritual stimulus. It has saved him from sacerdotalism and priestcraft. It supplied for him the place for every possible sort of intellectual or artistic or even professional activity, from which his peculiar religion on the one hand, and the intolerance of medieval society on the other, kept him effectively away. It was the study as well as the fulfilment of the law which prevented the Jews from sinking in the scale of manhood, throughout the middle ages, intellectually and even morally. Like every other ideal, it had its evil side, and was capable of lamentable perversions: ideally, the study of the law is the equivalent of the study of perfect truth: practically, it is often the study of puerilities: the evolving of juridic hair-splittings upon the one hand, and fantastic and disordered imaginings on the other. In this capacity for perversion and degeneration it shared the fate of other ideals, some of which were even nobler than itself.[32]

Avoiding legalism

How was Judaism, which undoubtedly went through a long and intense legal stage, from which it is only now emerging (while even we do not wholly evict law from religion), enabled to avoid, or, at any rate, if it did not wholly avoid, yet largely to triumph over . . . dangers [of legalism?] Perhaps partly because of the very nature of the Law itself, and partly because the Sacred Scripture, while it contained the Law (which was regarded as the best and most inspired portion of the whole), yet also contained the Prophets and the Psalms. Or, in other words, because the prophetic teaching was never wholly forgotten, or because the Prophets (inconsistent with the Law as their teaching partly was) had yet partly begotten and produced the Law. No priest, no law; but also, in this case, no prophet, no law.

Now the Law not only included a number of ceremonial enactments, both positive and negative, but as a code it did contain those moral and spiritual dangers which have already been pointed out. On the other hand, the Law included enactments which could only with difficulty be fulfilled in an outward, perfunctory, self-regarding, cheese-paring and selfish way. It asked for the love of neighbour and of the resident alien, it asked for the love of God. And these two laws were moved from early days (let it be noted, not merely by Jesus) to a position of superiority and of primacy. Again, the heart was not wholly quenched even in the Law! The neighbour was not to be hated in the heart; God was to be loved with all the heart. 'Thou shalt not covet': the tenth word could hardly be obeyed except from the heart.

But these are, perhaps, casuistical elegances. The real and fundamental reason I conceive why the dangers were so often and so largely avoided was because the Prophets and the Law together succeeded somehow in making the service of God into a passion. God and His Law were loved, and they were loved not merely because men were asked to love them. God and His Law were so loved that the fulfilment of the Law was carried out for its own sake, and not merely for the sake of reward. And pity and kindness are such characteristics of the Law that they, too, sank deep into the Jewish heart, and were performed for more than reward, and more than outwardly, and more than perfunctorily. God was so loved that the imitation of Him was sought for its own sake. And to imitate God meant pity, meant Chesed, meant a good and holy life, meant a tender and loving heart. Believe that God is good and love Him, and all the rest follows. Believe that He is pitiful and loving as well as just and holy, and whatever your system, be it legal or be it Pauline, so long as you love Him enough, true goodness and uncalculating unselfishness will ensue.[33]

Honouring the Law and God

[It is] the extreme simplicity of the Rabbinic religion, coupled with its variety, which specially appeals to us. There is no lack of ideas, and these ideas are conveyed in very simple words and forms. And this strange simplicity seems to be connected with another strange point about it, namely its odd combination of professionalism with the attitude of the common man. The literature was written by Rabbis for Rabbis; by the learned for the learned; by a class for a class, and yet, so far as its religious and moral teaching is concerned (apart from its laws and its legal discussions), it might be largely written for everybody. On the whole, the attitude is sane and simple and broad. It does not give religious and moral teaching for a class; on the whole, its teaching is for everybody. On the whole, the very virtues it expects the student of the Law to bring to, and to get from, his study are the virtues which all men ought to seek for, and which all men may practise. On the whole, the study of the Law ought to unite you with your fellows in humility and service rather than to separate you from them in pride and the spirit of caste. The Rabbis were very keen that the Law should be honoured, and so, too, God, by the good conduct of those who studied it. The name of God is to be made beloved by you, they say. If a man studies Torah, and is upright and is gracious and polite in his dealings with his fellows, they say of him, Such a one has learnt Torah: see how comely are his ways, how upright are his actions! It is an injury to the Law and a profanation of the name when a Rabbi's conduct causes his fellows to say the reverse.[34]

THE RABBIS AND THE NEW TESTAMENT

The Rabbis and Jesus (i): Priorities

He [Jesus] sought to bring back into glad communion with God those whom sin, whether 'ceremonial' or 'moral', had driven away. For him, sinners (at least certain types of sinners) were the subject not of condemnation and disdain, but of pity. He did not avoid the sinners, but sought them out. They were still children of God. This was a new and sublime contribution to the development of religion and morality. When tenderly nurtured women work in the streets of London, and seek to rescue the degraded victims of deceptions or cruelty, they are truly following in the footsteps of their Master. But it should be noted that there is nothing anti-Jewish in the bearing and teaching of Jesus on this matter. It is only a development of the best Old Testament teaching, and it fits in with the Rabbinic teaching upon repentance. But to deny the greatness and originality of Jesus in this connection, to deny that he opened a new chapter in men's attitudes towards sin and sinners, is, I think, to beat the head against a wall. Nevertheless, the Rabbis would not have condemned Jesus merely because he cared for the outcast, the poor, and the sinner. They too welcomed the repentant sinner. And they were intensely eager to relieve distress, to mitigate suffering. Any other description of them is untrue. But the Law came first. God came before themselves, even before their neighbour. And Jesus says that a man for the sake of the Kingdom must on occasion leave his father or hate his mother, so they would have said that all other relationships must be put lower than the Law of God. If your father bids you transgress the Law, do not obey him. The enactments by which they developed the written Law were not a benefit to themselves; they were honestly intended as a fence and honour to the Law.[35]

The Rabbis and Jesus (ii): Forgiveness

It would be very difficult to answer the question: which teaches, on the whole, a more forgiving conception of God – the Jesus of the Synoptic Gospels or the Rabbis. We have a number of exquisite and tender sayings such as Matt. 18:14,[36] but these are counterbalanced by Matt. 25:41–46[37] and similar passages, where 'aeonian' and painful hell is declared to be the lot of the wicked. We have also such a hard and gloomy utterance as that in Matt. 7:13–14,[38] which seems to teach that those who perish shall be far more numerous than those who shall be saved. We have a cruel denunciation and threat, such as Matt. 11:20–24.[39] But it has also to be recognised that the main strain of the Synoptic teaching is (a) sound as regards the purely ethical tests for salvation or destruction, as the case may be; (b) of a less nationalistic tendency than that of the Rabbis; (c) less burdened by verses in the O.T. of a low ethical quality; and (d) more definitely solicitous for the 'little ones' or the 'simple'. The new particularism of creed had hardly begun to rear its ugly head in the Synoptic Gospels. The Rabbis were more 'nationalist' than Jesus: their hostility to the idolator and the alien (who for them mean so largely and often the oppressors and the 'Romans') was more intense and more constant. As regards sinners in Israel, so long as these were not anti-Rabbinic 'enemies,' the Rabbis were, I should think, no less eager for their repentance than Jesus, though they did not, like him, seek them out and try actively to convert them to righteousness. The O.T. burden was, however, very grave for them. It reinforced the hatreds and animosities of the natural man. Jesus did not, I should imagine, know the O.T. in the same wonderful way that they did. Nor did he regard it in the same way. He had present in his consciousness and memory only those verses which had specially struck him, or which chimed in with his own teaching. He was more independent and inspired. The Rabbis knew the O.T. too painfully well, and to them, unfortunately, all the statements about God in the O.T. were almost equally true. Thus, if God is said to 'hate' Edom, if he is said to 'laugh at' the wicked, all of whom he will at the last 'destroy' (and we know that there are many similar passages), all these sayings must somehow be true – just as true as the loving and beautiful and tender sayings, and they all came in most conveniently, and were most 'handy', when nationalistic and particularistic animosities craved biblical sanction. On the whole, the Rabbis come out of this great difficulty fairly well; but if both Jesus and they equally believe in hell and in its eternity (and I see no difference here), there is, sometimes, in the Rabbinic conception, more zest attributed to God in the destruction of enemies who are both his enemies and Israel's.[40]

The Rabbis and Paul

Paul doubtless declared that in the Messiah Jesus there was neither Jew nor Greek: he made the new religion independent of race. He broke down the shackles which had so greatly hindered the diffusion of Judaism beyond the limits of a single nation. He showed that religion was something gloriously wider than any single people. But, in destroying one kind of shackles, he created another. In shattering old fetters, he forged new ones. And these new fetters, though related to morality, were yet distinct from it. All who believe in the Messiah Jesus are on an equality, be their race, their social condition, or their sex, what it may. But what of those who do not believe in him? These are left in, or relegated to, the outer darkness. And just as the Jews were tempted to declare (in order to save the moral situation) that every heathen was of necessity a sinner, so were Christians soon tempted to describe those who rejected – and even those who were ignorant of – Christ. The unbeliever not because he is of one particular race, but in virtue of his unbelief, is a child of perdition and sin. And, in some ways, this particularism, when 'faith' is partly degraded to an intellectual assent to certain theological dogmas and subtleties, is more shocking, more calumniating to the goodness of God, than the particularism of the Rabbis.

Moreover, the fetters of Pauline Christian particularism proved more heavy and powerful than the fetters of race. The Gospel became more pitiless than the Law. And the Christian fetters lasted, with small breaks and loosenings, till modern times.

Some dubious exceptions were made for Socrates and Plato, and a few others of the heroes of Greece and of Rome, but neither the ancient nor the Medieval Church ever enunciated the doctrine: 'the righteous, be their religious beliefs what they may, have a share in the blessedness of the world to come.'

The Rabbis, however, to their great credit and glory, broke down their nationalist particularism, even while the credal particularism of the Church was hardly penetrated by any serious breach. In an early Rabbinic treatise we find the immortal saying: 'The righteous of all nations shall have a share in the world to come.' In their words: not genealogy, but conduct, is the passport to heaven. It is true that a Rabbi could hardly have conceived a man as righteous who did not believe in One God. But, nevertheless, not religious belief, but conduct is made the condition. The righteous: he it is who is 'saved.' Righteousness – not race, not belief – that is what God cares for, looks to and demands.[41]

The future life and punishment

The growth and acceptance of the doctrine of the future life and of a judgement beyond the grave made many differences in the teaching about divine retribution, whether in the New Testament or in the Rabbinic literature. . . . The greater the prosperity here, the more assured can be the punishment hereafter, and the more poignant the earthly calamity, the more exquisite and the more permanent will be the bliss of the future and its felicity. Again, reward on earth tends to be material; reward beyond the grave is spiritual. 'Eye has not seen and ear has not heard.' The reward is neither proportionate to the virtue, nor is it of the same kind as the earthly prosperity of wickedness.

The doctrines of the 'world to come', of the resurrection, and of the future life tend by their very nature to modify the crudities of the old teaching of retribution and tit for tat. It is true that God rewards and punishes, but both reward and punishment are out of proportion to the deed. For my own part, I see in the punishment doctrine, both of the New Testament and the Rabbis, an ethical injustice. Finite faults receive infinite punishments; the New Testament especially seems to ignore the doctrine that punishment is disciplinal. If for any earthly sin, however heinous, the punishment is either to last for ever or to consist in complete annihilation (and both Jesus and Paul seem to have thought that the lot of the wicked would be either one or the other), it is hopelessly unsuited to, and unworthy of, a Deity who has created the souls of men, and is described as love. It is idle to defend the odious doctrine by saying that man's liberty to sin is a necessary corollary of his capacity to be really good, and that

112

when the will is fixedly hostile to the good, external exclusion from beatitude is inevitable. The God of Jesus and Paul did not work by formulae such as these. If He condemns certain people to eternal perdition, or to eternal absence from felicity, or to annihilation, He does so because He thinks it to be right and just. He need not do so. The responsibility for the perdition is as much His as it is the sinner's, and even more. Hence, so far as the wicked are concerned, the New Testament helps not at all. On the contrary. The material prosperity of the wicked on earth is a much less terrible puzzle than what is predicted of their fate by Jesus and by Paul. A loving God and a fiery hell from which there is, so far as we can gather, no return; out of which, so far as we are told, there is no escape – that is a worse inconsistency than anything in the pages of the Old Testament. There, at all events, God's punishments are ended by death![42]

Faith and works

The Rabbinic religion knows nothing of any opposition between faith and works. The difficulties and problems which are raised by Paul in the Epistle to the Galatians and to the Romans were unfelt by them and would hardly have been understood. As we have seen, the Law, so far from being a burden, was a joy. So far from being an incitement or stimulus to sin – by awaking a desire the satisfaction of which it forbade – the Law was regarded as a medicine which prevented such desires from becoming masterful and overpowering. It was never doubted that man could, as he ought to, fulfil – up to a point – the laws of God, laws which would not have been given to him, if the power had not also been given to him to fulfil them. To order men to fulfil laws which they cannot fulfil would have been cruel. But God was not cruel, but merciful. He gave the Law, not to show its futility, but its usefulness, its beauty, and its joy. It is true that man often fails to fulfil it – he often sins; but such sins are inseparable from the very constitution of a being who is set between the animal and the angel: half earthly and half divine. There would be no discipline and no joy (to say nothing of no merit!) in fulfilment if to fulfil were inevitable. There would be no educative obedience if there were not the possibility of disobedience. In spite of occasional complaints about the power of the evil Yetzer ['inclination'],

113

there was no feeling of despair. The cry, 'Who shall deliver me from the body of death?' is, on the whole, an un-Rabbinic cry. The Rabbis won their way to God on their own lines. And with their strong, but rarely unethical, belief in God's mercy and forgiveness, they were not daunted by failure and lapses. The Law remained medicine and joy, and not burden and poison. Indeed (but this, perhaps, was a direct polemic against Paul, and therefore less interesting), they wanted the desire to be felt in order that the Law should be the more purely and powerfully fulfilled. To abstain from eating the pig or from unchastity, what virtue and glory in that? But to abstain because the commandment bids you abstain, this is the right fulfilment of the Law and true service to God. The paradox is obvious – but no less obvious is its spirit. And just as there was little trouble as regards the Law because of human frailty, so there was little trouble because of any conflict between works and faith. There are few and rare indications in the Rabbinic literature of any theoretic unbelief, whether in the existence or in the power of God. It was needless to say: 'believe', because all the Rabbis did believe and no suffering made them sceptical. Belief or trust in God was as natural to the Rabbis as belief in the regularity of night following day. And faith in the sense of making the Law in any of its parts superfluous would have seemed absurd or unintelligible. This seems to be the reason why the references to faith occur with such comparative infrequency . . . the Rabbis were quite alert to its virtues, but they largely took it for granted: they did not theorise it, or dogmatise about it, and it would have greatly surprised them if they had been made to understand that the faith of Abraham, which they praised no less than the great antagonist, could actually be placed in opposition to the works of the Law.[43]

CHAPTER FOUR
MODERN JUDAISM

INTRODUCTION

Reform Judaism originated in Germany and quickly spread to America. Its appearance can be traced to nineteenth-century Jewish intellectual movements which responded to linguistic[1] and political emancipation. As a child of the Enlightenment Reform was an attempt to discover modern forms for an ancient faith. Increasing religious freedom in Western Europe and America had resulted in an ever-increasing adaptation by Jews of their local culture. Acculturalisation led many to believe that their Jewishness would no longer be an obstacle to being accepted into Christian society. Those who were disappointed with their slow progress in society felt that baptism might provide the 'emancipation' which being a Jew did not.

German Protestantism was one important influence upon Reform in its early stages. The synagogue and, in particular, the Sabbath service was contrasted by many with the order of Protestant services. The lack of beauty and decorum led to demands for changes including calls for a choir, organ accompaniment and use of the vernacular.[2] Christian influence or otherwise, the early reformers dealt with Jewish liturgy in such a way that the service was shortened and the vernacular was used, notably in sermons.[3] Actual systematic worship reform began in Hamburg where the new Israelite Temple Association was founded in 1817. The use of the word 'temple' indicated the community's acceptance of Germany as the homeland for German Jews. It was probably no coincidence that the temple was dedicated on the anniversary of the Battle of Leipzig, again emphasising the Jewish community's loyalty to Germany.

Throughout its early period (1780–1820), Reform was still groping for a clear viewpoint. More far-reaching changes than the use of the vernacular were needed if it were to make a positive impact upon much of the Jewish community. Those leaders who did embrace radical changes often did not recognise the implications of their own programmes. In addition, the rationalism of the Enlightenment offered few answers, it merely set forward many questions. Moses Mendelssohn managed to avoid conflict in his lifetime between traditional Judaism and the new world – succeeding generations, including his children, were not so fortunate. Like those of Israel Jacobson and thousands of others, Mendelssohn's children converted to Christianity.[4]

Most of the changes which the Reformers introduced during this period were external. However, the Jewish community, far from being the lifeless body some believed it to be, was immediately shaken by these changes. A huge controversy broke out over the subject of reform, the ramifications of which still affect Jewish life 150 years after the first Reform synagogue was established in Hamburg.

Various factors made the controversy more complex. First, the authorities involved themselves in the community's affairs, often backing the religious establishment who opposed the reformers.[5] Second, there were radicals among the reformers who alienated themselves, as well as much of the Reform movement, from the traditional community. They appeared to take a negative stance, fighting more for what should be left out of Judaism than for what should be kept in. These reformers, whose views were summarised in the Frankfurt Platform of 1843, will be discussed shortly. Third, and perhaps most importantly, Jews were tremendously ignorant of their religion and history. This was a major reason for the high assimilation and conversion rate. Emancipation combined with ignorance only led to stagnation. Jews had to be made acquainted with Judaism. Without much knowledge religious debates were bitter and inertia and conservatism were the consequences. The survival of Reform Judaism and the vitality of European Judaism appeared to be in jeopardy.[6]

In response to this ignorance among the majority of Jews Leopold Zunz founded the Society for the Advancement of the Science of Judaism ('Verein für die Cultur und die Wissenschaft des Judentums') in 1819. Zunz gave Judaism a scientific basis and spirit as well as a literary rebirth. It was he who offered Reform Judaism the lifeline it needed and some of his disciples became its most important leaders.[7]

Reform Judaism thus witnessed the rise of more scholarly leaders. External changes in the liturgy no longer dominated their thought but, with the powerful tool of the 'Wissenschaft', Reform Jews tried to answer the question: how can Jewish ways be adapted to modernity? It was essential to supply answers because, in ever growing numbers, their generation no longer tolerated the discipline which had maintained Jewish communities in the past. The older generation could furnish no philosophy which could hold the young and, consequently, Judaism appeared not as a path to modernity but as its obstacle. Assimilation and conversion became a temptation which many could not resist.

Under the leadership of Abraham Geiger, a disciple of Zunz, Reform rabbis, with university and traditional religious education, laid stress on what they understood to be the principles of Judaism. In order to provide the self-respect required to preserve the essentials of Jewish life they emphasised the need to increase among Jews knowledge of Jewish history and literature. This learning would also supply knowledge of, and the justification for, development in Judaism.

In Geiger's view Judaism was an evolving organism whose present and future were intimately related to its past.[8] For example, he and other reformers appealed to the Talmud as a source for their development of the liturgy.[9] The radical reformers, however, were not in favour of appealing to the Talmud. The Frankfurt Platform, which represented the views of the most radical Reformers, rejected its authority[10] and some rejected circumcision.[11]

The radicals made little impact upon German Reform with the exception of the Berlin community where the rabbi, Samuel Holdheim, led the service entirely in the vernacular with Sabbath services moved to Sunday.[12] Holdheim was a major opponent of Geiger and argued that Judaism should be understood as revolutionary and not evolutionary. His work and thought found little scope for growth in Germany but played a significant role in the American Reform movement.

Reform Judaism in America was expressed in scattered episodes until the appearance of Isaac Meyer Wise in 1846.[13] It was Wise's leadership and vigour which gave American Reform the stimulus it needed. The movement was heavily influenced by German Reform and most of its early leaders (including Wise himself) were immigrants from German-speaking countries. Wise was a moderate who hoped to unify American Jewish life. His friendship with many conservative Jews, such as Isaac Leeser, was part of an endeavour to maintain religious unity. He agreed with traditional Jews that the Pentateuch was the basic source for Judaism while the radical reformers emphasised the importance of the prophetical literature. Wise repeatedly advocated the foundation of an American Union of Congregations and a Rabbinical College.[14]

Wise was opposed by radical reformers who, under the leadership of David Einhorn, emphasised the gulf between Reform and Orthodoxy.[15] Before long a major split developed at a conference in Cleveland in 1855.

The initial confrontation centred around what should be the correct Reform attitude towards the Talmud. Samuel Holdheim represented the radical position when he stated: 'the Talmud speaks with the ideology of its own time and for that time it was right. I speak from the higher ideology of my time, and for this age I am right.'[16] The conference eventually decided that the Talmud 'contains the traditional and logical exposition of the Biblical laws, which must be expounded and practised according to the comments of the Talmud'.[17] This apparent victory for the moderates was short-lived and the major Reform conference of the century, which took place in Pittsburgh in 1885, clarified the Reform position for the next 50 years. The radicals dominated the conference and the wording of its declarations. Their success was marked by the publication of the Reform prayer book which was based upon Einhorn's work Olath Tamid (Eternal Light) rather than Wise's Minhag America (American Custom).[18] Decisive discussions were also held about the Sabbath. Unlike the German Reformers, many American Reform communities offered services on Sundays. Such synagogues included 'Har Sinai' (Baltimore), 'Kenesset Yisrael' (Philadelphia), and 'Emanuel' (New York). The Pittsburgh conference supported Sabbath services on Sundays where it seemed necessary to a congregation.[19]

American Reformers, like their German counterparts, held an ambivalent attitude towards Zionism. Their outlook was not dissimilar to that of their Orthodox brethren. Both rejected the idea of Palestine becoming a national homeland for the Jews.[20]

The rise of Reform in Britain has to be seen in the context of events in Germany and America as well as in the particular character of British life. Although Todd Endelman, in his study of Jews in Georgian England, has emphasised the primary importance of British history in understanding the history of Anglo-Jewry, we must equally bear in mind the history of Reform in Germany and America as discussed in the preceding pages.[21]

In the nineteenth century Anglo-Jewry was dominated by approximately six aristocratic families. Some were members of British cabinets and governments; all had integrated successfully into the economic, political and social life of the country. They represented the assimilated Jewish population which existed before the great immigration in the latter half of the nineteenth century. These 'Grand Dukes' of Anglo-Jewry have been described as the 'Cousinhood', for any 'member' who wanted to 'marry into his class or faith could hardly have avoided marrying a relative . . .'.[22] Until the 1920s the Anglo-Jewish establishment was dominated by this intertwined network of Jewish millionaires. Any major change in the structure of Anglo-Jewry could not occur unless it were supported by members of this elite.

It is thus no surprise to learn that the founding members of the West London Synagogue were all members, by some relation or another, of the Cousinhood. The success of the West London Synagogue can be traced directly to its support among members of the Cousinhood. The synagogue was bitterly attacked by the more traditional members of the community but its supporters were powerful enough to prevent its demise.[23]

It might be asked why this Reform community was so conservative, well behind the radicalism of Germany and America, and unwilling to shake loose from tradition. It appeared to be reformist in spite of itself.[24] Some might respond that it was British to be conservative.[25] What might be more important to remember is that the Reform synagogue was established not for religious but for social reasons. Although external changes were instigated, this split in Anglo-Jewry was not occasioned by religious arguments.

The Jewish Religious Union, on the other hand, was not only founded by two members of the Cousinhood, Claude Montefiore and Lily Montagu, but, in addition, was based upon religious disagreements with the Orthodox authorities. Without the support of the Cousinhood members, the Union would have met the same fate as the Sunday Movement and other radical religious groups who had no powerful supporters. With their support the Union survived to become the most radical force in Anglo-Jewry. Its radical basis was founded upon its antipathy for and opposition to the traditional Anglo-Jewish establishment. The Jewish Religious Union responded to what it saw as the failure of the United Synagogue and the stagnation of the West London Synagogue. Its foundation was based upon religion and not aristocracy. Thus, the Jewish Religious Union, perhaps even unknown to itself at first, had been established as the alternative religious movement in Britain.

THE BIBLE

The foundation of Liberal Judaism

However great and significant the changes in Liberal Judaism from many of the doctrines, or even from the prevailing doctrines of the Old Testament may be, still more remarkable, perhaps, is the fact that Liberal Judaism still finds in the Old Testament both its spiritual ancestry and its nourishment. It may be that, as I have shown, we have made the secondary primary, and the primary secondary, that we have put what was occasional and sporadic into the forefront and into the centre. It may be that we have expanded and curtailed, modified and spiritualised. But our very inspiration to do all this has been, in some measure, the Old Testament itself. We have had Amos and Isaiah for our teachers; they have pointed out to us the way. There is hardly a conception or a doctrine of ours which does not go back, even if only in germ, to the Hebrew Bible. It is true that we have to abandon certain prevailing doctrines, but we do not abandon, we only expand and deepen, strengthen and confirm, the most fundamental doctrines of all. God's unity and righteousness, the inseparable union of religion and morality, the election of Israel for a religious mission and service, the joy of communion with God – these doctrines, the essence of our Judaism today, are all found in the pages of the Hebrew Bible. The supreme revelations of the Hebrew Bible constitute the core of our Judaism, the core of our own religion, the core, as we believe, of the future religion of all mankind. We, too, can say of this book, as the gentile proselytes are to say of Zion, 'All my fountains are in thee.'[26]

Religion and the Bible

All the fundamental requisites of religion may be justly said to be found within the Hebrew Bible. Some of them are, as it were, fully worked out. For some of them there is much material; for others only a little. Some are stated with clarity that is adequate for all time; some are only hinted at: we have only pointings and indications. From the Hebrew Bible a grand religion can be adduced: upon it a grand religion can be built up. For the foundations, and for much of the superstructure. Our foundation; our superstructure. Jews ought to make themselves well acquainted with the foundation and superstructure. I do not say that they should stop there. The Rabbis added much to the building, and some of what they added is fine and everlasting. It is well worth knowing. Later generations added in their turn, and we are still adding today. The spirit of God moves among us still. Nor would I say that Jews should not study the religious documents of other religions, whether of ancient or of modern times. . . . We are free to develop and to add, but from our own basis. Firmly anchored in Judaism, and with a good knowledge of our Jewish treasures, we may legitimately explore what other religions and other literatures have to offer us. To add and develop is one thing: to splash about, or hunt about, vaguely is another. The highest teachings of the Hebrew Bible can give us a standard. We can test what we read outside by asking: How far do the 'outside' consort with those highest teachings? How far do they consort with the pure monotheism of the Prophets, the Psalms and the Rabbis when these three are at their highest and best?[27]

Divinity of the Bible

The divinity of the Bible can only be proved by the goodness and truth of the Bible. The Bible itself has played a very large part in educating us, and in enabling us to perceive its goodness and truth. Certain utterances, certain statements, are not good and true because they are found in the Bible, but the Bible by including them has been a chief means by which we have gained a knowledge of them, and by which we have, as it were, had our conscience so purified, so moralised, that it can now serve to us as a clearer and surer test than it might have done had there been no Bible to instruct us. Thus the Bible has helped us to prove its own divinity by its own excellence. For divinity means to us eternal righteousness and truth. If you ask me to believe that a book, a law, a saying, is divine, you must ask me to believe that it is divine because it is good and true, and I can only be asked to believe that it is good and true if my conscience, after sifting the matter as best I can, consulting other persons wiser and better

123

than I, and maturely weighing and considering the question all round, allows me to hold and believe that it is good and true. If goodness is the test of divinity, divinity cannot be the test of goodness. And, after all, for us today there is no meaning in divinity except goodness and truth. A bad or false God is a contradiction in terms . . .

Now, if this be so, if, namely, the measure of the divinity of the Bible is its measure of goodness and truth and of its influence for goodness and truth, then surely its divineness is very great. But it is not all divine, for it is not all perfectly good, and all perfectly true. There is a lower human element as well as a higher divine element, for though the Bible is all written by men, yet, in the light of what has already been said in this book, it is true to say that its goodness and truth are divine, and that its errors and inadequacies are human. Yet we have always to remember that what may be inadequate for us now and even erroneous, may in its own day have been a moral advance. Hence even in what is now recognised as an error there may be past inspiration.

What we get from examining the Bible itself is what we might expect before we began. For we could not expect to find perfection in any human product. Perfection is the inalienable quality of God, which even he cannot grant to the beings whom he has made. Perfect righteousness, perfect truth, are not capable of being embodied in any book, or of being contained in any single generation or in any human mind. The Divine spirit, as we believe, helps the human spirit in its growth and development. God reveals himself in different degrees to man, but the most inspired writer or speaker is still a man; his inspiration is no guarantee that he will not make mistakes. He will exaggerate; he will err; he will have his national limitations and prejudices. Even in his very conceptions of righteousness he will remain, in many ways, the child of his age. All this we should expect a priori, for the divine cannot be completely contained in a human brain, a human heart, a human will. God cannot make man his secretary or phonograph; in his perfection God remains alone. No human being can be invested with absoluteness. The errors and limitations which we find in every collection of words attributed to a man, however much also attributed to God, are just what we might expect.[28]

Inspiration

We can only say that such and such teaching, or that such and such a writing, is inspired by our estimate of the actual words, the actual contents. God has put no other test into our hands. When I say 'we', I do not mean, however, that the judgement of others, the judgement of our forefathers, and the judgement of the civilised world, is to go for nothing and that 'we' – each individual – must begin all over again. All I mean here is that the test of inspiration is the product of inspiration upon the human mind. The test of the beauty of a picture is not that it was painted by Watts: the test of the beauty of the picture is the picture itself. Nor do we say that because some of the pictures by Watts are adorably beautiful therefore everything which he painted must be equally fine. We cannot even say: such and such words of a prophet or teacher seem to us inspired; therefore all his words are inspired; or, therefore all his words which he thought inspired were inspired. The test of inspiration is not what he thought; still less is the test that his writing or words are included in a certain book, which many people have believed to be inspired in all its contents from beginning to end.

The gauge of inspiration can only be the actual content of the words together with their effects for goodness and truth: the content of the words, including their originality, power, beauty, influence, and so on. It is not the place where they are found which makes them inspired; it is themselves – their own value, importance, originality, excellence, truth . . .

[Consequently] we find in the Bible much which is sublimely true and great, and which – as we believe – will always be so regarded; much which teaches and helps and strengthens and comforts us, as it taught and helped and strengthened and comforted our forefathers; much which was, and is, and (as we believe) will always be, considered as the essential doctrines of our religion, its very kernel or foundation. On the other hand, we find in the Bible some things which we discern to be inconsistent with its best and sublimest portions, and others which, though they may have played their part, and have been of use, in days gone by, seem to us today no longer valuable or beautiful or true.

However much we may wish that we could discern no imperfection in the orations of a particular prophet, or in the laws of a particular code, we must never juggle with our conscience, or play fast and loose with our reason. For conscience and reason are the two noblest and divinest of all God's gifts, and it is our duty to follow whither they lead. Let us never seek to say: 'this is good and true,' unless we sincerely believe that it is good and true. Let us, moreover, never lower the level of the best by seeking to put what is less good upon the same height. People who have tried to maintain the equal excellence, truth and inspiration of the whole Bible, or of the whole Law, or of all the Prophets, have only done the Bible, Law, and Prophets an ill turn. We shall gain more general adhesion to the best and greatest by freely acknowledging the presence of the less good, or even, it may be, here and there, of the not good.[29]

The Old Testament and truth

The new conception of the Old Testament takes a very different view of it. Religious and moral truth, it holds, in their perfection and completeness, cannot be contained in any book. They are only progressively revealed to man's heart and understanding. The Old Testament is not homogeneous in faith or doctrine. It has higher and lower elements; permanently good and noble elements, together with other elements which were good in their own day, but are good no more. What is good and true in it is of God in the same sense that we hold that whatever is good and true has God as its author and source. Because of its good and true teachings, because of its transcendent originality and excellence in matters of religion, because of its immense issues for good we call it, and believe it to be, a divinely inspired book.

Clearly this view of it does not separate it by a great gulf from all other 'sacred' books. They too, in proportion to their originality, their excellence and influence for good, may be 'inspired' and 'divine'. The Old Testament contains much truth, but not all truth. Nor is it all true. God may have chosen that the sacred books of the other nations and creeds should also contain, together with much error, many elements of new truth, supplementary and complementary to the truths of the Hebrew Scriptures. There is nothing a priori unlikely or inconceivable in the

126

idea that he should have done so. In fact, the more we think of it, the more we consider analogies in other spheres of his rule and providence, the more is it unlikely that he should have desired all truth to enter into the world by a single gateway or channel.[30]

THE LAW

Is Judaism still a legal religion?

It is clear that our Judaism is a not a legal religion in the same sense as the Judaism of our forefathers. We no longer put the Pentateuch, as it were, between our consciences and God. We no longer accept all of its ordinances as binding and divine. We no longer think that to be religious means to fulfil a series of laws – a series of doings and avoidings. In our rejection of the absolute authority of the Pentateuchal code as a whole, in our insistence upon spirit and being and character as well as, even more than, upon doing and observance, we differ from the conceptions of many of our forefathers. Is our religion, then, no longer rightly to be characterised as a legal religion at all? Has the Law no place in our conception of religion? It is to these questions that we have now to address ourselves.

First of all, then, as regards the Pentateuch. No phase of Judaism can forget the place which that book, or collection of books, has held in history. The Law – the Law of the Pentateuch – has been a great source of Jewish heroism and of Jewish holiness. The Law, and the study of Law, have prevented the Jews from succumbing morally, spiritually and intellectually to persecution and degradation.

Nor can we forget that the framework of the Jewish religion has come to us through the Law, just as, in its narratives, the Law tells us of the origins of our race and of the beginnings of its history as a nation. We fill this framework with fresh meaning, but the framework itself comes to us from the Law. Passover, Pentecost, Tabernacles, the Day of Memorial and, above all, the Day of Atonement – all these owe their origin to the Law.

But there is much more still. As we pass from the Ceremonial to the Moral, we are arrested half-way by that remarkable institution, which in one aspect is ceremonial, in another aspect is moral – the Sabbath. Whatever the origin of the Sabbath may be, beyond and outside the Hebrews, its origin for us and for the world is the Pentateuch and the Decalogue. Who shall measure the beneficent effects of the Sabbath upon our own brotherhood and upon the world at large?

Then we pass from the Sabbath to the Decalogue in which it is contained. Are there not laid down here for all time some of the foundations of human society, of human law and order, of monotheistic religion? The sanctity of human life, the sanctity of marriage, the sanctity of truth – are these three not proclaimed here in no uncertain terms? What praise is not deserved for the Tenth Word, which sets a curb to human appetite, and demands that sin should be checked at its source? . . .

But the Pentateuch is not limited to the Decalogue. We remember, in devout homage and gratitude, that it contains also the famous declaration of the Divine Unity. Here too we need not worry our heads as to what the Hebrew words originally meant. That is a question of great interest truly to scholars and antiquarians; it is sufficient for us to know that for more than two thousand years they have meant little less than they mean for us today. They have meant that there is one God only, and that this sole God is One.

What follows upon this solemn declaration of Monotheistic faith? 'Thou shalt love the Lord thy God' – the injunction which lies at the basis of our theism, the injunction which implies there can be and is a communion between God and man, and that on man's side this communion can and should reach to the heights of love . . .

Though we have passed beyond many of the conditions and conceptions of the Pentateuch, we yet recognise that here we find the ideal of social righteousness, the ideal that here upon the earth, with divine help and sanction, man must seek to establish the kingdom of God.

'Justice, purity, compassion, combined with simple happiness and gratitude, these are the ideals of the Pentateuch, and these are the ideals (for earth) of Judaism today.'

The Pentateuch throws them into the form of laws. In the honour which we pay to the Pentateuch for all these reasons, in the place which we give to it in our worship and in our synagogues, we may still rightly denominate Judaism as, in that sense at all events, a 'legal' religion even today.

But this is not all. There is another and a deeper, a more

'inward' and essential, sense in which it can be rightly said that Judaism is, partially at any rate, a legal religion . . .

[Judaism holds that] man has to recognise a Must, a Compulsion, a Law, which by his own efforts, and by the help of God, he can more and more completely fulfil and obey. He has to bow down in homage and reverence to that Law – the Law of duty – and in the reverence, and in the free fulfilment of it, he has to find, and he will find, his true human freedom.[31]

God and the Law

The consciousness, the conviction, that the moral Law is both God's Law and my Law, not merely mine and not merely his, help me to fulfil it. If it were only the mere arbitrary Law of the stronger – to be executed on pain of punishment and hope of reward – I should have no inward desire to perform its enactments; I should not bow down in willing surrender to its compulsion, and do glad homage to its majesty. If it were merely the Law of my own being, however much I might recognise that in its fulfilment I best realised myself, I might be more indifferent to its commands. Why should I not do as I please with my own will? But it is in the combination of its aspects – God's Law is my Law, and my Law is God's Law; the Law within is the Law without, and the Law without is the Law within – that is where its seductive compulsiveness lies. Here is the secret of its success; the key to its sweet and persuasive constraint; here is the realisation that bondage to the law is also the highest freedom, and that he who is the most devoted servant of God is also His child, that servitude is liberty and submission is independence.

Thus to us too, adherents to Liberal Judaism, the Law is still precious. It is the symbol of our free surrender to the God who is our Master and our father, joyful acknowledgement that His will must be ours. The Law, we admit, does, in one sense, create sin. If we had no consciousness of right, we should have no consciousness of wrong. The acceptance of the Law implies the possibility of breaking it. But, in a higher sense, the Law helps us, as the Rabbis taught and rightly taught, to dominate the evil inclination, and to resist its solicitations. If we do wrong because of the Law, much more do we do right. The Law pulls us up, and drives us forward, by its attractiveness. Majestic and beautiful, winning and severe, it is, after all, only God Himself, revealing to us His will, and beckoning to us on the way. The sense of wrong doing is the consciousness of the violated Law: but that very Law itself, because it is divine, creates the balsam for the wound which it has made. In adoring it we are helped to obey it. Our worship of it prompts us to its fulfilment.[32]

The Law in Liberal and Orthodox Judaism

To Orthodox Judaism the Law is primary, and the Prophets are secondary: secondary both in importance and date. To Liberal Judaism the great prophets (Amos, Hosea, Isaiah, Jeremiah) are primary: the Law is secondary; secondary both in importance and in date. This does not mean that the Law is not important at all. If there were two mountains, one of 15,000 feet and one of 12,000 feet, the second is lower than the first. But the second is also high. So it is with the Prophets and the Law in the scheme of Liberal Judaism. The Law is honoured; but the Prophets are honoured still more. Liberal Judaism recognises the place of Law in religion and of the Law in Judaism. But if Liberal Judaism is partly 'legal', it is yet more prophetic. It accepts as the deeper and greater portion of its faith, the famous utterances: 'I desire love and not sacrifice, and the knowledge of God rather than burnt offerings.' 'What does the Lord's command require of thee, but to do justice, and to love mercy, and to walk humbly with thy God.' It accepts them and draws the consequences.

Unlike Orthodox Judaism, it can, and it does, cheapen Leviticus 19:19[33] in comparison with Leviticus 19:18.[34] And I may even say that, as regards some details of the old ceremonial law, this cheapening is not merely comparative, but also positive – positive, at all events, in relation to our present knowledge and our present life. Liberal Judaism, e.g., can perceive, and is able to recognise, the needlessness and pettiness of many Rabbinical prescriptions about the Sabbath or about food. It recognises that laws about food are world-wide, and common to innumerable races. It realises that these laws do not pertain to what was new and specific in Judaism, but to what was common to it and many other religions; that they belong not to what separated Judaism from endless pagan tribes, but to what united it to them; that they are not the creations of its prophets or even of its lawgivers, but old customs and taboos, adopted by the lawgivers and given a fresh religious sanction and reference.[35]

Issues of Observance: the dietary laws

The Pentateuchal dietary laws must be followed, if at all, as a whole. If we pick and choose, avoid rabbit but eat prawns, we are simply following personal predilections or the doctor's advice. Even if we observe them all from the sanitary point of view, we are imposing a purely modern and secular interpretation upon an ancient and religious code. It may, indeed, be argued that care for bodily health is part of religion, and that no man who grossly neglects his body can expect to do justice to his soul. He is an incomplete man unless all his faculties are brought to their best. But these principles are only true when stated as principles. Translated into detail, they cease to be part of religion, just as, though it may be said that recreation and physical exercise are part of a man's moral duty, no modern system of ethics would lay down precise rules as to what exercises are to be practised and what exact forms of recreation are right and wrong.

Again, as these laws do not concern the public life and worship of the community, it may be questioned whether their observance tends to maintain the corporate spirit or the consciousness of Judaism. That consciousness must depend on nobler methods, as it is required for nobler ends. The dietary laws, both Pentateuchal and Rabbinical, have kept the Jews together through the dark ages of persecution and disability, but they have undoubtedly exercised an influence for evil, as well as an influence for good. In the first place, they have directly tended towards an unnecessary and unsocial separation. In the second place, they have tended to make personal piety a question of food, cooking, and dishes. A 'pious' Jew has too often been one who observed extraordinary precautions in the minutiae of the dietary laws. The taunt that Judaism is a 'kitchen religion' has not always been without its grains of truth.

It may be more reasonably argued that, as these laws exist, and as on the whole they operate for health, and as on the whole they hinder the centrifugal tendencies of the age and help to bind the atoms of the community together, they should be observed, even by liberals, as a discipline. They are a practice in self-denial. I would not seek to minimise their importance from this point of view. The Pentateuchal dietary laws can usually be obeyed without violating any higher civic duty. Under such circumstances, their observance may act as a reminder of our special duties to God and man, and as a simple exercise in self-control and self-denial. When combined with the Rabbinical laws, this exercise has often been purchased at too heavy a cost.[36]

A Sunday Sabbath?

How we are to observe the Sabbath is a question which each one must settle for himself. The details cannot be considered here. But, broadly speaking, two things are desirable: the first is that there should be a day of rest; the second is that we should spend, wherever possible, one or two hours of it in the public worship of God. Now the present conditions of life sometimes prevent both the one and the other. The Christian day of rest being Sunday, a large number of Jews, and a considerable number of Jewesses, are more or less bound to 'work' upon Saturdays. One of the most important questions which Liberal Judaism has to consider is, what attitude it should take up towards this urgent and complicated problem.

It would not be irrational to advocate a transference of the Sabbath from Saturday to Sunday. There is no divine virtue in one particular day. The old orthodox view was that God created the world in six days and rested on the seventh, and it was undoubtedly believed that if the Saturdays were followed back far enough, you would ultimately come to the very Sabbath upon which God rested. 'Time' began on Sunday. If this were so, and if we still believe that God Himself directly ordered us to observe the Sabbath (that is, the seventh day, the Saturday), and to rest upon it, it would be monstrous to suggest any change or transference. Such suggestion would amount to blasphemy. But for 'liberal' Jews this supernatural sanction for the Sabbath has passed away. Thus, if the whole of European and American Jewry could transfer the Sabbath from Saturday and Sunday, and if all Jews were faithfully to observe the Sunday by rest and prayer and worship, and if they did not lose their Jewish consciousness by the transference, but, on the contrary, deepened and vivified it, then the change, so far from being a loss, might be a benefit.

It is, however, exceedingly doubtful whether these provisos could be carried into effect. It is commonly alleged that where a 'Sunday Sabbath' has been attempted, the speedy result is that neither Saturday nor Sunday is properly observed. In other words, average human nature (I will not say average Jewish human nature) has not the self-sacrifice, the strength of mind and tenacity of purpose sufficient to make the change of religious effectiveness and value. For it is a question of will power. It would need strong resolution and fixed determination for any Jew to transfer to Sunday the feelings which his early training and the lives of his ancestors have centred upon Saturday. Yet by sufficient doggedness and sacrifice, and above all by the most patient care devoted to the education of children, there seems no absolute or overwhelming reason why a new generation could not arise who would observe Sunday with a full and eager Jewish consciousness, and in all religious solemnity and fruitfulness.

Meanwhile for the present – and this book is written to meet present needs – there is no question of transference of the Sabbath from Saturday to Sunday. We have to consider things as they are, and to make the best of them.[37]

The Sabbath

We are no less eager to sanctify the Sabbath than our Orthodox brothers and sisters, but we feel that the sanctification must be effected in a living way, though also at the cost of sacrifice. We can no longer just refer to the paragraphs of a code. We ask that every Liberal Jew should himself consider whether a given action is or is not consistent with Sabbath sanctification, with making the Sabbath a day of peace and joy, different from other days to some extent even in its pleasures. Two questions have to be put. First, is a given pleasure, e.g., in accordance with the spirit of the Sabbath? The reply might condemn such pleasures as card-playing, visiting cinemas or races. Secondly, is a certain pleasure or action undesirable on Saturday for me? If my circumstances never enable me to play cricket except on Saturday, that is a good reason for playing cricket on Saturday. If my circumstances (of which I take advantage) enable me to play cricket on other days, that is a good reason for abstaining on Saturday. The mind must be used in these matters, not a mere rule of thumb. Then as to work. Orthodox Judaism seldom seems to be able to preach a higher point of view. To work on the Sabbath is a sin, be the consequences of abstention what they may. So many an Orthodox Jew works on Saturday because economic pressure compels him, but he says that it is a sin. The result is often unfortunate. What you continue habitually to do, while you yet regard it as a sin, becomes in the end no sin. The sin is acknowledged with the lips in a purely formal manner. Religion gradually drops out of the man's real life and out of his heart. Liberal Judaism says definitely: to work on the Sabbath because of economic pressure is no sin. Your relation with God can remain as good and pure as before. But all the more important does it make it become how you use the hours on Friday evening and on Saturday when you are free. And the ideal of Liberal Judaism is hard and severe. If you have a few free hours on the Sabbath, all the more careful should you be how you employ them. If a suitable service is arranged on Saturday afternoons for those who work on Saturday mornings, it is really a misuse of words to say that we ask the Sabbath workers to come to this service because it is held at a convenient hour. It is held at a possible hour, if you like, but, we would be quite open and frank, not necessarily by any means for all persons at a convenient hour. I wish I could think so! Then on Saturday afternoon services would be fuller than they are! For Liberal Judaism demands sacrifice: in this case the sacrifice (and this is hard) of some leisure and quiet. But we believe in public worship; we believe in the religious advantage and utility of congregational prayer. And so we ask the Jew who works on Saturdays to make a sacrifice of his hard-earned leisure, and to acquire the taste and habit of worship. We will provide the service, if he will come to it, if he will sacrifice his convenience, and make the effort to come. 'No suitable service' is the excuse which just suits the man who has to work on Saturdays and does not want to sacrifice his convenience.[38]

CHRISTIANITY

Judaism's concern with Christianity

We today want to know . . . are there Jewish equivalents for certain Christian conceptions? Do, or should, any of these conceptions form part of our modern Jewish religion, and if so, how have we obtained them, or how should we mould them? Have these Christian conceptions Jewish origins or parallels, or were these dropped out of the Jewish consciousness or the Jewish religion when the more deliberate opposition to Christianity began to grow up? A certain Christian conception may be in the forefront of the Christian religion and of Christian theology: in its specific Christian form it may be inconsistent with Judaism, whether orthodox or liberal; nevertheless, it may have distinct Jewish parallels in old Jewish thought or in old Jewish literature. But because the conception became predominantly Christian, and a characteristic of Christianity, did it drop out, or was it deliberately excluded, from Jewish religion and Jewish theology? What was the result? This must be considered and decided in each particular case. It may be that Judaism was rendered in some given point one-sided. The conception in question may have provided a certain balance. The lack of it may have tended to exaggeration, aridity, one-sidedness. Again, it may even be that a certain Christian conception may supply a corrective to a particular Jewish inadequacy, or a supplement to a particular Jewish doctrine. The conception, being cast in Christian form, was repellent to Jewish thinkers, and the result may have been that Judaism was rendered still more one-sided. For if a certain religion X lacks a certain conception Y, the omission may not for X be of any great consequence, or again, it may easily be supplied. But if a rival religion, Z, adopts this conception, and gives it a place of prominence in its own system, what may happen? The religion X may now make a dead set against Y; it may declare Y to be false, dangerous and antithetically opposed to itself. Instead of finding out the truth about Y, X may set itself to caricature and contemn Y, with the result that X becomes consciously one-sided, which is far more serious than being unconsciously one-sided . . . It may be of importance to find out what, if any, are the Christian conceptions which have no old Jewish parallels, but which, nevertheless, are not essentially opposed to Judaism, but which on the contrary, in a modified form, could be adopted with profit and consistency. Such additions might merely add volume and depth to Judaism, and correct any existing one-sidedness, exaggeration, or roughness of edge. There seems to me little doubt that Judaism has suffered from Christianity in a very different way from what has usually been supposed! It has suffered in keeping half an eye on it. In some respects, Judaism would have developed more freely and naturally, if it had never known that there was such a religion as Christianity existing in the world. It would have mattered less if Christianity had been a tiny religion in an out-of-the-way portion of the globe. But Christianity became a universal religion: the religion of Europe and of Western civilisation; partly the creator of that civilisation. It partly absorbed, and was itself partly modified by, the best thought of Greece and Rome. Hence, the rejection by Judaism, of all Christian conceptions may have meant that it rejected a great body of thought which was not merely and purely Christian. It may have rejected much that was, or could be made, supplementary and complementary to itself. By too wholesale rejection it may have rejected what was true as well as what was false, and it may have narrowed its own outlook and its own doctrines more than was needful or desirable. And it may have done all this in modern times more than in ancient times; it may even be doing this today. It may be that Talmudic Judaism is more full of living, varied, sometimes, I admit, inconsistent ideas than is the Judaism of our modern textbooks or sermons. Instead of being more one-sided than they are, it may be in some ways less one-sided, more alive, more responsive to, more expressive of, various aspects of truth, various sides of experience.[39]

A call for Liberal Jewish theologians

We need philosophic theologians who shall neither be afraid of Christian doctrine on the one hand, nor be on the constant search for contrasts on the other. Problems connected with transcendence and immanence, with omnipotence and creation, with the relation of God to suffering and evil, still need much examination; Jewish teaching on these subjects needs development and expansion. So, too, as to the divine character; as to wrath and love, righteousness and love, holiness and love; here, too, there is much work to be done, and much room for theologians and philosophers, who will not wish to impoverish Judaism by insisting on differences and contrasts, but will rather seek to enrich it by finding out what the great minds of other religions have thought and taught, and how much is consistent with Judaism, and valuable and worthy of adoption and incorporation, and how much must be rejected; how much can be translated into Jewish terminology (for, after all, what a large amount is a question of terminology!), and how much is untranslatable, undesirable, and untrue. We need theologians who do not want to sit in corners and erect peculiar systems of their own, but who are willing to profit and learn even from those whose traditions and accents are other than their own. We have done a góod deal but much remains to do.[40]

Liberal Judaism and the New Testament

Nobody should be more qualified for a calm and impartial investigation of this book than Liberal Jews. We need have no difficulty in accepting from it whatever is good and true. We need not be excited about it, whether to refute or advocate. What is good and true in it is divine, because what is good and true is of God. Liberal Judaism does not teach that all goodness and truth in religion are or can be contained in one book; its equilibrium and fundamental tenets are not upset if the Jews who composed the New Testament, amid much error, said also several things that were new and true. The Jews who wrote the Talmud did the same . . .

But all this does not commit us to any particular view of the central hero. Jesus, so far as we can gather, was a great and inspired teacher but what he precisely thought and taught will always remain obscure. The Gospels were written by the disciples of his disciples for purposes of edification. They idealise on the one hand; they darken on the other. To increase the lonely greatness of the hero, the disciples must be made stupid, the people ungrateful, hardhearted, wicked. To estimate the Jewish religion (as Christian theologians do) from the New Testament is to produce a caricature; to find a portrait of Jesus in the Gospels is to look for a photograph in an idealised picture, painted several years after the subject's death.

Nor can the New Testament be acknowledged by Jews as a part of their own Bible. The Hebrew Scriptures remains by itself; it is the charter of Judaism. The New Testament is, after all, the charter of another creed. So things must remain for many a year. To read a chapter of the New Testament in a 'liberal' synagogue would provoke misunderstanding, even though a piece of a modern religious poem, such as 'In Memoriam' which could not have been written outside of the New Testament, does not. But, outside the synagogue, it is right for liberal Jews to read the New Testament; it is their duty, and it is within their power, to appraise and estimate it correctly without prejudice or passion. What on these lines we appropriate and admire can never make us less devoted to Judaism, because what we admire and what we appropriate will itself be Jewish, the 'supplement and complement' and the expression of Jewish doctrine and of Jewish truth.[41]

Jesus and the Rabbis

Modern Judaism needs both Jesus and the Rabbis. It can, as it were, absorb them both. Both are bone of Jewish bone and spirit of its spirit. The teaching of Jesus in the Synoptic Gospels could not suffice for a new religion. A religion needs body as well as spirit. Hence, Christianity had to create a quantity of dogmas, of ceremonies, of institutions, many of which were in antagonism to the teaching of its founder. Modern Judaism can combine what is best and truest in the two strands:[42] in the prophetic, inward teaching of Isaiah and Jesus; in the institutional, outward system of the Pentateuch and the Rabbis. For the second itself was based upon the first, and included considerable portions of it, while it also breeds the first as a perpetual corrective and limitation. Rightly regarded, the two are not antagonistic, but complementary. If Modern Judaism may rightly claim Isaiah as one of its founders, it may also claim Jesus. He too is ours.[43]

Appropriation of Christian teaching

The Christian culture and conception of life contain much that is congruent to Judaism or which is essentially Jewish; they contain some things which are supplementary and complementary to the best and highest Jewish ideas; they contain a few things which are antipathetic to Judaism. As regards, then, the first class, there can be no objection to our assimilating it all. As regards the second I hold that Liberal Judaism will be all the richer and truer for assimilating it. As regards the third, it can be trusted to be alive enough and strong enough to reject the food which is discordant with its own organism and unsuited to its own life. Moreover, if I read the signs of our age aright, the third class is slowly diminishing. There is much in modern culture and in the modern conception of life which is more sympathetic to Judaism than to the medieval conception of Christianity. On the whole, the modern conception of life tends to become not less Jewish, but more Jewish. If this statement is true, it is most important . . . that there is little in our modern environment or 'culture' which is disintegrating to Judaism in general or to Liberal Judaism in particular, but that, on the contrary, there is much which may deepen and enrich it.[44]

LIBERAL JUDAISM AND HELLENISM

A Jewish re-examination of Hellenism

Only now in modern times, only today, can Hellenism and Judaism meet together in a perfectly conscious and satisfactory way. Only now, and only, I think, by Liberal Judaism, can a fusion be effected in a perfectly free way, with independence and an open mind. Twice before did Jewish and Greek thought meet together and bear fruit. First, in Alexandria, just before and just after the beginning of the Christian era. And then, again, many hundreds of years later in the Middle Ages. Philo is the record or embodiment of the first meeting; Maimonides with many others is the record and embodiment of the second. Nor can the imperfections of either Philo or Maimonides be rightly used to constitute an argument against the need and propriety of the meeting. In no way do their imperfections show that Hellenism and Judaism, or rather, that Hellenic and Jewish spirituality, cannot be combined, and from that combination some fresh spiritual creations cannot be achieved. We need not be discouraged. The conditions are for us far happier than for them. It is true that Philo had the possibility (how far he availed himself of it is another question) of reading certain Greek books which we can never read, but this was but a poor set-off to his disadvantages. His attitude towards the Pentateuch; his odd ignorance or neglect of the prophets; the necessities of his allegorical interpretation of the Pentateuchal text; his defective knowledge of Greek philosophy in the higher, more historic, and also more philosophic manner in which we know it today: all these, and several other limitations and imperfections, contributed to the limited and imperfect results. It is needless to catalogue the very grave, though very different limitations of that meeting of Greek and Hebrew thought which spoiled the philosophic and spiritual elements of Maimonides and the other Jewish schoolmen. Neither group of imperfections affect us. Therefore Liberal Jews of today, and, far more truthfully, Liberal Jews of tomorrow, though much lesser men than Philo or

Maimonides, have the power and possibility of achieving much more spiritual results. Judaism and Hellenism are both revealed to them. They possess the sources. They can catch and learn the spirit of both. They can stand above the sources, and possess that true detachment, combined with that reverence, humility, and appreciation, which are the condition of all fruitful religious work of this particular kind.[45]

Liberal Judaism and Hellenism

As in things political, and in the doctrine of the state, men have learned from Greece the value of ordered freedom, of the liberty of obedience, so in morality and religion we can, I think, learn from Greece the nobility and worth of a certain reverent independence, a certain self-sufficiency, a certain conquest of circumstance. Man wills the divine will, and all that befalls him – so far as it is not his own fault or alterable by his own action – he regards as the will of God. If he can do that, he is 'independent in the face of the storms of fortune', and desire and fear are extinguished. Reasoned courage in the hour of danger when the call of duty, or the command of the state, or the will of God, summon you to peril and to death – the courage of Leonidas at Thermopylae – is peculiarly Greek. The Hebrew order seems to be, God enjoins and man obeys: the Greek order seems to be, Man freely puts himself into harmony with God. Both are true and both inspiring; in some moods we may like to use the first order, in some moods the second. The Hebrew bidding to righteousness comes from without: the Greek bidding comes from within. Neither Hebrew nor Greek condemns the world and the things of the senses: both are sane and sober realists, but both are idealists as well. Both ask for an enjoyment of the things of sense which is other than the enjoyment of the animal. Personal sanctification and the glory of God – that is how the Hebrew uses the world and triumphs over it: self-control, temperance, the cultivation of the mind, inward refinement and good taste, these are the ideals and the ideals we have won from Hellas.[46]

LIBERAL JUDAISM AND ZIONISM

Liberal Judaism and a national religion

Liberal Judaism believes in, aims at, a universal Judaism, universal in doctrine and in form. Liberal Judaism holds that a national religion is an absurdity, or, at any events, an anachronism. Just as Buddhism, Christianity, Mahommedanism have adherents of many races, and by this very fact have shown their universality, so must it be ultimately with Judaism. The one universal God cannot fitly be worshipped by a national cult. The national ceremonial has become too narrow for the universal God. The clothes do not fit the religion. Moreover, the national references do not fit in with the consciousness of the worshipper. If the English Jew had to compress his religion in the strait-jacket of national forms, those forms should be English. Thus, whichever way one looks at it, a national religion, whether in cult or creed, becomes to the Liberal Jew an obsolete and outworn conception, from which his faith must gradually be more and more completely divested and freed; it must be gradually so freed as regards its forms.[47]

Nationalism and religion

The stress, therefore, by foes without and by Zionists within, is being laid upon nationality, and not upon religion. And if religion is also mentioned, it is, at any rate, combined with nationality. Thus religion is depressed; nationality is exalted. Judaism takes a secondary place, a back seat; it is the Jewish 'people', the Jewish 'nation', which is put in the front rank. To all those (whether Liberals or Orthodox) to whom Judaism is dear, these results are inexpressibly sad. But saddest of all are they to those who desire to universalise Judaism, to exalt its place in the hierarchy of the religions. Zionism and Zionistic activities not only depress Judaism by putting nationality first and religion second, but they injure Judaism by combining religion and nationality. What does Judaism become according to such a combination? It becomes the religion of one particular nation: in other words, it becomes a hopeless anachronism. For the days of national religions are over. No national religion can have any distinguished future before it. No national religion can hope to influence the world. No national religion can any longer be thought to possess a charge, a calling, a mission. The Jews outside Palestine are wronged, and their religion is wronged.[48]

The emancipation

It can now be easily realised why Liberal Judaism has ever been intensely and doubly keen as to complete Jewish emancipation. Its keenness was not merely on humanitarian grounds, but on grounds of religion. Without political emancipation the Jewish religion itself could not be emancipated. Unless the Jews became a religious community, neither less nor more, Judaism could not become a religion, neither less nor more. Hence it was that even in bad days, at the risk of seeming indifferent to the woes of brethren in faith, we sought to keep staunch to the religious conceptions of our brotherhood, that we refused to lower our aspirations and ideals. Therefore, it was that the rise of Jewish nationalism was even more a bitter disappointment to us than the diffusion of anti-Semitism. For the bitterest disappointment is ever the internal disappointment: the disaffection, the alienation of your own party hurts you more than the hostility of outsiders. Hence it is that though, individually, Liberal Jews and Jewish nationalists may be good friends to one another, the antagonism of the two sections is so pronounced. For each justly recognises in the other its keenest and most uncompromising opponent. Jewish nationalism tends to thrust back and depress Judaism once more to the level of a national religion, both in the eyes of the Jews themselves and of the world. For the separation between religion and nationality, which I indicated above as a theoretical, though hardly realisable solution of the great antinomy, is never (so far as I know) put forward or suggested. Hence what bids fair to happen is that religion tends to be neglected and ignored and pushed into the background. What moves the minds, and stirs the feelings of the nationalists is not religious, but political. 'Our people', 'our nation', national and racial considerations – these are in the forefront. Or if religion comes in at all, it is given a back seat. Religion is turned into the handmaid of the nation. All the national elements in ancient Judaism: all the material and racial features of the Prophets and the Old Testament, tend to come to the fore. Nobody denies that the Prophets were, in one sense, nationalists; but they were very much more. The universal elements – 'God's house a house of prayer for all nations' – were in conflict (though the Prophets could not realise it) with their nationalism. We were liberating the higher from the lower. But now the lower has sprung back up again.[49]

A Jewish state and religion

It would be best in accordance with modern and enlightened views as to what constitutes a nation if Jewish nationalists were to purge Jewish nationalism from every trace and particle of religion. And this is what a large and very important section of them actually desires to do. They are Jewish secularists. They do not want to have anything to do with religion, which no longer interests them. They would, therefore, I imagine, have no difficulty in granting that for full Jewish citizenship in a Jewish state there should be no religious tests whatever. A Jewish 'national' might be of all religions or of none. If he professes the Jewish religion, and then becomes a Christian, he would none the less remain a full Jewish 'national', and would no more lose any fragment of his national rights than an English Christian who became a Jew (by religion), or a French Jew (by religion) who became a Christian, would lose a fragment of his. A Christian Dane could become a Jewish 'national' precisely in the same purely secular manner as he could become an Englishman. His Christianity would have nothing to do with the matter of naturalisation one way or the other . . .

But if Jewish nationalists desire to retain some measure of religion and of Judaism, then the odious monster of religious tests again rears up her hoary and antiquated head. Then a Jewish 'national', who formally abandons the Jewish religion, would *ipso facto* cease to be a Jewish national any longer and a French Christian who sought to obtain naturalisation could only do so if he became a Jew by religion as well as a Jew by nationality.

May not this result justly be called Charybdis?[50]

Would not this kind of Jewish nationalism be justly considered too entangled with religion?

The truth is that the conception 'Jew' is so inextricably mixed up with religion that it is extremely difficult to free it from any religious connection. And the argument shows that there can be no compromise. There can be no via media. There can be no half-way house. Either the Jews must be a religious community – if you like to use the words in a non-natural sense, a priest-people – and that only. Or they must be a nation, the men and women of which (like the men and women of every other modern nation) may belong to all religions or to none . . .

Religion has become so integral a part of the Jew that if an attempt were made to form a new Jewish state, it would be exceedingly difficult to know how to deal with it. Nothing could be more abhorrent to the modern spirit, nothing could be more opposed to all that we have claimed and fought for, than to make religion the test of citizenship. And yet in a Jewish state what other test could there be? If ten French Christians immigrate into Palestine and live there for five or seven years, are they to be refused the rights of citizenship and naturalisation? Will they not be allowed to become Jews? If they are so allowed, how curious; if they are not so allowed, how monstrous! The truth is that the Jewish religion has made a Jewish state almost inconceivable.[51]

Zionism and anti-Semitism

Is it not, to begin with, a suspicious fact that those who have no love for the Jews, and those who are pronounced anti-Semites, all seem to welcome the Zionist proposals and aspirations? Whence this welcome, if it were not that Zionism fits in with anti-Semitic presuppositions and with anti-Semitic aims? Nor is it a matter of great difficulty to show why the welcome is given.

Let us assume that a Jewish state is founded in Palestine. Is it not natural and specious that the anti-Semite should say: 'The Jews now possess a country and a state of their own. Let them all go thither. Let us show them clearly where their true place is: in Asia and not in Europe, among their own people and not among ours.' The number difficulty will be conveniently ignored. That five-sixths of the total Jewish population must remain outside Palestine can be hushed up and suppressed. What, however, can be emphasised and trumpeted abroad is that there is a Jewish country, there is THE Jewish national home! Why, then, should not all Jews, if things are not completely to their liking elsewhere, betake themselves to their own home, which the generosity of England has given unto them? And why should all other countries suffer these Asiatic foreigners gladly, when they now have their own shelter, their own country, their own National Home? It seems as clear as noonday that the establishment of a specific Jewish home for Jews will, on account of this alone, and on this argument alone, enormously strengthen the plausibility of anti-Semitic machinations, and increase the volume of anti-Semitic activities. In every country, but more especially in Austria, Germany, Poland, Romania and Russia, the position of the Jews will tend to become worse instead of better.

But the foregoing argument will not be the only argument. The Zionist agitation among the Jews themselves, and the unrestrained and short sighted hilarity with which Mr. Balfour's declaration has been greeted by Jews, has provided another argument of which the anti-Semites will not be slow to avail themselves. 'At last', it will be said, 'the Jews have shown themselves in their true colours. We anti-Semites always knew, always declared, that their supposed desire to be Italians, Russians or Romanians, etcetera, was mere hypocrisy. We know that they felt themselves always to be, what, indeed, they were – an alien body in an alien environment, separated in ideals, aspirations and character from the nations who had to endure them. Now when this opportunity has arisen, they have, at last, shown their true colours: they have confessed themselves to be an alien nationality who long to start a national life of their own. Let us be all the less disposed to listen to the few remaining hypocrites who fawn upon us, and whine about their patriotism, or about their desire to become, or to remain, citizens of the countries where now they are. Let us take measures of protection: let us make things as unpleasant as we can, so that the new Jewish home in Palestine may be the more rapidly filled.' Is it not clear that this argument lies ready to the anti-Semites' hand? Why should they not avail themselves of it?[52]

Anti-religion and anti-Semitism

My slogan, 'The Englishman of the Jewish faith' is the solution of anti-Semitism and the answer to it. Such a person is a reality, and in no wise a baneful reality. It is for Jews, in spite of all temporary discouragements, to stick to the slogan through thick and thin. It is their one salvation; their charter; their watchword. It is for Christians to make it possible. It is for Christians to show their desire to be Christians by helping to cure any faults among some Jews with Christian charity, and by not helping to increase and intensify them with hatred, persecution and wrong. It is for Jews to remember that we carry, each one of us, the reputation of the entire brotherhood in the conduct of every individual; that minorities are necessarily marked out for observation and criticism, so that to escape a whipping, even if only a whipping of words, we should not merely be as good as the majority, but better. Our honour, the happiness of our religious brotherhood, the Sanctification of the Holy Name of God, whose witness we dare claim to be, should be our encouragement and our stimulus.

For countries with racial and national minorities, such as Poland and Romania, the problem is more difficult. In these countries Jews tend to be regarded, and to regard themselves, as racial minorities, as sub-nationalities. I have desired to avoid Jewish polemical questions as far as possible, but I cannot entirely conceal my considered and deliberate opinion that Jewish nationalism, or any Jewish consciousness of Jewish nationalism, in the countries of the west, Holland, France, Italy, Germany, England and America, is an evil, not unconnected with anti-Semitism, and inimical to its mitigation and disappearance. In countries such as Poland and Romania, the best one can hope for is, I fancy, two distinct patriotisms or national consciousnesses, one smaller and one larger, one Jewish and one Polish, one Jewish and one Romanian. The parallel might be the two national consciousnesses of a Welshman or a Scot, one for Wales or Scotland, and one for the United Kingdom. It is not an entirely satisfactory solution, but it seems to be the best in the circumstances, and it is no use blinking one's eyes to facts, whether one likes the facts or no.

One last word about religion. In medieval days religion was, as I have said, the primary cause of the hatred of the Jew. When the Crusaders waded to their knees in Jewish and Mussulmen blood through the streets of Jerusalem, killing every man, woman and child in their wild lust for slaughter, it was done in the cause and in the name of Christianity and of religion. Things are different now. Religious hatred has not wholly ceased, but it is generally secondary. And we may go further, and say that the trouble now is, not the Jew who believes in Judaism and practises it, whether he be Orthodox or Liberal, not even the Jew who, though by stress of doubt religiously agnostic, is yet of high moral excellence and spirituality, but the Jew who disbelieves in, and is hostile to, religion altogether. The atheistic, Bolshevist Jew supplies anti-Semitism with priceless fuel, nor can we say that the attack, however exaggerated – and however easily to be explained – is yet entirely without justification. The solution lies in Jewish hands. Orthodox Jews will say it lies in Orthodox Judaism. Liberal Jews will say that it lies in Liberal Judaism. Perhaps for many generations it may lie in both. In any case, it is for Jewish parents, whether Orthodox or Liberal, to do their utmost to prevent the increase of the atheistic, anti-religious Jew. He is without value; he has no meaning; he is a danger. He breeds anti-Semitism; the least worthy and the least unjustifiable anti-Semitism is caused by him.[53]

A meeting with Theodore Herzl

On a visit to England he [Herzl] asked me for an interview, and made the request that I should become his English Zionist Lieutenant . . . By every possible means, by flattery, cajolery, argument, threat, he sought to gain his end. And I admit, that so charming was the man, so powerful and winning his personality, that I had to pull myself together in order to keep straight, and to refuse him. As for his theory, it was this. He compared the Jews in the various countries to water in a sponge. A sponge can hold a certain, very limited quantity of water. Pour a little more water into the sponge, and the water trickles out at the other end. He compared the Jews in the various countries in the world to water in a sponge . . . the countries of the world can endure a certain number or percentage of them. Put some more in the country, what trickles out is anti-Semitism. This, Herzl said, had always been. It was an iron and immutable law. The only remedy was to get all the Jews, over and above the permissible percentage, away into a country of their own. As Herzl put it, it seemed to me at the moment, sadly convincing. But then I reflected: 'Not so: at least the percentage must vary greatly in different countries, and, then, is nothing to be allowed for any progress in toleration, in understanding, in appreciation, in good-will? Must these hatreds continue for ever?' So I rejected the defeatist, sponge theory, and I reject it still . . .

On the Jewish side, the Mandate led to an enormous increase and development of Jewish nationalism; on the gentile side, to an increase in anti-Semitism, and an increasing misapprehension and denial of the old Jewish position – of my once ordinary, now, alas, die-hard position . . .

You see before you a disillusioned old man, a sad and embittered old man. But yet, not a hopeless old man, for he still believes in God. He refuses to bow the knee to the fashionable Zionist Baal. He refuses to succumb to Jewish nationalism, on the one hand, or to Gentile anti-Semitism on the other, even though these powerful forces so powerfully react upon, and stimulate one'another. He is an extremist, a die-hard, a fanatic, if you will, but he has not lost his faith. His old ideal of the Englishman of the Jewish faith shall yet, as he believes, prevail.[54]

Jews and Palestine

To avoid misconception, it should be added that Liberal Jews are in no wise opposed to the free settlement of such Jews in Palestine as may desire to go thither and to make Palestine their home. Such opposition would be churlish and foolish. Jews have as much right to settle and reside in Palestine as anywhere else, and if they become the predominant element of the population in that country, they must obviously exercise a predominant voice in the administration and government. We must be as hostile to any restriction upon Jewish immigration into Palestine as we are hostile to any restriction upon Jewish immigration into America. Nor can Liberal Jews, any less than Orthodox Jews, be uninterested in the future development of a land and of a city, in which long ago their ancestors lived, where the Prophets spoke, and the Psalmists sang, the Sages taught. But the religious dangers of a Jewish State remain, and for the various reasons given Liberal Judaism, looking at the matter from a purely religious point of view, is bound to regard Jewish nationalism with much concern. It cannot harmonise any movement to make

Judaism more of a national religion with its own movement and impulse towards universalism, towards catholicity. The Lord's house of tomorrow must be a house of prayer for all peoples.[55]

AUTHORITY

The authority of traditional literature

We recognise no binding outside authority between us and God, whether in man or in a book, whether in a church or in God, whether in a tradition or in a ritual. Most, if not all, of our differences from the traditionalists spring from this rejection of an authority which they unhesitatingly accept. The fact of our rejection of the supreme and binding authority of a book and a code is due to two causes which support and co-operate with each other. The first is philosophical; the second, historical. We cannot conceive the perfection of God enshrined in, or precipitated into, a book or code. A book or code is something human. However 'inspired' it may be, it must nevertheless possess its human limitations. It must have been written down by mortal hands, and have passed through human brains. It must bear the impress of time and locality, of race and environment. It cannot from the very nature of the case be perfect, for it must bear the stamp of the man or men by whom it was written – touched, even though they were by the spirit of God. We cannot curb and confine the infinite God within the paragraphs of a code. No book or code, therefore, can stand between us and God. We must bring our God-given reason to criticise, accept, or reject any human production, however much we may rightly say of such a 'human' production that it is also 'divine'. Thus, even before we open the Book, before we open the Code, we know that it cannot be for us an infallible and eternal authority. Even if the whole Pentateuch were unquestionably the work of Moses, we should still declare that no book, be its human author who it may, can be for us an unquestioned and binding authority.

To free ourselves from the heavy bondage of the Rabbinical law and of the Shulchan Aruch may be, and indeed is, desirable and necessary. But the bondage of the written law of the Pentateuch, or the view that the 'Bible, and the Bible alone', is the religion of Judaism may be even heavier, or at all events more fossilising, than the Bible plus the interpretations and additions of Tradition. The written word remains: it is the same for all ages; it can never grow, expand, develop. But we stand for the conception that religion is progressive. However much we owe to and draw from the past, we cannot be bound to it, or to a certain product of it, in the sense that we are to see exactly as it saw. Religion grows. The Judaism of today will, we trust, be found inferior in many things to the Judaism of two hundred years hence. Our descendants will profit from our thoughts and feelings and experience; they will advance upon them and beyond them. The idea of development, for which we stand, is inconsistent with the absolute authority and final perfection of a particular Book.

We, therefore, do not take up the attitude of the earlier Jewish reformers towards the Bible and Talmud. We do not allow the authoritative power to the former, and deny it to the latter.[56] We recognise the Spirit of God in the Talmud as well as in the Bible. Though the second is a much greater 'book' than the first, it too has its human, just as the other has its divine, elements. For the Talmud also contains many good and true words, and what is good and true has its source in God. We cannot, therefore, allow any abstract and rigid separation between the Biblical and the Rabbinic codes.[57]

Authority in Liberal Judaism

We stand for a modern view of inspiration, for a modern attitude of free inquiry and critical investigation. What reason and conscience tell us to be good, that only can we accept. For these, and not the book, are the supreme authority. They investigate the book; it is not the book which dictates to them. The inward moral law recognises no authority between itself and God. Yet it may and does recognise as the words of God the moral laws of a code, be they ten or be they fifty. And so recognising them, it does them homage, and freely accepts their divine authority.

This combination of reason and the conscience of the individual with the gathered and sifted wisdom and experience of the past, whether enshrined in books, codes or institutions, provides an excellent mixture of stability and progress. It recognises the joint claims of the present and the past; of tradition and criticism; of society and the individual. It establishes a harmony between the ultimate authority of conscience and the secondary authority of the Sacred Book. It recognises the divine element in both. So far from producing chaos, it produces strength.

THE SURVIVAL OF JUDAISM

The puzzling progression of humanity

[Liberal Judaism] declares and believes that the course of human history is, in spite of set-backs, a divinely intended course of progress from ignorance to knowledge, from savagery to civilisation, from crude and low ideas about goodness to purer and nobler ideas, from superstition and cruelty to enlightenment and compassion. What some people call development, and others call evolution, we accept as the deliberate will of the divine Ruler. The development or evolution is the deliberate will.

We know that this progress has been terribly slow, and that it has been accompanied, so far as we can judge, by serious set-backs and by appalling waste. Comparatively civilised nations have been ruined by savages and barbarians; and many barbarous and savage races have never developed into civilisation at all; while recent investigation has shown us that human history is far older than used to be supposed, and that, therefore, the development of righteousness and of the knowledge of God has been painfully and puzzlingly slow . . .

Why all this long development? Why all this apparent waste? Why all this long painful history of slow movement from animal to lowest savage, and from lowest savage to civilisation?

We do not know. We cannot tell. Still it is, I think, much more cheering and comforting to believe that man has slowly risen than to believe (as has been widely believed) that he suddenly fell. A slow ascent fits in better with our conception of God than a sudden fall. An enduring golden age in a far-distant future is a more comforting and bracing idea than a transitory golden age in a far-distant past. There is comfort, too, in the very thought that human nature has in it the power to grow and improve, and to reach ever nearer – by whatever gradual stages – to the perfect ideal. It makes us think more and not less of human nature when we realise that in some early savage there was a germ of a Socrates or an Isaiah.[58]

The mission of Israel

A chosen people: a consecrated brotherhood. Chosen for others, and not for themselves. But if chosen for others, chosen with a certain end and purpose: hence, we may equally well say, invested with a special mission, a peculiar calling . . .

That the Jews have any religious work still to do is a doctrine largely limited to the Jews themselves, and I fully admit that it is a daring thing to hold to a doctrine which is rejected by a very large majority of the civilised world. Still we must not be frightened at being in a minority. We may, nevertheless, in the long run, find the truth we champion more and more generally acknowledged.

Why do we still believe in the continuing and unaccomplished mission? For several reasons. Mainly, I think, because our religion and our religious experience have not yet become the religion and religious experience of mankind, and we possess the faith that in their essentials they are destined to become so. If it be said: 'Even if your religion is to become in its essentials the religion of mankind, what are you doing, and what do you expect to do, towards the diffusion of it?' – then I would answer: 'I am not sure that we are doing nothing now; still less am I sure that we shall do nothing in the future. They too may serve their mission who, even for long stretches of time (and to our Master a thousand years are as a day), only stand, and suffer, and wait.'

We, believe, moreover, in our general mission because of our history and because of the general history of mankind. We hold that the preservation of the Jewish race from A.D. 30 to A.D. 1912 is not due to chance, and that it has not been effected without the will and intention of God. We venture, in all humility, to suppose that the purpose of this preservation is religious; that is to say, we hold that the preservation of our race and brotherhood has some religious object. In other words, the religious work which the Jewish brotherhood has to do for the world did not cease at the birth of Christianity. For my part I share these opinions. That Christianity was intended by God to play a great religious part in the world, I firmly believe, but I also believe that its appearance in the world did not betoken the end of Judaism as a religion of value. Christianity itself seems to Jews only a stage in the preparation of the world for a purified, developed, and universalised Judaism . . .

In its deeper essentials then – in its conception of God and his unity, of his relation to man and of man's to him, of the true service of God and of the consecration of life – Judaism, as we believe, stands at the head of God's religions in value and truth, and these deeper essentials have not yet been wholly adopted by the world, or even by that large section of the world with which we, in England, are immediately concerned. Our special conceptions of God and of his relation to man have, in some respects, still to make their way.[59]

The mission of Liberal Judaism

Conscience and reason, duly trained and disciplined, would not lead, and have not led, to the existing religious chaos which we all deplore in Judaism. There are classes of persons who drift and 'observe' nothing, but it cannot be said that they live under the conscious and severe rule of conscience and reason. Liberal Judaism is the absolute antithesis to drift; hence Liberal Judaism, with its solemn appeal to personal responsibility, would alone seem capable of arresting drift and of establishing order out of chaos.

There are those who, 'observing' nothing themselves, yet seem to belong to the orthodox section of the community, in so far as they would, and do, oppose any change in the synagogue ritual. They would like to think (from afar) of the unbroken chain which binds the modern service of their ancestors. This thought appeals to their antiquarian sense. But it does not exercise a constraining influence upon their conduct. They clearly have no living belief in a Divine Law; obedience to the Pentateuchal code has no claim upon their lives. They neglect it cheerfully. Therefore they have no right to shield themselves under the cover of orthodoxy. They have no right to prevent changes which would make no difference whatever to their own lives.

There are also some who call themselves Liberal, but have deliberately set themselves to test the value and the effect of Jewish religious observances and practices. They could not truthfully say that they have tried to study the Bible, or attempted to sever the lower from the higher. Nor have they sought to discipline their lives by consecrating them to the service of God. Such people who neglect observances in a haphazard and whole-sale manner, cannot be said to follow the dictates of conscience and reason. They have no right to shield themselves under the cover of Liberal Judaism.

There are others again who say that they have a sentimental attachment to the ancient faith, but can, to their sorrow, find in it no spiritual satisfaction. But have they honestly tried? Have they read? Have they attended synagogue? Have they even sought to find the best religious teachers for their children? It is doubtful whether they have a justified right for their grievances against Judaism.[60]

The agenda of Liberal Judaism

Large and important is the work which Liberal Judaism has accomplished. If we recognise that its own edges are still rough, though less rough than the edges of the Old Testament, we yet believe that it is capable of smoothing them. Much we can see which remains to be done: much doubtless will be done which we cannot see. That which remains and which we can see is mainly to complete what has already been achieved, and to do so on the same lines. We have gradually to let our ideas shine forth more perfectly from our institutions, to let our forms reflect our doctrines more completely. That must be a long and difficult task, in which it is better to go too slow than too fast. It is not easy, though sometimes the attempt may have to be made, to retrace a false, or even an inexpedient step. We may, however, be fairly satisfied with the work, all imperfect though it may be, which has already been achieved. Liberal Judaism has taken up again, on distinctive Jewish lines, the teachings of the Prophets. It has, we may truly say, put Prophets and Law in a new position and relation to each other. It has religiously emancipated women, and in this respect, as in some other respects, it has become a religion suited to, and fitted for, the western world. It has attempted to denationalise Judaism and to universalise it. It has fashioned or adopted new ideas of much moment and signifi-cance concerning revelation and inspiration, as well as new ideas concerning authority and freedom. It has boldly and openly faced the new conclusions of history and criticism, and sought to find new adjustments to them. It has attempted to fashion a Judaism which can look Science in the face without flinching, which is independent of the dates and authorships of the Biblical books and of the miracles recorded in them. It has sought to free Judaism from absolute priestly conceptions. It has abandoned the Talmudic theory of the ukas[61] as applied to the ceremonial enactments of the Pentateuchal Code, a theory which, while, as must be gladly admitted, it largely got rid of superstition, yet rested upon the hypothesis that, for various good reasons, the perfectly wise and perfectly good God had directly ordained and commanded all these enactments, whether one could find parallels for them in many other races in certain stages of civilisation or not. Liberal Judaism has deliberately restricted the idea of religious purity and impurity of states of the soul, in other words, to virtue and to sin. Physical ailments and bodily conditions are, religiously, neither pure nor impure, and the physically clean is to be distinguished from the religiously clean: in other words, ritual cleanness or uncleanness is abolished. Yet Liberal Judaism no less than Traditional Judaism, and with greater success and efficacy for the modern world, seeks to make religion coterminous with life. It gives to cleanliness – even physical cleanliness – a religious value, but a value very different from the priestly ideas of cleanliness which have hitherto prevailed. Liberal Judaism seeks to fashion a Judaism which shall be broad enough and humble enough to believe that its own truths, its own treasures, can be enriched and added to from the truths and treasures which may have been vouchsafed to other than Jewish teachers. It does not attempt to fashion a Judaism which shall be a mere medley of pretty notions gathered from every source. But it attempts to make its own doctrines still richer and fuller, and no less harmonious and consistent, by selected garnerings from without. One set of garnerings, however, can hardly be rightly held to come from without. So far as we can learn from Jesus and even from Paul, we learn from Jews, and not from aliens. While Liberal Judaism must not hesitate to differ from these illustrious men, it need not hesitate also to learn from them. From their teaching, too, it may adopt and adapt what suits it, and what appears to it to be true. Free in respect of the Old Testament, it may claim a similar freedom as regards the New. Fearless it is and unperplexed 'what weapons to select, what armour to imbue'. So does it go forth into the battle of life, in hope and joy, trusting to truth and to God.[62]

Freedom of choice

Only Liberal Judaism possesses liberty – conscious, reasoned and deliberate. Only Liberal Judaism has nothing to fear. Only Liberal Judaism can stand above the facts, and examine its own house reverently, tenderly, lovingly, but freely. For by the conception of progressive revelation, by the conception of the spirit of God giving light to all generations and to all mankind, so that no one religion, and no one stage of that religion, is in possession of perfect truth in all its fullness and completion – only by these conceptions Liberal Judaism has won its power to smooth the 'rough edges', to fill the gaps, to strengthen the weak points and generally to expand and to modify, to adapt and to adopt, to curtail or to reject. It has won the power and the capacity to do this in happy freedom and in the full light of day. It is a grand and solemn power, a power to be made use of in all soberness and caution, in all reverence and care; it is a power in the exercise of which some mistakes are bound to be made, and some ephemeral conclusions to be drawn, but it is a power which, in spite of its dangers (and what high gift of God has not its dangers?) must yet be used, and in the use of which a distinctive feature, privilege and glory of Liberal Judaism are to be found. Liberal Judaism need not explain away: it need not turn molehills into mountains, or mountains into molehills. It need not regard the exceptional as usual, or the usual as exceptional. It need not make a single saying mean more than it really meant, or less. In a word, it can be honest, historical, and free. If it is to make the best use of its freedom, it must and dare not be anything but honest . . .

Liberal Judaism makes use of its freedom in four or five main directions or ways.

(1) It modifies or enlarges the doctrines of the past – the doctrines which it inherits and finds – so as to make them consistent with each other and in harmony with the highest conceptions of truth to which it can attain. And some ancient doctrines may have to be dropped altogether, and some

doctrines may have to be added. It further seeks to make the private and public institutions of religion the purest possible manifestations and expressions of its doctrine.

(2) Liberal Judaism deliberately aims at universalism and universalisation, though the goal may be distant and the pathway long. It would not merely desire to possess and teach only such doctrines as may be fervently held by all races, and as are fully coexistent with the fundamental dogma of the One God who is the impartial father of all mankind, but it would desire that its religious rites and institutions should, as far as possible, harmonise with its universalist doctrines. It would wish to magnify and exalt the purely religious elements in Judaism, and to depreciate and minimise the purely national elements; it would wish, so far as practicable, gradually to disentangle the first from the second, and, so far as any national rites and institutions are retained, to clothe and suffuse them with new spiritual and universalist values and meanings.

(3) Liberal Judaism sets out to emphasise the 'prophetic' elements in Judaism, and to minimise or negate the 'priestly' elements. Thus it abandons priestly conceptions of clean and unclean; it rejects the idea of 'holiness' as attaching to things as well as to persons in a real, serious, and outward sense; it gives up praying for the restoration of the Temple and of animal sacrifices.

(4) Liberal Judaism tends to exalt the 'prophetic' elements in Judaism, and to depreciate, though not to abandon, the purely legal elements. It sets the Prophets above the Law. It desires to make Judaism no longer a predominantly legal religion, though it does not desire to deny or ignore the place of Law and of the Law (i.e. the Pentateuch) in the Jewish religion as a whole.

(5) Liberal Judaism seeks to construct a Judaism which is independent of the dates and authorships of the Biblical books, which is free to accept the assured conclusions and results of Biblical criticism, and which does not require any belief in the 'miracles' of the Pentateuch.[63]

Liberal Judaism and the West

Judaism was, it is true, born in Asia, and its fundamental truths were developed upon Asiatic soil. Nevertheless, I believe that Judaism – or Liberal Judaism, at any rate – can be a religion for the

161

West, and that in the West it can flourish and bear fruit. It is by no means certain that the impact with other civilisations or with other products of thought does not, or may not, cause special efflorescence of Jewish thought. Two or three salient names in Jewish history strike the mind immediately in that connection – Philo, Maimonides, Mendelssohn. Dr. Abrahams reminds me that of very Rabbinical tradition itself the same observations may be made. The Babylonian Talmud (as its name implies) was not developed on Palestinian soil. It grew up in what is now glibly called an 'alien environment'. Within the Talmud are elements derived from many cultures. After its close, we find Judaism again and again flourishing in non-Jewish countries, assimilating, to some extent at least, the good of these countries, and yet growing fuller, richer, and even more influential, just because of its wider horizon. Judaism throughout has seemed to flourish best when it has been able to absorb into itself other ways of looking at things. It may even be said (and this is by no means a mere paradox) that the Hebrew Bible itself is an instance of the manner in which Jewish genius, taking much from other Semitic cultures, managed to stamp its own impress upon its borrowings. I see no reason why the process should stop. I see no reason why from the very midst of the emancipated life important contributions to the Jewish religion may not arise. The days are still early, too early for an adverse decision in any case. Nor do I fear so greatly adjustments, approximations, interchange of ideas. I do not believe that all truth and all goodness have shone into our own windows, and that outside Judaism there is nothing but darkness and falsity. That is an antiquated standpoint. We may have much to give, but something also to receive; much to teach, but something also to learn. It may be said that the mixture of ideas can only lead to universal flabbiness, a common measure of feebleness and vagueness. But why may not the competition of ideas lead to the evolution of the truest and the best?[64]

THE FUTURE OF RELIGION

An optimistic future for Liberal Judaism[65]

I desire to confess to my rash belief in the distant victory of Liberal Judaism with certain important reservations ... I can only picture that distant prevailing religion as my own religion, purified, developed, enriched. It cannot be the actual Liberal Judaism of today or tomorrow, not my Liberal Judaism nor my son's. And secondly, it seems to me absurd and ridiculous to suppose that the great drama of Christianity will pass away, if it ever does pass away, without leaving deep traces and influences upon the religion of the distant future. Thus I plead that there is no inconsistency in believing that Liberal Judaism has a part to play in the religious history of the world, and that its fundamental religious conceptions (purified, developed, enriched) will ultimately prevail, without, at the same time, dogmatizing, or even having any opinion, as to the name or names of the religion or religions of the far future, or as to the names and the nature of the buildings in which the public worship of God may then be carried on.[66]

The religion of the future

The future will do justice both to the protest of the Jew and to the new outlook upon religion and life which Jesus introduced to the world. For, on the one hand, thought and criticism alike are tending to the recognition of the fundamental Jewish doctrine, which Jesus like every Jew believed in and taught. God is One, and no man is God. What the Jews have died in thousands to protest against was not the teaching of Jesus, but the teaching of the Church – the incarnation, the Trinity, the worship of the Man-God, the mediation of the Messiah, the worship of the virgin, the doctrine of transubstantiation and so on. And when some liberal Protestant German theologians, of today, who are practically Unitarians, though they do not call themselves by that name, write about Rabbinism and Judaism with disdain and disapproval, they forget that what they directly depreciate and contemn, they indirectly justify and exalt. They abandon, as not originally or specifically Christian, all those doctrines against which, from the very birth of Christianity, the Jews rebelled and protested. They have come round to our position. For surely, as regards their conception of God and His relation to the world, the orthodox Christian of every age would dub them Judaizers and heretics. If their conceptions of Christianity conquer and prevail, great is the victory of Judaism . . .

The religion of the future will be, as I believe, a developed and purified Judaism, but from that developed and purified Judaism the records which tell, however imperfectly, of perhaps its greatest, as certainly of its most potent and influential teacher, will not be excluded. The roll-call of its heroes will not omit the name of Jesus. Christianity and Judaism must gradually approach each other. The one must shed the teachings which Jesus did not teach, the other must acknowledge, more fully, more frankly than has yet been done, that what he did was for religion and for the world.[67]

CONCLUSION

THE HEBREW BIBLE:
MONTEFIORE THE ECLECTIC SCHOLAR

Claude Montefiore started his first major scholarly exercise when he was invited by the Hibbert Trustees (nudged by Benjamin Jowett) to deliver the Hibbert Lectures in 1892. He was the first Jewish scholar to receive this honour. His subject was entitled 'The Origin and Growth of Religion as illustrated by the Religion of the Ancient Hebrews'. The first portion of the lectures traced the historical development from Moses to Nehemiah while the second dealt with the relation of the Law and its observances with the Jewish religion.

The lectures were one of the first attempts on the part of a Jew to interpret the history of the Bible in accordance with the conclusions of the Higher and Lower criticism.[1] They attracted enormous attention for three reasons: firstly, Montefiore accepted many of the results of modern scholarship; secondly he paid tribute to the teachings of Jesus; thirdly, he vigorously defended Judaism from Christian criticism concerning the Law. In the Jewish community this overshadowed any sentiment of alarm which his opposition to the Mosaic authorship of the Pentateuch and the value of the Synoptic Gospels might have aroused.

His Biblical research led to another book entitled *The Bible for Home Reading*. This two-volume work was written partly for the benefit of his son and partly for the use of Jewish parents who wanted to teach the Bible to their children in a manner which took into account modern scholarship.

His work on the Biblical period was based upon the critical researches of Stade and Wellhausen of Germany, Keunen of Holland and Cheyne of England. He attempted to evaluate the conclusions made by these scholars and to assess their impact for Jews and Jewish interpretation of the Bible. His work was not an attempt by a Jew to add to the criticism but to interpret it.

Montefiore was not concerned with the more primitive aspects

167

of religion in the Hebrew Bible, but with the more sophisticated or higher elements. 'Are you most yourself at your best or your worst?' he asked, 'When you yield to your weaknesses, or when you struggle against them and overcome them? If my answer be sound, then the Old Testament is also most itself, its true essence is most truly shown, at its best, and not at its worst; its true tendency and issue are displayed, not in Esther but in Jonah.'[2] He never ceased to expound on the significance of the religion of the prophets. He approached the Bible with what might be described as reverent criticism and he was not prepared to expound Biblical themes on conventional grounds. It was on account of his criticism of the Bible that he came into conflict with the Orthodox Jewish authorities. His lineage and influence in Jewish communal life were of no avail.

He concluded that the Bible contained the highest truth but that it did not contain all truth. No book could be completely true in word and thought. The Bible was built up during several generations and different sections revealed different degrees of knowledge, faith and culture. This did not diminish the value of the Bible but rather undermined the traditional Jewish understanding of it as perfect and divine. At the heart of Montefiore's approach to the Bible is this crucial point: its value did not depend upon its divinity, but its divinity depended upon its excellence for truth. The Bible was divine 'because of its religious excellence, because of its righteousness and truth, because of its effects for righteousness and truth.'[3]

CONCLUSION

CHRISTIANITY AND THE NEW TESTAMENT: MONTEFIORE THE RADICAL THEOLOGIAN

Montefiore then turned his thoughts to Christianity and, in particular, to the New Testament. In 1909 he published *The Synoptic Gospels*, a two-volume work which consisted of an introduction, translation and commentary on the first three Gospels. His other major works included *Some Elements in the Religious Teaching of Jesus* (1910) and *Judaism and St Paul* (1914). His views were met with dissent within the Jewish community and provoked a great deal of discussion in Christian circles.

Throughout his writings he expressed the view that it was time for Jews to abandon their traditional negative attitude towards Christianity. At the heart of his approach to Christianity was the Liberal Jewish understanding of progressive revelation which viewed revelation as something that did not just exist in the Pentateuch but also in the Prophets, Writings and Rabbinic Literature as well. This was not all. Revelation could be discovered in other religions. According to Montefiore, Liberal Judaism denied that God had 'enabled the human race to reach forward to religious truth so exclusively through a single channel.'[4]

This openness allowed Liberal Jews to select the highest elements of all religions as well as to omit the more crude and primitive elements of Judaism. Consequently, Liberal Judaism became the justification for Montefiore's freedom in criticising both Christianity and Judaism.

The appropriate moment had arrived for a Jewish reappraisal of Christianity and a Christian reappraisal of Judaism. It was time for these two religions to stop judging each other from their defects; instead they should examine their qualities. Montefiore felt that he had an understanding of both points of view and was in a good position to appreciate both religions. With hope and optimism he consistently believed that Judaism was on the threshold of a new age and that this age would mark a turning point in Jewish attitudes towards Christianity.

Montefiore was heavily influenced by nineteenth century liberal Christian theology, and particularly important in this regard was his mentor Benjamin Jowett. In an article entitled 'The Religious Teaching of Jowett' Montefiore admitted that he had tried to incorporate some of Jowett's ideas into Judaism. The following words of Jowett provide an insight into Montefiore's approach to Christianity: 'The Jew must be able to put himself above the documents and estimate them as they truly are. He occupies a delightful vantage ground of liberty. He is not fettered by the letter. He has not to swear by the words of any human master or to the sentence of any book.'[5] Jowett encouraged Montefiore to devote himself to Judaism and to investigate its relations with other religions.

Like most scholars of his age, Montefiore was optimistic that he might attain objectivity in his writings and his attempt to act as impartially as possible was a landmark in Jewish approaches to Christianity. Previously, it was the norm for Jews to look for defects in Christian works or for parallels in Rabbinic writings. 'What was true could not be new and what was new could not be true.' This phrase summarised contemporary Jewish attitudes towards Christianity. Scholars such as Joseph Salvador, Abraham Geiger and Heinrich Graetz emphasised Rabbinic parallels while others such as Leo Baeck and Samuel Hirsch stressed the superiority of Judaism over Christianity. Montefiore took a much more sympathetic position and offered a balanced approach. As far as Christians were concerned Montefiore did not have to assume that Jesus was always right; with Jews he did not feel obligated to defend the Rabbis.

Is there something special about Montefiore that elevated his work above others? I would not claim that his writings were based entirely on objective scholarship. However, in comparison with Jewish and Christian scholarship of the day, Montefiore was the least tendentious. The fact that Christian scholars attacked him for being too Jewish and Jewish scholars for being too Christian is one indication that he approached the neutral position which he sought.

Montefiore was a bitter opponent of the negative Jewish attitude towards Christianity and attacked the tendency of Jewish scholarship to denigrate the Gospel teaching through cold analysis and dissection. He argued that the atomistic treatment of Christian writings had as its goal the denigration of Christianity. Judaism was unable to approach Christianity with impartiality. This was Judaism's loss and he wanted to rectify it. He made it clear that anti-Christian bias had affected modern interpretation of the 'Old Testament' itself to the detriment of its value and truth. He gave as an example the Suffering Servant of Isaiah. This portion which concerns voluntary and vicarious suffering had been neglected by Jewish writers because it came to be identified with Christianity.

Montefiore also opposed Christian misconceptions about Judaism and pointed to crudities in the New Testament such as the Judgement in Matthew 25. His demolition of the ignorant view that the God of the 'Old Testament' was 'jealous' and 'violent' and that the God of the New Testament was 'loving' and 'merciful', was quite devastating.[6]

He often compared the central characters of the New Testament with the Rabbis. Concerning the problem of the relationship between Paul and the Law, Montefiore argued that in one sense God's Spirit was opposed to the Law but, in another, the Law was spiritual. Paul could write with validity that 'the letter kills but the spirit gives life' but the Rabbis could write with as much validity that there was no freedom except through the Law. This apparent paradox or tension allowed Montefiore to show the value of both views – he did not attempt to reconcile them. It was useful to be reminded by Paul that grace was important but at the same time the Rabbis were correct to emphasise the value of good works.

Montefiore attempted to introduce the New Testament to his people. He knew that the task would be hard and the response bitter – but this did not deter him. The New Testament, he argued, was part of Jewish literature. There were no Christian elements; it was entirely a Jewish book. He was in favour of Jews studying the whole work and stressed that they were not to be put off by anti-Jewish sentiment. This should be understood in its historical context for early Christians suffered persecution from many quarters including the synagogue and consequently, the authors of the New Testament showed little neutrality when writing about Jews.

The New Testament in general and the characters of Jesus and Paul in particular fascinated him. Montefiore argued that Paul could not have known the 'near Rabbinic God who longs to forgive his erring children.'[7] The peace, happiness and presence of God, all of which Rabbinic Jews found in the Law, were not discovered by Paul. Montefiore tried to show that there was no similarity between Rabbinic Judaism and the Judaism attacked by Paul. Paul's writings would have been inconceivable if Paul had been a Rabbinic Jew with a knowledge of the concepts of repentance and forgiveness. Paul was led to a new truth which was not the complement of the old religion but its opposite. Consequently the Law became identified with sin and Christianity identified with the end of the Law. The main goal of Montefiore's work on Paul was not to offer new and original interpretations (he admitted this was unlikely) but rather to discuss those elements that he, a Jew, could admire and extol. He spent less time explaining Pauline theology and more on how Paul could be made comprehensible to Jews. As in his other writings on Christianity, Montefiore made a conscious effort to interpret Paul for Jews and Judaism.

His sympathy for Paul was outweighed by his admiration for Jesus whose teaching was 'a revival of prophetic Judaism' and in some respects pointed forward to Liberal Judaism.[8] This was the key reason for Montefiore's admiration. Jesus emphasised precisely those values which Liberal Judaism wanted to bring out. The great value of the Synoptic Gospels lay in the teachings ascribed to Jesus. He was less concerned with Jesus' personality or life. Consistent with his approach to the Hebrew Bible Montefiore emphasised the 'higher' elements of the New Testament. The more scholarly questions such as those concerning historical criticism were not so important. It was not the miracle that mattered but the teaching, not the authenticity but the meaning.

Jesus viewed the Law in the manner of the Prophets and emphasised inward goodness rather than outward forms. Montefiore showed that all the important teachings of Jesus which differed from those of the Rabbis concerned the Law. The conflict between them arose because Jesus drew certain practical conclusions from his emphasis on inward goodness and this led to his transgression of the Law. Jesus, Montefiore argued, was to be seen as a great and wise teacher, but in no sense God. Part of the significance of Jesus lay in the fact that 'he started the movement which broke down the old barriers and brought about the translation of Judaism into the Gentile world – the translation of Judaism with many modifications, curtailments, additions both for the better and worse, good and evil.'[9]

Unlike most scholars of his time Montefiore emphasised the originality of the Gospels and argued that not only did there exist some of the greatest Biblical teachings but there was also 'a further development . . . of certain truths which were only implicit or not fully drawn out [in the Hebrew Bible].'[10]

It will be worthwhile asking what Montefiore meant when he used the words 'development' and 'originality'. He seems to have had in mind the 'fresh expression of universal truths'. Seeds planted in the Hebrew Bible were developed and grew to maturity in the teachings of Jesus. Referring to the parable of the leper, Montefiore wrote that the 'new note' of the ministry of Jesus was his intense compassion for the outcast. Yet a few lines later he described this compassion as an 'exquisite manifestation of the pity and love which the prophets demanded.'[11] The seeking out of sinners was another example of how a teaching in the Hebrew Bible was built upon and carried forward to become part of the originality of Jesus. Is there a contradiction in this understanding of Jesus? We should refer to Montefiore's emphasis on prophetism and the prophetic teachings of Jesus. Montefiore argued that Jesus' clash with the Law resulted both in a 'new' teaching and also in a 'continuation of Prophetic teaching'. There existed a bond between the two and the demands of Jesus were seen as the demands of the Prophets.[12]

Montefiore's writings on Christianity reached their climax in a call for the introduction of a Jewish theology of Christianity. Jews should start asking themselves what ought to be the correct relation of Judaism towards the teachings of Jesus. What is the place of the New Testament? To find the answers to these and other related questions was one of the most important duties that lay before modern Judaism.

There was a need to look at Christian ideas – were there Jewish equivalents? Were they dropped out of Judaism deliberately because of the existence of similar ideas in Christianity? By too wholesale a rejection of all concepts Christian, Montefiore felt that Judaism might have discarded what was true as well as what was false. It narrowed its own outlook more than was desirable. A theological study of Christianity could lead to the re-discovery of Jewish truths and so to a greater understanding of Judaism. This was a major justification for a Jewish theology of Christianity.

However, there was also another. It is likely that Montefiore had in mind the grafting on of Christian elements which had no parallel in Judaism. Perhaps this was at the forefront of his mind when he called for the Hellenisation of Liberal Judaism. The Jewish religion was constantly evolving and could only gain from a meeting between Jewish and Greek thought. One of the results of such a meeting would be the acquisition of Greek ideas. This was nothing short of appropriation: 'we need to find what the great minds of other religions taught and how much is consistent with Judaism and worthy of retention. How much can be translated into Jewish terminology and how much is untranslatable, undesirable and untrue.'[13]

It was clear that Montefiore wanted to appropriate some forms of non-Jewish thought whilst remaining within a Jewish context. He argued that there were 'new excellences' in other religions and truths outside of Judaism. It would be helpful to contrast Montefiore's approach with that of Maimonides and especially the latter's tendency to incorporate the Aristotelianism of his day into a Jewish framework. For Maimonides any statement that was true had to have a divine origin and its source could be found in Torah. In the Mishneh Torah, for example, he included four chapters of Aristotelian physics. Truths outside of Judaism were incorporated into Judaism and, consequently, not everything outside would be considered untrue. The same process can be found with Montefiore. Truths outside of Judaism were to be incorporated within and become Jewish. Potentially Judaism possessed all truth but 'the fabric was still to be completed'. It was not by chance that in his call for another meeting between Jewish and Greek thought Montefiore noted that the two had met twice before. The results of these meetings were to be found in the writing of Philo and Maimonides.[14]

Throughout his writings on Christianity and the New Testament we find Montefiore influenced by both Jewish and

Christian thought. It was the fusion of such thought that led to Montefiore's important position in Jewish – Christian relations and in the Jewish study of Christianity. Israel Zangwill once described Montefiore as a 'queer mixture, half-Jew, half-Christian'[15] and we must conclude that it was this 'queer mixture' which allowed the controversial Jewish scholar to gain the respect, if not the approval, of both Jews and Christians. Montefiore did not inaugurate a new era in Jewish–Christian relations but there can be little doubt that his life and work contributed towards a more positive relationship between the two religions.

RABBINICS:
MONTEFIORE THE CRITICAL DEFENDER

Naturally, the study of the New Testament led Montefiore to a close investigation of the parallel developments in Judaism itself. He produced two major works in which he was helped by Herbert Loewe, Reader in Rabbinics at Cambridge. A comparison between the two religions was the essence of *Rabbinic Literature and Gospel Teachings* (1930). In addition, towards the end of his life, the two produced a huge anthology of Rabbinic literature. Both wrote separate introductions to *A Rabbinic Anthology*, which was an excellent example of an Orthodox and Liberal Jew working together although disagreeing in many places. The anthology allowed the Rabbis 'to speak for themselves', but Montefiore was keen to stress the differences between Rabbinic teachings and those of Liberal Judaism.

Although Montefiore had been interested in Rabbinic Judaism during the early period of his life, particularly at the time he was studying under Solomon Schechter, it was not until 1930 that he published his first major work. This was perhaps because Christian interest in Rabbinic Judaism had increased during his lifetime. This interest was closely connected with the 'search for the historical Jesus' and the study of the New Testament. German scholars led the way and Montefiore, with a good knowledge of German, easily followed the discussions in German colleges and seminaries. Indeed, he once wrote that 'my German masters . . . led me to defend the Rabbis'.[16]

It was particularly in Germany where anti-Rabbinism in hand with anti-semitism came to the fore of scholarship. For example, Wilheim Bousset was ever keen to stress the antithesis between the teachings of Jesus and Rabbinic Judaism. Bousset insisted that Judaism viewed God as no more in the world and the world no more in God. This was a direct consequence of the prophetic exaltation of the uniqueness of God which had been formalised into abstract transcendent formalism. Bousset's argument typified a general feeling in Christian scholarship that by the end of the Biblical period God had become too transcendent and remote and had almost been purified away. For Christians this 'void' had been filled by Jesus because he caused the transcendent and unique God to become the indwelling and immanent God.

Montefiore responded to this criticism by arguing that the nearness of God was effected partly by the Law. He showed the extent to which the Law had been venerated, and stressed that it had been a blessing, and not a curse. The Rabbis believed that God, in perfect wisdom, had given the Law to Israel and that Israel, by its faithful obedience, would itself become wise and holy. The Law was the will of God and to study it was Israel's supreme joy and brought God near, 'with every kind of nearness'. Montefiore compared the position of the Law in Rabbinic Judaism to the position of Jesus in Christianity – both supplied the motive for love and passion; both became mediators between God and the people and the means of bringing God close to the people. In effect, the Law was the means of maintaining Israel's closeness with God.

Another Christian criticism of the Judaism of Jesus' day was propagated in the writings of Ferdinand Weber and Emil Schurer. To both Judaism was synonymous with legalism and legalism was 'the hated red rag and unclean thing to Lutheran theologians'.[17] In Judaism, God had become isolated and transcendent and was to be obeyed blindly. Consequently, the Law became a burdensome yoke which caused suffering among the people. Those who defended it (the Pharisees, and later, the Rabbis) were apparently spending their whole time thinking up new restrictions to add to the helplessness and hopelessness of the people. The Law became merely outward and ceremonial and lost its inward and moral value.

The particular aspect of Rabbinic legalism which angered these scholars most was the doctrine of 'merit and reward'. In their view, this doctrine taught that God, as Israel's King and Giver of the Law, must be obeyed. Those who were disobedient were to be punished and those who were not were to be rewarded. Thus, it was argued, the Rabbinic motive for obedience was the fear of punishment and the yearning for the reward: a terror of hell and a longing for the paradise of heaven.

In response to these criticisms Montefiore argued that the Law deepened the life of the Jew. It was false that the Law was an outward taskmaster which demanded fear and not love. No one could understand the Rabbinical religion with these presuppositions. He agreed that Rabbinic Judaism was legalistic but the fundamental reason why the dangers of legalism were so often avoided was that the Prophets and the Law had succeeded in making the service of God into a passion – God and God's Law were so loved that the fulfilment of the Law was carried out for its own sake and not merely for the sake of reward.

Montefiore stated that there were dangers to legalism and to such doctrines as 'merit and reward', but he also emphasised that these dangers were minimised by a love for the Law and its observance (simhat shel mitzvoth). The Law did not become a 'burden' but a joy. As for the additional 'restrictions', Montefiore replied that the 'spinning out of legal distinctions, developments and minutiae in the Law was as much an intellectual delight to the Rabbis as the spinning out of metaphysical and theological distinctions to any of the schoolmen'.[18] Another benefit of the Law was that it associated knowledge with religion and kept the intellect alive. Its intellectual value became a major element of his defence of and justification for Jewish legalism.

Montefiore argued that a Jew might be a legalist, observing every detail of ritual and ceremony, and could still be, and often was, sincere, loving, cheerful and good. Legalism did not necessarily spell formalism, self-righteousness and despair. Those who followed the Law could be as free as those who believed in the Gospel. In essence, Montefiore showed that the constant antithesis between the outward command to be obeyed (of Jews) and the inward disposition to be acquired (of Christians) was false and unhistorical.

Montefiore tended to explain Rabbinical concepts such as Law in quasi-Christian terminology. This was partly the result of his position of interpreter of Jews and Judaism to Christians. He attempted to educate but not convert. He wanted people to discover true Jewish values and teachings and not to believe in the bias in some Christian scholarship. He responded to Christian criticism by describing the 'higher' elements of Rabbinic Judaism. His attempt to show Jewish (and Christian) writings in the best possible light was often misunderstood. His Jewish opponents felt he was too influenced by Christianity and Christian opponents saw his Jewishness as a weakness.

It is interesting to examine the charge that Montefiore was overly influenced by Christian teaching. Can one explain his use of Christian language as merely an attempt to make himself understood by a Christian audience? Jowett and other Liberal Christian scholars held a strong influence over him but was there something more? We have already mentioned Zangwill's description of him as a 'queer mixture, half-Jew, half-Christian'.[19] Montefiore himself wrote that those Jews who lived in Christian societies were so 'Christianised' that '5/6ths of their conception of life is Christian'.[20] There is a similarity between Montefiore's statement and the position held by Franz Rosenzweig who was also fascinated by the relationship between Judaism and Christianity. Rosenzweig wrote that 'we are Christian in everything. We live in a Christian state, attend Christian schools, read Christian books, in short our whole 'culture' rests entirely on Christian foundations.'[21] Montefiore's 'Christianisation' led him to explain some Jewish concepts by describing their Christian 'counterparts'. He did this purely as a means of clarification. He tried in this way to elucidate Jewish concepts. If Christian forms of expression were part of this process so much the better – this approach allowed him to show that many concepts in the two religions shared similarities; indeed, some were almost the same although they might be called by different names.

A great deal of Montefiore's discussion centred on the role of Law. In the New Testament the Law was described as interfering with mercy and loving-kindness. It led to pride and self-righteousness. Yet in the Rabbinic writings the Law was treated in a totally different way where it became the source of joy and the means of obtaining 'reconciliation with, and forgiveness from, God'.[22] The conflict between Jesus and the Rabbis, as we saw earlier, centred on Jesus' interpretation of the Law and the conclusions which he drew from it. For Montefiore the conflict was tragic but inevitable. Both sides were right, but Montefiore's sympathies lay more with Jesus than the Rabbis. Although the

Rabbis were 'logically' right, the teachings and actions of Jesus were of a 'higher' order. For the Rabbis the ceremonial and moral were equal. For Jesus the moral came first.

Montefiore was much more critical of Paul's attitude towards the Rabbis. The Law did not awaken the desire to sin but rather acted as the medicine which prevented such desires becoming masterful. The Law was entrusted to Israel not to show its futility but its usefulness. The cry, 'Who shall deliver me from this body of death?', was an unrabbinic cry and suggested that Paul was no Rabbinic Jew. One could only understand Paul when one realised that his 'pre-Christian religion was poorer, colder, less satisfying and more pessimistic than Rabbinic Judaism.'[23]

Montefiore thus distinguished between Rabbinic Judaism and the Judaism with which Paul had been brought up. He did not accept Solomon Schechter's thesis that 'either the theology of the Rabbis must be wrong, its conception of God debasing, its leading motives materialistic and coarse, and its teachers lacking in enthusiasm and spirituality or the Apostle to the Gentiles is quite unintelligible.'[24] For Montefiore, neither was Paul unintelligible, nor were the Rabbis wrong. Paul merely originated from a Hellenistic Jewish background which could hardly have been conceivable in Palestine and which was almost antithetical to Rabbinic Judaism. For Paul the Law became the strength of sin and Christianity became the end of the Law. At the same time for Rabbinic Jews the Law could make for reconciliation and joy.

Montefiore's tendency to contrast New Testament writings with those in Rabbinic literature was paralleled by similar contrast between the Hebrew Bible and the Rabbinic literature. He asked and attempted to answer the question, how far had the Rabbis advanced beyond the Bible? He argued that there was both progression and regression. Some of the 'imperfections and crudities of the Hebrew Scriptures were elaborated and hardened by the Rabbis',[25] such as the doctrine of merit and reward. The Biblical doctrine was simple and unreflective, which was preferable to Rabbinic elaboration. There was far too much of an emphasis on merit and reward and this resulted in the 'ugly doctrine that such and such punishments are directly sent by God as the punishments for such and such deeds'.[26]

The major reason why the Rabbis developed some of the

'lower' Biblical concepts was because of the Rabbinic conception of the Bible itself. The burden of the Bible was the greatest burden the Rabbis had to bear for they believed that the whole Bible, and especially the Pentateuch, was divine and true. The Rabbis knew the Bible 'almost too painfully well' and to them almost all the statements were equally true. What concerned Montefiore most was that the 'lower' sayings, such as those concerning God's hatred for Edom, became convenient when nationalistic animosities craved Biblical sanction. He concluded that Rabbinic religion was similar to the religion of the Bible – full of inconsistencies and rough edges. Rabbinic Judaism 'lives on the Old Testament and suffers from it'.[27]

Montefiore also criticised the particularism of the Rabbis. He did not ignore the universalistic elements and accepted the view that the expression, 'the righteous of all nations shall inherit the Kingdom of God', eventually became the dominant view although it was a later development. Montefiore's criticism is closely linked to his anti-Zionism. Anything related to nationalism was an anathema. He was unable to distinguish between modern Jewish nationalism and ancient Jewish particularism.

Montefiore's criticisms engendered fierce opposition. He was attacked as much for the manner in which he put his criticisms as for the criticisms themselves. For example, he called the anthropomorphisms which are prevalent in Rabbinic writings 'childish'.[28] Although Montefiore was supported by many Reform Jews he would not go as far as some of the radical reformers. He rejected Holdheim's position and argued against cutting oneself off from the Jewish community. Violent change was as dangerous as rigid orthodoxy. A new development in the evolving religion of Judaism was the answer – something that had regard for the continuity of Judaism.

Montefiore's struggle with the position of Halakhah is a case in point. It is certainly true that he had little appreciation for Halakhah and found many of the Rabbinic discussions distant and obsolete. Yet, at the same time, he was the first to admit that students of Halakhah did not find the subject dull but delighted in the intellectual pursuits it provided. Montefiore realised that modern Judaism was the heir of the Rabbis and that legalism could not be wholly rejected. Law was an integral element of

Judaism although 'the Law' and the belief in the perfection of the Pentateuch had to be revised and some of the results of Biblical criticism accepted. The result of his reasoning was not the rejection of the Law. Rather, it was essential to ask what was going to become of the Law. Montefiore never succeeded in answering his own question except in the most general of ways. Judaism was a legal religion because 'man must recognise ... a Law, which by his own efforts, and by the help of God, he can more and more completely fulfil and obey'.[29] This interpretation allowed little room for traditional Rabbinic legalism.

MODERN JUDAISM:
MONTEFIORE THE LIBERAL LEADER

So far, we have described Montefiore's concern with the development of Judaism in the past. But all the time he was pondering the question: How can Judaism be developed today? Many Jews were becoming indifferent to their religion – something had to be done which would take into account Biblical criticism; which would be thoroughly universalistic, elevating the Prophets above the Law; which would expand the concept of progressive revelation and reject the idea of the one perfect revelation that required only adequate interpretation to secure religious truth; which would develop a theology of other religions and incorporate or graft on to Judaism suitable elements. Liberal Judaism was the answer: it had taken up again, on distinctively Jewish lines, the teaching of the Prophets.

> Much as we reverence the Law, we reverence the Prophets more, much as we recognise that the soul of religion needs a form or an embodiment, and that doctrine requires a 'cult', we yet look upon the 'ceremonial law' with other eyes than that of our forefathers. So Liberal Judaism, while preserving a true connection with all phases of Judaism which may have preceded it, is yet enormously different from any of them.[30]

In 1903 he wrote *Liberal Judaism*, which was his manifesto for a Liberal Jewish movement. A more comprehensive and systematic account of Liberal Judaism was published a few years later under the title *Outlines of Liberal Judaism*. It was during this time that Montefiore wrote numerous pamphlets published by the JRU called 'Papers for Jewish People'. They aimed at disseminating knowledge about Liberal Judaism. He also published a series of essays about the new movement, *Liberal Judaism and Hellenism*. His most important work on Liberal Judaism was the final chapter of *The Old Testament and After*.

Montefiore offended the sensibilities of the majority of the

Jewish community. A cause of this offence was his leaning towards Christianity. It was obvious to all that Montefiore was heavily influenced by Christian scholarship and theology. His admiration for and acceptance of German Protestant scholarship was regarded as treason to the Jewish cause.[31] He was understood by many to be looking forward to a future religion which would be a fusion of the best of both Judaism and Christianity. Although he would not place the New Testament on the same pedestal as that of the Hebrew Bible he still felt it was time for Jews to read the New Testament and to allow it an honoured place in Judaism.

Another controversial and, to many people, an offensive side of his work was his emphasis on universal Jewish teaching at the expense of nationalism. His universalistic fervour led him to become a vigorous opponent of Zionism because it was diametrically opposed to his concept of universal religion. The Jews did not constitute a nation but the tie which bonded them was solely one of religion. The most criticised incident of his career centred around his anti-Zionist activity. In 1917 *The Times* published a manifesto criticising Zionist aspirations, which were then in sight of practical realisation. Montefiore, the chairman of the Anglo-Jewish Association, and D.L. Alexander, president of the Board of Deputies, both signed the manifesto. This unleashed a storm of controversy and Alexander was forced to resign. Montefiore refused to take back anything he wrote and stayed on for four more years. Montefiore was afraid that if a Jewish State did come into existence Jews would no longer be able to freely participate in the social, cultural and political life of their respective countries. It should be added that he was not alone in this fear and that many Jews, Liberal and Orthodox alike, held similar opinions.

Montefiore was an aggressive opponent of Zionism. For instance, when the Balfour Declaration was being discussed by the Cabinet, the text was privately submitted to six Jewish leaders of whom Montefiore was one. He particularly objected to one phrase of the suggested version which described Palestine as 'the national home for the Jewish people' and it was his influence which forced a change. The wording in the final draft was altered to 'a national home for the Jewish people'.

He believed that a Jewish state in essence would be secular. It would possess inhabitants of all religions and therefore could not be a Jewish state. On the other hand if it became a Jewish theocracy, citizenship would be dependent upon the Jewishness of an individual. What would happen, Montefiore asked, if a 'Christian Jew' applied for citizenship?[32] In 1962 that theoretical problem became reality for the Israeli government during the 'Brother Daniel affair' when a Jew who had converted to Christianity applied for, and was refused, citizenship. This case brought out tensions and inconsistencies in Israeli civil law which Montefiore had predicted 50 years earlier.

In opposing Zionism Montefiore was also responding to the rise of anti-semitism. He argued that anti-semitic hatred had in some quarters inclined some Jews to despair – hence the growth of Zionism which, at bottom, was 'a surrender to our enemies, and to their contention that the Jews themselves admit that they cannot become, and that they do not want to become, citizens of the countries in which they dwell'.[33] Zionism had 'put the clock back' and had only fuelled the anti-semitic hatred. He once wrote that 'Weizmann is abler than all the other Jews in the world lumped together . . . He is a Jewish Parnell, but even abler . . . Hitlerism is, at least partially, Weizmann's creation.'[34] If there was one point to which his tolerance did not stretch, this was Zionism. He predicted that it would bring great evil upon Jews and his last days were darkened by its growth.

Montefiore's most important contribution to the development of Anglo-Jewry was his leadership of Liberal Judaism. Western in philosophy, Liberal Judaism was a response to what Montefiore saw as the irreversible decline of Orthodox Judaism. Although Montefiore respected Orthodox Judaism and accepted that for many Jews Orthodoxy was the vehicle through which they drew near to God, he felt it was becoming more and more unacceptable to the majority of Jews.

There were two reasons for this eventual decline – the character of observance and worship and the nature of doctrine. Concerning observance he noted that Hebrew was still used in the synagogue although the younger generation hardly understood the language. Men and women sat apart and consequently the family was separated. Some Jews had little choice but to work for a living on Saturdays and little effort was made to offer services at different times. Sabbath restrictions such as driving made service-going more difficult. The dietary laws hindered social intercourse between Jew and Christian.

Doctrinally there were other factors. If Jews really believed that God ordered Jews never to eat oysters, or to keep men and women apart during services, surely every Jew would make the necessary sacrifices. Yet how could Jews believe this to be so? How could Jews believe that the Pentateuch was wholly inspired and divine? Was the command 'you shall love the neighbour as yourself' no more authoritative than the command 'a garment of two kinds of stuff mingled together shall not come upon you', which immediately succeeds it? Montefiore felt that most Jews could not follow the practices of Orthodox Judaism because they did not believe in them and in the perfection and authority of the Pentateuch. The unbelief helped the unobservance and the unobservance was rooted in unbelief. This vicious circle was the fundamental reason why Montefiore was certain of the decline in Orthodox Judaism, be it in his lifetime or in the future.

If Orthodox Judaism was not satisfying those Jews who went to synagogue or those Jews who did not, what could take its place? The answer, quite obviously, was Liberal Judaism. He believed it would attempt to save all that was true and valuable in Orthodox Judaism and release all that was moribund and obsolete. There were five aspects of Liberal Judaism which gave it the ability to face the future with optimism.

The first was its freedom as regards the results of criticism and history. It did not have to worry whether there was one, two or three Isaiahs. It was almost lifted above historical scholarship. It had to concentrate less on authorship and more on meaning and significance.

Second, Liberal Judaism had the capacity to expand and absorb. Montefiore had no objections to the appropriation of some aspects of Christian thought, for example, as long as they were not inconsistent with Jewish fundamentals. A living religion was never too old to learn. Judaism could learn from its daughter religions as well as those of India. The critical factor, as we saw earlier,[35] was what Montefiore understood by Jewish fundamentals.

Third, Liberal Judaism was still a historical religion. It was the heir to many ancestors, including the Rabbis, and although it was separated from them in some points, it was united with them in the deeper issues.

Fourth, Liberal Judaism was a matter of faith. It was a faith in Judaism and a belief in God. Faith illumined the past, sanctified the present and guaranteed the future. Israel had been charged with a certain mission and this charge had never been cancelled.

Fifth, Liberal Judaism had the capacity to universalise and spiritualise what was national and particularist. Liberal Jews no longer saw Israel as a race but a religious community, the borders of which were not limited by ties of kinship or blood.

Liberal Judaism was a crucial phase in the development of Judaism. It offered hope for the future and maintained a link with the past. In Montefiore's mind, Liberal Judaism appeared to be the most dynamic form of Judaism. Only Liberal Judaism could ensure Judaism's long term survival and health. There were many aspects to Judaism at the time but there was only one which could make the Jewish religion a significant force among the religions of the world.

NOTES

INTRODUCTION

1. Lucy Cohen, *Some Recollections of Claude Goldsmid Montefiore* (London, Faber and Faber, 1940), p.47.
2. *Hibbert Lectures on the Origin of Religion as Illustrated by the Ancient Hebrews* (London, Williams and Norgate), p.x. Note the use of the word 'Law' for a translation of 'Torah', which is derived from the root 'to teach'. 'Torah' means much more than 'Law'. It means literally: 'instruction', 'path', or 'way'. More generally, it refers to the entire body of Jewish writing. It is impossible to translate 'Torah' with one English word and the use of 'Law' tends to mislead the reader. The word 'Law' derives from the Septuagint translation (*Nomos*), translated by Jerome as *Lex*. In recent years, Christian and Jewish scholars have begun to grapple with this problem together. The best solution may be just to leave it without any translation. This difficulty went unnoticed in Montefiore's day and we find in his, and in other contemporary Jewish writings, frequent use of the word 'Law' as a translation of 'Torah'. For further information, see Charlotte Klein, *Anti-Judaism in Christian Theology* (Trans. Edward Quinn) (London, SPCK, 1978), p.39ff.
3. Cohen, *Some Recollections*, p.115.
4. In 1910 the work became too much for the Editors (especially Israel Abrahams) and all rights were transferred to Dropsie College in Philadelphia, where it is still published today.
5. *Outlines of Liberal Judaism* (London, Macmillan, 1912), p.212.
6. *The Synoptic Gospels*, Vol. 1 (London, Macmillan, 1909), p.cxxxv.
7. 'The Significance of Jesus for his Own Age', *Hibbert Journal*, 10 (1911–12), p.773.
8. *The Old Testament and After* (London, Macmillan, 1923), p.561.
9. *Synoptic Gospels*, Vol. 2 (London, Macmillan, 1909), pp.326–27.
10. Cohen, *Some Recollections*, p.189.
11. *A Rabbinic Anthology* (London, Macmillan, 1938), p.xxiv.
12. *Ibid.*, pp.xxxv–xxxvi.
13. 'Some Reflections on the Rabbinic Religion', *The Quest* (1927), pp.21–2.
14. *The Old Testament and After* (London, Macmillan, 1923), p.299.
15. *Jewish Chronicle*, 8 September 1909, p.15.
16. Charles Singer, whose father, Simeon Singer, was the editor and translator of the Orthodox *Authorised Daily Prayerbook*.
17. Cohen, *Some Recollections*, p.98.
18. 'Anti-Semitism in England', *Hibbert Journal*, 19 (1920–21), p.345.
19. Cohen, *Some Recollections*, p.253.

THE HEBREW BIBLE

1. Astruc argued that Moses actually wrote the Pentateuch but that he used different sources. See *Conjectures sur les mémoires originaux dont it paroit que Moyse se servit pour composer le livre de la Genèse* (1753).
2. Johann Eichorn, *Einleitung in das Alte Testament* (Leipzig, 1787).
3. Wellhausen's *Prolegomena zur Geschichte Israels* (Berlin, 1882, translated into English 1885) was the most important work on Biblical criticism in the 19th

century. Wellhausen published other valuable writings including *Geschichte Israelite* (1878). See Herbert Hahn, *The Old Testament and Modern Research* (SCM, London, 1956), pp.11ff.

4. The *Grundschaft* (the primary source) had been associated with the 'Priestly document' but Vatke proved that the latter was, in fact, a much later document.

5. (i) 'E' source – derived from the divine name, Elohim; (ii) 'J' source – derived from the German spelling of the Tetragrammaton; (iii) 'P' source – the Priestly code, apparently written by members of the priesthood; (iv) 'D' source – the author of Deuteronomy. These four sources were fused together by a redactor ('R') or redactors.

6. John Rogerson, *Old Testament Criticism in the Nineteenth Century* (Cambridge University Press, Cambridge, 1985), p.250.

7. See *The Old Testament and the Jewish Church* (1881) and *The Prophets of Israel and their place in History to the close of the eighth century B.C.* (1882). In addition, he wrote an introduction to the translation of Wellhausen's *Prolegomena*.

8. Preface, *Lex Mundi*. See Owen Chadwick, op. cit., pp.101ff.

9. 'It is an infelicity of the modern German mind that it is acute in observing detached differences rather than comprehensive in grasping deeper resemblances. It has been more busied in discovering what is new, than in observing the ground of what is true.' (*Minor Prophets*, pp.510–11).

10. See *Introduction to the Old Testament* (in The International Theological Library, 1891) which was very much dependent upon the results of German scholarship.

11. Louis Jacobs, *Principles of Jewish Faith* (Vallentine, Mitchell, London, 1964), pp.216–302.

12. Louis Jacobs writes:

> The passage under discussion is a cryptic one and is not easily deciphered, but this is its meaning according to Spinoza: In the verse: 'These are the words which Moses spoke to all Israel behond the Jordon' the words 'beyond the Jordon' are puzzling. In Moses' day the Israelites had not yet entered Palestine so that in those days the words 'beyond the Jordon' would refer to Palestine itself, not to the land in which the Israelites were encamped when they heard Moses' farewell address. On this Ibn Ezra says. 'If you know the secret of the twelve, and of "And Moses wrote", "And the Canaanite was then in the land", "Behold his bedstead was a bedstead of iron" you will discover the truth'. Spinoza in his Theological and Political Tract, published in 1670, explained this as follows. 'The secret of the twelve' means the last twelve verses of the Penteteuch which deal with the death of Moses and could not have been written by Moses himself. Similarly, the words 'And Moses wrote' presuppose another author. 'And the Canaanite was then in the land' is hard to explain if this verse was written by Moses because in his day they were sill in the land. 'Behold his bedstead was a bedstead of iron' speaks of the bedstead of Og, king of Bashan, who was slain by Moses near the end of the latter's life, while the words appear to suggest that the bedstead was pointed out as a landmark many years after Og had been slain.

We Have Reason to Believe (Vallentine, Mitchell, London, 1956), p.65.

13. 'Orthodox Judaism's stance is based upon a passage in the Talmud. "Who wrote the Scriptures? – Moses wrote his own Book and the portion of Balaam and Job. Joshua wrote the Book which bears his name and the book of Judges and Ruth. David wrote the Book of Psalms, including in it the works of the elders, namely Adam, Melchizedek, Abraham, Moses, Haman, Yeduthan, Asaph, and the three sons of Korah. Jeremiah wrote the Book which bears his name, the Book of Isaiah, Proverbs, Song of Songs, Ecclesiastes. The Men of the Great Assembly wrote Ezekiel, the Twelve Minor Prophets, Daniel and the Scroll of Esther. Ezra wrote the Book that bears his name and the genealogies of the Book of Chronicles

up to his own time." Hag 6a–b; Sot. 37b; Zeb. 115b.' Louis Jacobs, *We Have Reason to Believe*, op. cit., p.60.

14. He argued against a separate Holiness Code in Leviticus, inserted by 'P', and asserted that Ezekiel was dependent upon the Pentateuch and not vice versa. See *Die Wichtigsten Instanzen gegen die Graf-Wellhausenische Hypothese* (Berlin, 1903).

15. See *The Study of the Bible Today and Tomorrow*, ed. H. Willoughby (University of Chicago, Chicago, 1947), pp.98ff. Montefiore was also aware of these anti-Semitic tendencies:

> They [the critics] freely use the language of mocking irreverance . . . in Wellhausen, who is responsible for this ugly fashion, brilliance and even genius cover the gravity of the descent from the language of Ewald. But in the hands of the ordinary clever and industrious German professors, this laborious humour is quite unendurable, and the anti-Semitic prejudice which is presumably at the bottom of it all is only too easily and clumsily revealed.

Jewish Quarterly Review, Vol. 19, p.281.

16. *Affirmations of Judaism*, p.41.

17. Preface to the first edition of his commentary to Pentateuch and Haftorahs. He also wrote that 'every attack on the Torah is at the same time an assault against Israel as well as a revolt against the Spiritual and Divine in history and human life'. *Affirmations of Judaism*, pp.29ff.

18. Isadore Epstein, *The Faith of Judaism* (London, 1954), pp.112–13. It is certainly true that Biblical criticism is not as sure today or even 30 years ago as it was in the 19th century. Many views of Wellhausen have been challenged, such as the division of the documents. However, the central tenets, such as the conclusion that Moses did not write the Pentateuch, are not now questioned by scholars. Jewish scholars who have modified the Wellhausen position include U. Cassuto (*Torat ha Te'udot*, 1941; translated, *The Document Hypothesis*, 1961); Y. Kaufmann (*Toldot ha Emunah ha Yisrael'elit*, 1937–57; translated, *The religion of Israel*, 1960); M.H. Segal (*The Pentateuch, it Composition and its Authorship*, 1967).

19. Solomon Schechter, *Studies in Judaism* (Philadelphia, 1945), Vol. 1, pp.40–1.

20. Ibid., p.xiv.

21. Morrish Joseph, *Judaism as Creed and Life* (London, 1903), p.19.

22. *Liberal Judaism and Hellenism*, pp.20–1.

23. *The Old Testament and After*, pp.285–8.

24. 'A Plea for the Old Testament', *The Nineteenth Century*, pp.832–3.

25. Ibid., pp.836–7.

26. *Some Introductory Remarks on the Psalter*, pp.17–19.

27. *The Old Testament and After*, pp.118–23.

28. Leviticus 19:34. 'The stranger [*ger*] who sojourns with you shall be as the native among you, and you shall love him as yourself.'

29. *The Old Testament and After*, pp.183–5.

30. Amos 5–24.

31. Proverbs 22:2. 'The Old Testament and its Ethical Teaching', *Papers for Jewish People*, pp.10–11.

32. The Hibbert Lectures on *The Origin and Growth of Religion as illustrated by the Ancient Hebrews*, pp.156–8.

33. *Liberal Judaism*, pp.96–8.

34. *The Old Testament and Judaism*, pp.11–14.

35. Lev. 19:18 'You shall love your neighbours as yourself'; Lev. 19:34 'The stranger [*ger*] who sojourns with you shall be as the native among you, and you shall love him as yourself.'

36. *A Short Devotional Introduction to the Hebrew Bible*, pp.49–50.

37. It is interesting to note Montifiore's reliance upon Kant at this point. Morality as

Kant expounds it involves autonomy of the will and such autonomy makes sense only with freedom. We are to think of the will as free and at the same time as subject to the moral law, i.e., under obligation The autonomy of the will ensures the centrality of the individual in contrast to the community. One or two examples from the writings of Montefiore make his dependence clear:

> The Law which man is to obey and fulfil is both human and divine; God is at its source and God enjoins it. It is independent of man and outside him, but it is also within him. He realises himself in accepting the Law. He is most a slave when he is most lawless; when he is most lawful he is most free.

Liberal Judaism, p.117.

> Judaism, I take it, holds that man to be as good as he can be must be rule by law. He must be ruled by a law which he accepts, but the source of which he recognises as outside of him and greater than he. He must feel the compulsion of law, and yet, through that compulsion, he must rise to a higher freedom . . . The constraint of law is the beginning of the higher freedom; the human freedom which leads up to the freedom of God. For God we may regard as completely free or completely bound. He is bound in his own freedom. He never wants to do anything but what he does. He is the subject of law, but the law is his own law. Man is never wholly free or wholly bound. The external law never wholly becomes his own law, and for two reasons. First, because it is God's law, and therefore man is always subject (however freely) to a law which is not wholly his own, seeing that its source is outside him. Secondly, because man is never completely moralised. He is always straining towards an ideal, which is ever receding. He can never become so good that there is no possible conflict with temptation or desire. Nevertheless, his freedom, the realisation of himself, the fulfilment of his being, reside and consist in the free acceptance and execution of the moral law. The more he freely fulfils that law, the more man he becomes, and the more he becomes like unto God. The outward must also become inward, but however inward it becomes (however much the ideal of Jeremiah 31:33 is realised), it still always remains the law of God.

Outlines of Liberal Judaism, pp.223–4.
38. *The Old Testament and After,* pp.137–40.

CHRISTIANITY AND THE NEW TESTAMENT

1. For example, on a verse in the Mishnah, *Avodah Zarah* 1:8, 'One should not let a house to a Gentile,' Ha Me'iri commented that 'this prohibition applies fundamentally only to those idolators who kept their idols in their house, and sacrificed to them there' (cf. Beth-Ha-Bekhirah on *Avodah Zarah.* Also see J. Katz, *Exclusiveness and Tolerance,* Schocken, New York, 1962, pp.114–28). This later became the basis for today's traditional (Orthodox) Jewish attitude towards Christianity.
2. It is true, however, that Rashi felt Christians were not 'versed in the worship of idols', but this was merely an attempt to exempt the wine of Christians from being regarded as 'libation wine' and therefore prohibited to a Jew. Jacob Katz understands it to have been primarily a change in a particular custom rather than a change in Jewish theology. See Jacob Katz, op. cit., p.34.
3. His polemical writings were mainly based on the *Sefer ha-Berit* of Joseph Kimhi. He attacked various christological interpretations by demonstrating Christian 'corruption', cf. comments on Isa. 2:22, Ps.22:57, and on the inapplicability (Isa. 7:14, Ez.44:2) or irrationally of the interpretation (Ps. 87, Ps. 110).

4. Cynical conversions included that of Heinrich Heine who said that the 'baptismal certificate is the ticket of admission to Europe culture'. cf. Paul R. Mendes-Flohr and Jehuda Reinharz, *The Jew in the Modern World* (Oxford University Press, Oxford, 1980), p.223.
5. Samuel Hirsch is one example of the attempt to demonstrate that Judaism, not Christianity, was the superior religion. See *Das Judentum* (Leipzig, 1843).
6. Schechter termed anti-Jewish bias in Christian scholarship as the 'higher anti-Semitism'.
7. George Foot Moore and more recently Charlotte Klein and E.P. Sanders have examined the works of these scholars and have made clear their bias. They have proved that these scholars made an inadequate and one-sided selection of Jewish sources and possessed an a priori biased attitude towards those sourses. In addition, their method of comparison depreciated all things Jewish and exalted all things Christian. See George Foot Moore, *Christian Writers on Judaism*, op. cit., Charlotte Klein, *Anti-Judaism in Christian Theology*, op cit.; E.P. Sanders, *Jesus and Judaism* (SPCK, London, 1986), pp.24ff.
8. Their emphasis upon the Jewishness of Jesus was an attempt to diminish, or even reject, any of the originality of Jesus. See Walter Jacob, *Christianity through Jewish Eyes* (Hebrew Union College Press, 1974), pp.42ff.
9. R.T. Herford was a Liberal Christian scholar who devoted his life to researching the Judaism of the Second Temple and Talmud. He was fascinated by and sympathetic to the Pharisees. His most important works included *Christianity in Talmud and Midrash* (1903), and *The Pharisees* (1924). George Foot Moore dealt with Tannaitic teaching and although he neglected the variety of views in Judaism, his three-volume work *Judaism* (1927-1930) contributed to the study of Rabbinic Judaism. Solomon Schechter spent most of his life examining Jewish Tradition and his works included *Studies in Judaism* (3 vols, 1896-1924) and *Some Aspects of Rabbinic Theology* (1909). Israel Abrahams was Reader in Rabbinics at Cambridge and a major exponent of Jewish scholarship in England. Adolf Buchler concerned himself particularly with the history of the Second Temple period and responded to the writings of E. Schurer. See *Studies in Sin and Atonement in the Rabbinic Literature of the First Century* (1921). This is not a comprehensive list but merely mentions some of the most important contributors to the scholarship of this period all of whom dealt with the negative portrayal of Judaism.
10. It is difficult to appreciate the controversy that dogged Montefiore throughout his life. We live today in an ecumenical and reasonably tolerant society. Leslie Edgar wrote that

> at one point in his long discussion with me, I saw – for the first and only time – something approaching anger, and certainly scorn, when he [Montefiore] told me that many Jewish friends had said to him: 'You know, Montefiore, I would join your movement if you would only give up your pre-occupation with Jesus and the Gospels.' I can still hear the ring of Montefiore's voice as he said: 'Of course I wouldn't.'

See Leslie Edgar, *Claude Montefiore's thought and the present religious situation*, p.21.
11. Jesus did not intend to separate all material-legalistic elements from religion and ethics but to de-emphasize the particularistic needs of the nation and to cause them to be forgotten; thereby he negated unconsciously Judaism as the particular philosophy of life of the Israelite nation. For a religion that stresses a concept of God and ethics that is universal and generally human, shatters the fences of nationalism consciously or not. But, Judaism wanted to live and to survive as the bearer of a great national-human ideal, for which the time was not yet ripe in the time of Jesus. For the sake of humanity in the future, Judaism had to survive in its national distinctiveness. Feeling the danger to its particularism that is contained in the ethical teaching of Jesus, Judaism rejected his teaching with both hands.

NOTES

See J. Klausner, *History of the Second Temple*, Vol. 4, p.260. This paragraph shows Klausner's intention to explain the split between Judaism and Christiniaty solely in nationalistic terminology. He attempted to justify the position of the modern nationalist Israeli through the retrojection of Christian Universalism and modern Jewish nationalism into ancient times.

12. 'The "problem" of Jesus for modern Jews is not only religious and psychological, but also cultural and sociological. It is especially rooted in matters of history, and in what partakes of folk experience and folk wisdom, even in modern and cosmopolitan situations.' See S. Sandmel, *We Jews and Jesus* (Oxford University Press, New York, 1965), p.6.
13. *The Synoptic Gospels*, Vol. 1, pp.cxxxvi–cxxvii.
14. Ibid., pp.xx–xxi.
15. Ibid., pp.xxiv–xxvi.
16. Amos 3:2.
17. Reward.
18. *The Synoptic Gospels*, Vol. 1, pp.cxvii–cxx.
19. *The Old Testament and After*, pp.229–32.
20. Ibid., pp.239–41.
21. Ibid., pp.244–4.
22. *The Synoptic Gospels*, Vol. 1, p.xx.
23. Ibid., p.cxxxv.
24.   It [Mark 7:15] was a noble, a liberating utterance. When we remember the immense burden which material conceptions of clean and unclean had imposed upon humanity in earlier primitive relitions; when we think of these conceptions in their relation not merely to food, but to the sexual life, or to intercourse between the members of one faith and race and the members of another; or when we bear in mind the many troubles of the priesthoods and the vanities of priestly purity – can we laud too highly, can we appreciate too gratefully, the grand and prophetic principle that only that which comes out of a man can make him unclean? Things cannot defile persons . . . The spiritual personality can only be spiritually defiled.

Some Elements of the Teachings of Jesus, pp.49–50.
25. Matt. 5:18, 'For truly I say to you, till heaven and earth pass away not an iota, not a dot, will pass from the law until all is accomplished.'
26. Matt. 11:13–15, 'Truly, I say to you, among those born of women there has been no one greater than John the Baptist; yet he who is least in the Kingdom of Heaven is greater than he. From the days of John the Baptist until now the Kingdom Of Heaven has suffered violence, and men of violence take it by force. For all the prophets and the law prophesised until John; and if you are willing to accept it, he is Elijah who is to come. 'Luke 16:16: 'The law and the prophets were until John; since then good news of the Kingdom of God is preached, and every one enters it violently.'
27. Edicts.
28. *The Synoptic Gospels*, Vol. 1, pp.130–1; 156–60.
29. Ezekiel 36:25ff.
30. *The Old Testament and After*, pp.252–3.
31. Luke 6:27–8: 'But I say to you that hear, Love your enemies, do good to those who hate you, bless those who curse you, pray for those who abuse you.'
32. Luke 23:34: 'And Jesis said, "Father, forgive them for they know not what they do."'
33. Matt. 11:20–24: 'Then he began to upbraid the cities where most of his mightly works had been done, because they did not repent. "Woe to you, Chorazin! Woe to you Bethsadai! For if the mighty works done in you had been done in Tyre and Sidon, they would have repented long ago in sackcloth and ashes. But I tell you it shall be more tolerable on that day for Tyre and Sidon than for you. And you

Capernaum, will you be exalted in heaven? You shall be brought down to Hades. For if the mighty works done in you had been done in Sodom, it would have remained until this day. But I tell you that it shall be more tolerable on the day of judgement for the land of Sodom than for you."'

34. *Rabbinic Literature and Gospel Teachings*, pp.103–4.
35. *The Synoptic Gospels*, Vol. 2, p.456.
36. Amos 3:2.
37. *The Synoptic Gospels*, Vol. 1, pp. 395–6.
38. *Hibbert Journal*, Vol. 3, p.779.
39. *Judaism and St Paul*, pp.126–9.
40. *The Bible for Home Reading*, Vol. 2, pp.778–81.
41. *The Old Testament and After*, pp.210–11.
42. *Liberal Judaism and Helllenism*, pp.127–8.
43. *The Synoptic Gospels*, Vol. 2, pp.326–7.
44. Hibbert Lectures on *The Origin and Growth of Religion as Illustrated by the Ancient Hebrews*, pp.409–13.
45. *Some Elementss of the Religious Teachings of Jesus*, p.31.
46. *The Synoptic Gospelss*, Vol. 2, pp.40–1.
47. *Hibbert Journal*, Vol. 1, pp.636–45.
48. *A Rabbinic Anthology*, pp.612–16.

TORAH AND RABBINIC JUDAISM

1. Halakhah is the name given to the body of rules forming a coherent system embracing personal, social, national, international relationships and all other practices and observances of Judaism. It is often translated by the term 'Jewish Law'.
2. Hillel nullified the Biblical law about the remission of debts in the Sabbatical years (Deuteronomy 15:2; Sevi'it 10:4); Yohanan ben Zakkai suspended the ordeal of jealousy (Numbers 5:11–31; Sotah 9:9); Joshua ben Chananyah rendered inoperative the prohibition against the Ammonite and Moabite prosellytes marrying into the Jewish community (Deuteronomy 23:4; Yadayim 4:4). The Rabbis were aware of exactly what they were doing and it was common to read in the Rabbinical literature that laws in the Oral Torah were 'like mountains suspended by a hair', i.e. that the scriptural pegs on which they hung were very slight (Hagigah 10a).
3. Cf. Shabbat 112b.
4. Solomon Freehof, *Reform Jewish Practice* (Union of American Hebrew Congregations, New York, 1963), p.10.
5. We should mention the famous Orthodox rabbi in Pressberg, Moses Sofer (1762–1839), who virtually declared war on liberal interpretations in Judaism. He coined a famous phrase which became the banner of strict Orthodoxy – 'Anything new is forbidden by the Torah.' According to his understanding any innovation was strictly forbidden because it was an innovation.
6. Solomon Freehof, *Reform Responsa* (Ktav, 1973), p.15.
7. *Rabbinische Gutachten*, I, 71. See David Philipson, 'Samuel Holdheim, Jewish Reformer' in *Central Conference of American Rabbis Yearbook*, 1906, pp.305–33.
8. The influence of Protestant Biblical scholarship and nineteenth-century romanticism is noticeable in these views.
9. See Samuel S. Cohon, 'Authority in Judaism', *Hebrew Union College Annual*, Vol. 11, 1936, pp.636ff.
10. See J.J. Petuchowski, *Hebrew Union College Annual*, Vol. 31, 1960, pp.223–50.
11. *Nachgelassenen Schriften*, I, Berlin, 1875, p.448.
12. Montefiore's tribute to his teacher in the preface to the Hibbert Lectures makes

clear his respect and admiration for Schechter.

13. It might also be suggested that Montefiore's growing radicalism was connected to Schechter's departure to the United States to lead the Conservative Movement. Schechter was opposed to the Anglicised and almost Anglicanised aspects of Liberal Judaism as envisaged by his student. Cf. 'Four Epistles to the Jews of England' in *Studies in Judaism*, Second series, London, 1908, pp.182–201.

14. Similar negative views were held by many influential German Protestant writers, among them, Ferdinand Weber and Wilhelm Bousset. See George Foot Moore, 'Christian Writers on Judaism', *Harvard Theological Review*, Vol. 14, 1927, pp.198–254.

15. 'For three transgressions women die in childbirth: because they have been negligent in regard to their periods of separation, in respect to the consecration of the first cake of the dough, and in the lighting of the Sabbath lamp.'

16. *A Rabbinic Anthology*, pp.xxiii–xxv.

17. *The Old Testament and After*, pp.365–6.

18. Ibid., pp.377–8.

19. *A Few Rabbinic Ideals*, pp.15–20.

20. *A Rabbinic Anthology*, pp.xxxv–xxxvi.

21. Numbers 25:1–18:

> While Israel dwelt in Shittim the people began to play the harlot with the daughters of Moab. These invited the people to the sacrifices of their gods, and the people ate and bowed down to their gods. So Israel yoked himself to Ba'al of Pe'or. And the anger of the Lord was kindled against Israel; and the Lord said to Moses, 'Take all the chiefs of the people, and hang them in the sun before the Lord, that the fierce anger of the Lord may turn away from Israel.' And Moses said to the judges of Israel, 'Every one of you slay his men who have yoked themselves to Ba'al of Pe'or.' And behold, one of the people of Israel came and brought a Midianite woman too his family, in the sight of Moses and in the sight of the whole congregation of the people of Israel, while they were weeping at the door of the tent of meeting. When Phineas, the son of Eleazer, son of Aaron the priest, saw it, he rose and left the congregation, and took a spear in his hand and went after the man of Israel into the inner room, and pierced both of them, the man of Israel and the woman through her body. Nevertheless those that died by the plague were twenty four thousand. And the Lord said to Moses, 'Phineas, the son of Eleazor, son of Aaron the priest, has turned back my wrath from the people of Israel, in that he was jealous with my jealousy among them, so that I did not consume the people of Israel in my jealousy. Therefore say, "Behold I give to him my covenant of peace; and it shall be to him, and to his descendents after him, the covenant of a perpetual priesthood, because he was jealous for his God, and made atonement for the people of Israel."' The name of the slain man of Israel, who was slain with the Midianite woman was Zimri the son of Salu, head of a fathers' house belonging to the Simeonites. And the name of the Midianite woman who was slain was Cozbi the daughter of Zur, who was the head of the people of a fathers' house in Midian. And the Lord said to Moses, 'Harass the Midianites, and smite them; for they have harassed you with their wiles, with which they beguiled you in the matter of Pe'or, and in the matter of Cozbi, the daughter of the prince of Midian, their sister who was slain on the day of the plague on account of Pe'or.'

22. Montefiore was commenting on Numbers Rabah 21.1:

> It is written, 'I make with him [Phinehas] a covenant of peace' (Num. 25:12). Great is the peace which God gave to Phinehas, for the world is governed only with peace, as it is said, 'All her pathss are peace' (Prov. 3:17). And if a man comes back from a journey, they greet him with peace, and they ask for

peace evening and morning, and after the reading of the Shema, they end with 'who spreads the tent of His peace on His people' (Prayer Book pp.53, 94, 114).

And the daily prayer ends with peace (ibid. p.54), and the priestly benediction likewise. R. Simeon b. Halafta said: 'There is no way to bless except through peace, as it is said, "The Lord blesses His people with peace" (Ps. 29:11).'

23. Numbers Rabah 21.3.
24. Deut. 23:3-6:

> No-one misbegotten shall be admitted into the congregation of the Lord; none of his descendents, even to the tenth generation, shall be admitted into the congregation of the Lord. No Ammonite or Moabite shall be admitted into the congregation of the Lord; none of their descendents, even to the tenth generation, shall ever be admitted into the congregation of the Lord because they did not meet you with food or water on your journey after you left Egypt and because they hired Balaam son of Pe'or, from Pithor of Aramnaharaim to curse you. But the Lord your God refused to heed to Balaam; instead, the Lord your God turned the curse into a blessing, for the Lord your God loves you.

25. A Rabbinic Anthology, p.534.
26. The Old Testament and After, pp.299-300.
27. A Short Devotional Introduction to the Hebrew Bible, pp.116-17.
28. The Old Testament and After, pp.371-4.
29. A Few Rabbinic Ideals, pp.4-6.
30. Liberal Judaism, pp.107-8.
31. Aboth 2.2; 4.14.
32. The Hibbert Lectures, The Origin and Growth of Religion as illustrated by the Ancient Hebrews, pp.494-6.
33. The Old Testament and After, pp.140-2.
34. Ibid., pp.461-2.
35. The Synoptic Gospels, Vol. 1, pp.55-6.
36. Matt 18:14: 'So it is not in the will of my Father who is in heaven that one of these little ones should perish.'
37. Matt. 25:41-6:

> Then he will say to those at his left hand, 'Depart from me you cursed, into the eternal fire prepared for the devil and his angels; for I was hungry and you gave me no food, I was thirsty and you gave me no drink. I was a stranger and you did not welcome me, naked and you did not clothe me, sick and in prison and you did not visit me.' Then they also will answer, 'Lord, when did we see thee hungry or thirsty or a stranger or naked or sick or in prison, and did not minister to thee?' Then he will answer them, 'Truly, I say to you, as you did it not to one of the lease of these, you did it not to me.' And they will go away into eternal punishment, but the righteous into eternal life.

38. Matt. 7:13-14: 'Enter by the narrow gate; for the gate is wide and the way is easy, that leads to destruction, and those who enter by it are many. For the gate is narrow and the way is hard, that leads to life and those who find it are few.'
39. Matt. 11:20-24:

> Then he began to upbraid the cities where most of his mighty works had been done, because they did not repent. 'Woe to you Chorazin! Woe to you Bethsaida! For if the mighty works had been done in Tyre or Sidon, they would have repented long ago in sackcloth and ashes. But I tell you, it shall be more tolerable on the day of judgement for Tyre and Sidon than for you. And you Capernaum, will you be exalted to heaven? You shall be brought down to Hades. For if they mighty works done in you had been doen in Sodom, it

would have remained until this day. But I tell you that it shall be more tolerable on the day of judgement for the land of Sodom than for you.'

40. *Rabbinic Literature and Gospel Teachings* pp.261-2.
41. *Liberal Judaism and Hellenism*, pp.120-1.
42. *The Old Testament and After*, pp.215-17.
43. Ibid.., pp.384-5.

MODERN JUDAISM

1. 'We, God's people who are dispersed in all the lands of greater Germany and grew up under the impact of the language of the dominant peoples, "came down wonderfully" and there is "none raising us up". For the ways of our holy tongue have been forgotten in our midst; the elegance of its phraseology eludes us; and the loveliness of its poetry is hidden from us. No one takes care to render the Tora in the German tongue as spoken today among our own people.' These words of Moses Mendelssohn from his work *Álim ha-Terufa* (1778) not only describe the sad situation in German Jewry but also underscore the importance of his translation of the Bible into German. Cf. Alexander Altmann, *Moses Mendelssohn* (Jewish Publication Society, Philadelphia, 1973), pp.368-83.
2. Marvin Lowenthal, *The Jews of Germany* (Jewish Publication Society, Philadelphia, 1936), pp.242ff.
3. The influences of Christianity and Rationalism are noticeable in the words of Israel Jacobson (1768-1828), one of the earliest reformers, who wrote that 'our ritual is still weighted down with religious customs which must be rightfully offensive to reason as well as to our Christian friends.' W. Gunter Plaut, *The Rise of Reform Judaism* (World Union for Progressive Judaism, New York, 1963), p.30.
4. 'Adapt yourselves to the customs and the constitution of the land in which you live; yet at the same time, adhere firmly to the religion of your ancestors. Carry both burdens as well as you can.' Cf. W. Plaut, op. cit., p.78. Uplifting as these words may be, they did not offer practical solutions to the problems facing Jews.
5. In 1817 the Prussian Government ordered all private synagogues to be closed. This action was apparently directed against Reform synagogues in Berlin, established by Israel Jacobson and Jacob Herz Beer. David Philipson has suggested that the reason for official intervention lay in the government's inability, or unwillingness, to accept that there 'was still life in the religion'. David Philipson, *The Reform Movement in Judaism* (Cincinnati, 1930), p.25.
6. It is interesting to question whether the conflict in Eastern Europe between the Hasidim and the mitnaggidim had an impact. Some of the grievances the reformers nursed paralleled complaints of the Hasidim. Perhaps the traditional community, learning from the failure of their fellow traditionalists in Eastern Europe to stamp out the Hasidic movement, decided to oppose any Jewish group immediately they demanded reforms similar to those of the Hasidim. However, very little work has been devoted to this subject and one must await further study before attempting a conclusion.
7. Zunz did not fail to offer the reformers advice although he refused to speak at their conferences. 'The closest attention in the movement for improvements in the service of the synagogue should be given to the removal of faults and abuses, and to the reintroduction of the regular sermons. Let the speaker be called what he will, preacher or rabbi, teacher or orator so long as he understands how to expound the word of God, to extract the pure gold from the old and new fields, to teach the present generation its true work and to reach all ears by skilful speech.' *The Homilies of the Jews, Historically Developed* ('Die Gottesdienstlichen der Juden Vortrage Historish Entwickelt') (Berlin, 1832), p.451. Cf. David Philipson, op. cit., pp.28ff.

8. 'Every era in the history of Judaism is of importance, the present can break with the past as little as every separate limb can separate itself from the body without suffering serious injury. Such a connection with the past means not the dominance of dead custom, but the persistence of the living idea which permeates all ages with vigour and if it leads to different developments, this does not justify a disregard of its origins.' *Nachgelassene Schriften*, I (Berlin, 1875), p.205.

9. The early period of Reform was also marked by a discussion of whether changes were supported by the Talmud. The Hungarian rabbi Aaron Chorin (1760–1844) supported the demands of the reformers. He issued a pamphlet in 1814 entitled *Kin at ha-Emet* (Zeal for the Truth) where he argued that the Talmud permitted services to be held in the vernacular. By appealing to the authority of the Talmud reformers showed their desire to avoid sectarianism. Many justified their changes in the traditional Jewish manner and perhaps hoped to maintain unity in Judaism.

10. 1. We recognise the possibility of unlimited progress in Mosaism.
    2. The collection of controversies, dissertations and prescriptions commonly designated by the name Talmud possess for us no authority either from the dogmatic or practical standpoint.
    3. A messiah who is to lead the Israelites back to the land of Palestine is neither expected nor desired by us; we know of no fatherland except that to which we belong by birth or citizenship.
    David Philipson, op. cit., pp.122–3.

11. It is interesting to note that Geiger, although he never expressed his views publicly, also opposed circumcision. In a letter to Zunz he wrote, 'I cannot comprehend the working up of a spirit of enthusiasm for the ceremony [circumcision] merely on the ground that it is held in general esteem. It remains a bloody barbarous act.' W. Plaut, op. cit., p.209.

12. 'All our effort for the restoration of a worthy celebration of the Sabbath is fruitless and there is unfortunately no thorough remedy whereby the conflict between the Sabbath and the demands of daily life can be removed other than the transfer of the Sabbath to a civil day of rest.' From a speech at the Breslau conference, 1846. See David Philipson, op. cit., p.208.

13. There had been attempts at Reform in Charleston during the mid-1820s. However, due to lack of leadership it collapsed a few years later. Just before Wise arrived, the Baltimore 'Har Sinal' congregation was established (1842) and three years later a New York congregation followed, called 'Emanuel'.

14. When these organisations were established with the support of Wise it was no coincidence that in their names there was no mention of the word 'reform' – Central Conference of American Rabbis and the Hebrew Union College. Cf. W. Plaut, *The Growth of Reform Judaism* (World Union for Progressive Judaism, New York, 1965), p.xxi.

15. Orthodoxy was the title by which the opponents of Reform became known. It later came to designate those who believed in, and acted accordingly from, the divine nature of Torah.

16. W. Plaut, *The Rise of Reform Judaism*, op. cit., p.123.

17. David Philipson, op. cit., p.353.

18. W. Plaut, *The Growth of Reform Judaism*, op. cit., pp.31–41.

19. For a complete list of synagogues which offered Sabbath services on Sundays see David Philipson, op. cit., p.374. Cf. W. Plaut, *The Rise of Reform Judaism*, op. cit., pp.184–95. The conference adopted this resolution:

    Whereas we recognise the importance of maintaining the historical Sabbath as a bond with our great past and as a symbol of the unity of Judaism the world over, whereas, on the other hand, it cannot be denied that there is a vast number of working men and others who, for some cause or another, are not able to attend the services on the sacred day of rest, be it resolved that there is nothing in the spirit of Judaism or its laws to prevent the introduction of Sunday services in localities where the necessity for such services appears or is felt.

20.   We naturally favour the facilitation of immigration to Palestine to Jews who, either because of environmental necessity or political or religious persecution desire to settle there. . . . We do not subscribe to the phrase in the declaration which says, 'Palestine is to be a national homeland for the Jewish people'. . . . We hold that the Jewish people are and of right ought to be at home in all lands. Israel, like every other religious communion, had the right to live and assert its message in any part of the world.

Response to the Balfour Declaration. *Central Conference of American Rabbis Yearbook* (1918), Vol. 28, pp.133–4. The overwhelming majority of Orthodox Jews saw in the efforts for the restoration of Jewish nationhood an affront to the command to wait for the Messiah. They also disagreed with the definition of Jewry as a modern nation which accepted religious and non-religious Jews as equal. They also feared a Jewish homeland would call into question the loyalty of Jews outside of Eretz, Yisrael.

21. Todd Endelman, *The Jews of Georgian England* (Jewish Publication Society, Philadephia, 1979), pp.ix–x.
22. Chaim Bermant, *Troubled Eden* (Vallentine, Mitchell, London, 1969), p.62.
23. Moses Montefiore, a great opponent of Reform, would not allow any representatives of the West London Synagogue to participate in the activities of the Board of Deputies for 30 years. Chaim Bermant, *The Cousinhood* (Eyre and Spottiswoode, London, 1971), p.75.
24. Chaim Bermant, *Troubled Eden*, op. cit., p.228.
25. The words of Rabbi Louis Jacobs, quoted by Howard Morely Sacher, *Diaspora* (Harper and Row, New York, 1986), p.159.
26. *The Old Testament and After*, pp.587–8.
27. *A Short Devotional Introduction to the Hebrew Bible*, pp.155–6.
28. *Outlines of Liberal Judaism*, pp.207–9.
29. *Outlines of Liberal Judaism*, pp.175–82.
30. *Liberal Judaism*, pp.169–60.
31. *What is Judaism?*, pp.47–51.
32. *Liberal Judaism and Hellenism*, pp.159–60.
33. Leviticus 19:19: 'You shall keep my statutes. You shall not let your cattle breed with a different kind; you shall not sow your field with two kinds of seed; nor shall there come upon you a garment of cloth made of two kinds of stuff.'
34. Leviticus 19:18: 'You shall not take vengeance against the sons of your own people, but you shall love the neighbour as yourself: I am the Lord.'
35. *The Justification of Liberal Judaism*, pp.19–20.
36. *Liberal Judaism*, pp.129–31.
37. *Liberal Judaism*, pp.135–7.
38. *Liberal Judaism and Convenience*, pp.4–5.
39. *The Old Testament and After*, pp.164–6.
40. *The Old Testament and After*, pp.560–1.
41. *Liberal Judaism*, pp.158–81.
42. 'I find my position as a liberal Jew so eminently comfortable and satisfactory. I am free. I can praise Jesus and the Rabbis when they deserve praise. I can criticise them when they deserve criticism. I can see both their strength and their weakness; where Jesus is a child of his own age is no more trouble for me to understand than it is for you or me to see where the Rabbis are the children of theirs.' *The Synoptic Gospels*, Vol. 2, pp.122–3.
43. *The Synoptic Gospels*, Vol. 2, p.646.
44. *Liberal Judaism and Jewish Nationalism* (PFJP), pp.23–4.

45. *The Old Testament and After*, pp.470–1.
46. *Liberal Judaism and Hellenism*, pp.222–3.
47. *Outlines of Liberal Judaism*, pp.9–10.
48. *The Dangers of Zionism*, pp.9–10.
49. *Liberal Judaism and Jewish Nationalism*, pp.14–15.
50. One of two perils or extremes (Scylla and Charybdis) which it is hard to avoid without running into the other.
51. *Liberal Judaism and Jewish Nationalism*, pp.310–25.
52. *The Dangers of Zionism*, pp.5–6.
53. *Anti-Semitism*, pp.16–18.
54. Lucy Cohen, *Some Recollections of Claude Goldsmid Montefiore*, pp.226–7.
55. *Liberal Judaism and Jewish Nationalism*, pp.26–7.
56. Am implicit rejection of the position held by the West London Synagogue.
57. *The Jewish Religious Union: Its Principles and Future*, pp.9–10.
58. *Outlines of Liberal Judaism*, pp.115–17.
59. Ibid., pp.162–5.
60. *Liberal Judaism and Authority*, pp.12–13.
61. Edicts.
62. *The Old Testament and After*, pp.588–90.
63. Ibid., pp.555–9.
64. *Assimilation: Good and Bad*, pp.15–17.
65. These words were written in response to the question: Do you mean that, in the far future, you hope and believe that the religion of all Europe, America and Australia (to put Asia and Africa on one side) is to be Liberal Judaism, and that the Synagogue is finally to overcome the Church?
66. *The Place of Judaism among the Religious of the World*, pp.33–4.
67. *The Synoptic Gospels*, Vol. 2, pp.162–3.

CONCLUSION

1. Liberal criticism examined the text, comparing and correcting it with ancient manuscripts. Higher criticism inquired into the authorship and dates of different books and weighed their value as historical documents.
2. 'A Plea for the Old Testament', *The 19th Century*, p.835.
3. *Outlines of Liberal Judaism*, p.212.
4. *Liberal Judaism and Hellenism*, p.76.
5. See *Jewish Quarterly Review*, Vol. 12 (1900), pp.337ff. Also cf. F.C. Schwartz, *Jewish Quarterly Review*, Vol. 55 (1965), pp.52ff.
6. *The Synoptic Gospels*, Vol. II, pp.326–7.
7. *The Old Testament and After*, p.275.
8. *The Synoptic Gospels*, Vol. I, p.cxxxv.
9. 'The Significance of Jesus for his Own Age', in *Hibbert Journal*, Vol.. 10, p.773.
10. *Bible for Home Reading*, Vol. II, p.779.
11. *Some Elements in the Teaching of Jesus*, p.47.
12. *The Synoptic Gospels*, Vol. I, p.cxix.
13. *The Old Testament and After*, p.561.
14. Ibid.
15. Lucy Cohen, *Some Recollections of Claude Goldsmid Montefiore*, p.189.
16. *Liberal Judaism and the Law*, p.3.
17. *Some Elements in the Teaching of Jesus*, p.31.
18. *A Few Rabbinic Ideals*, p.9.
19. Lucy Cohen, *Some Recollections of Claude Goldsmid Montefiore*, p.189.
20. *Liberal Judaism and Jewish Nationalism*, p.19.
21. Cf. Nahum Glatzer, *Franz Rosenzweig: His Life and Thought*, p.19.

22. *A Few Rabbinic Ideals*, p.4.
23. *Judaism and St Paul*, pp.126-7.
24. Solomon Schechter, *Some Aspects of Rabbinic Theology* (Macmillan, 1909), p.18.
25. *A Rabbinic Anthology*, p.xxiv.
26. Ibid., pp.xxxv-xxxvi.
27. *Some Reflections on the Rabbinic Religion*, pp.21-2.
28. *The Old Testament and After*, p.299.
29. *What is Judaism?*, p.51.
30. Lucy Cohen, op. cit., p.98.
31. The comments on Wellhausen by Chief Rabbi Dr. H. Hertz in his preface to the translation and commentary of the Pentateuch and Haftorahs showed tremendous antipathy towards historical criticism and German Protestant scholarship. This view was representative of much of Anglo-Jewry.
32. See *Liberal Judaism and Jewish Nationalism, PFJP*.
33. 'Anti-Semitism in England', *Hibbert Journal*, Vol. 19, p.345.
34. Lucy Cohen, op. cit., p.253 (italics added).
35. See p.167ff.

BIBLIOGRAPHY

A. WORKS BY CLAUDE MONTEFIORE

1. PUBLISHED WORKS

1882 'Is Judaism a Tribal Religion?', *Contemporary Review*, Vol. 42
1885 'A Justification of Judaism', *Unitarian Review*
1887 *The Wisdom of Solomon*, London: Jewish Chronicle Office
1889 'Many Moods in Hebrew Scripture', *Jewish Quarterly Review (JQR)*, Vol. 2
     'Mystic Passages in the Psalms', *JQR*, Vol. 2
     'Proverbs: Notes upon the Date and Religious Value of the Book of Proverbs', *JQR*, Vol. 2
1890 'Recent Criticism on Moses and the Pentateuchal Narratives of the Decalogue', *JQR*, Vol. 3
     'Retribution: the Doctrine of Divine Retribution in the Old Testament', *JQR*, Vol. 3
     'A Tentative Catalogue of Biblical Metaphors', *JQR*, Vol. 3
1891 'Dr. Friendlander on the Jewish Religion', *JQR*, Vol. 4
     'Some Notes on the Effects of Biblical Criticism upon the Jewish Religion', *JQR*, Vol. 4
1892 *Hibbert Lectures on the Origin of Religion as Illustrated by the Ancient Hebrews*, London: Williams and Norgate
     'Retribution – Hebrew and Greek Ideas of Providence and Divine Retribution', *JQR*, Vol. 5
1893 'First Impressions of Paul', *JQR*, Vol. 6
     'Inspiration', *JQR*, Vol. 6
     'Miss Smith: a Possibility', *JQR*, Vol. 6
     'Miss Smith: Notes in Reply' (with Israel Abrahams), *JQR*, Vol. 6
1894 'The 4th Gospel – Notes on its Religious Value', *JQR*, Vol. 7
     'Philo : Florilegum Philonis', *JQR*, Vol. 7
1895 *Aspects of Judaism* (with Israel Abrahams), London: Macmillan
     The Bible for Home Reading, London: Macmillan
     'On Some Misconceptions of Judaism and Christianity by Each Other', *JQR*, Vol. 8
     'Dr. Wiener on the Dietary Laws', *JQR*, Vol. 8
1896 'Unitarianism and Judaism in their Relation to Each Other', *JQR*, Vol. 9
1899 'Liberal Judaism in England: its Difficulties and its Duties', *JQR*, Vol. 12
     'The Religious Teaching of Jowett', *JQR*, Vol. 12
1900 'Rabbinic Judaism in the Epistles of Paul', *JQR*, Vol. 13
1901 *The Book of Psalms*, London: Macmillan
     'The Desire for Immortality', *JQR*, Vol. 14
     'Motives of Moral Action', *Parents Review*

BIBLIOGRAPHY

1903 'Jewish Scholarship and Christian Silence', *Hibbert Journal* (*HJ*), Vol. 1
Liberal Judaism, London: Macmillan
'Rabbinic Conceptions of Repentance', *JQR*, Vol. 16
1904 *Jewish Addresses*, London: Brimley Johnson
'The Weakening of Jewish Religious Life', London: Jewish Chronicle Office
1905 'Biblical Criticism and the Pulpit', *JQR*, Vol. 18
'The Synoptic Gospels and Jewish Consciousness', *HJ*, Vol. 3
'There is a Time to Keep Silence and a Time to Speak', London: Jewish Religious Union (JRU)
1906 *Truth in Religion and Other Sermons*, London: Macmillan
1907 'Liberal Judaism', *JQR*, Vol. 20
1908 'Judaism, Unitarianism and Theism', *Papers for Jewish People* (*PFJP*)
1909 'The Jewish Religious Union: its Principles and its Future', London: JRU
'Let me not be ashamed of my Hope', London: JRU
'The Profit of Religion', London: JRU
1910 'The Liberal Movement in English Jewry' (an address to the Central Conference of American Rabbis), Michigan: CCAR
The Mystic Element in Religion, New York: Block
Some Elements of the Religious Teaching of Jesus, London: Macmillan
The Synoptic Gospels, London: Macmillan
1911 *Judaism and St. Paul*, London: M. Goshen
1912 *Outlines of Liberal Judaism*, London: Macmillan
'The Significance of Jesus for his own Age', *HJ*, Vol. 10
'The Witness of Judaism', in *The Unity of Faith*, ed. G. Rhodes, London: Macmillan
1913 'Mr Landa and the Future of Judaism', *HJ*, Vol. 13
'Modern Judaism and the Messianic Hope', *HJ*, Vol. 11
'What would you have us do?', *PFJP*
1914 'The Meaning of Progressive Revelation', *PFJP*
1915 'Assimilation: Good and Bad', *PFJP*
'Jewish Apocalypses and Rabbinic Judaism', *The Quest*, Vol. 7
'Judaism and Authority' (with Lily Montagu), *PFJP*
1916 'The Perfection of Christianity – a Jewish Comment', *HJ*, Vol. 14
'The Place of Judaism in the Religions of the World', *PFJP*
1917 'Immortality' in *Judaism and the War*, London: Liberal Jewish Synagogue (LJS)
'How to spread the Message of Liberal Judaism', London: LJS
'Judaism and Democracy', *PFJP*
'The Old Testament and its Ethical Teaching', *PFJP*
1918 'The Dangers of Zionism', *PFJP*
'The English Jew and his Religion' (with Basil Henriques), London: LJS
'The Jewish Religious Union', *PFJP*
Liberal Judaism and Hellenism, London: Macmillan
'Liberal Judaism and Jewish Nationalism', *PFJP*
'The Old Testament and its Ethical Teaching', *HJ*, Vol. 16
The Place of Judaism among the Religions of the World, London: The Lindsey Press
'The Psalter: its Contents and Dates', *The Quarterly Review*
'Race, Nation, Religion and the Jews', Keighley: Wadsworth & Co.

1919 'An Ancient Arraignment of Providence', *HJ*, Vol. 17
'Contemporary Jewish Religion', in *A Commentary on the Bible*, ed. A.S. Peake, New York: T.C. & E.C. Jack
The Justification of Liberal Judaism', *PFJP*
'Liberal Judaism and Authority', *PFJP*
'Modern Judaism', *HJ*, Vol. 17
1920 'Is there a Middle Way?', *PFJP*
'Has Judaism a Future?' *HJ*, Vol. 19
The Spirit of Judaism', in *The Beginnings of Christianity* (Part 1, Volume 1), eds. F.J. Foakes-Jackson and K. Lakes, London: Macmillan
1921 'Anti-Semitism in England', *HJ*, Vol. 19
The Passing of an Old Controversy – The Jewish Law and its Effects', *Holborn Review*, Vol. 12
'A Plea for the Old Testament', *The Nineteenth Century*
1922 'The Higher Freedom', *Child Life*
The Religious Teachings of the Synoptics', *HJ*, Vol. 20
1923 'Judaism and Europe', *HJ*, Vol. 21
The Old Testament and After, London: Macmillan
The Originality of the Teaching of Jesus', *Contemporary Review*, Vol. 123
'Some Rough Notes about Liberal Judaism' (with Israel Abrahams), *PFJP*
1924 'Liberal Judaism and Convenience', *PFJP*
'What Constitutes a Jew?', *PFJP*
1925 Two Devotions', *The American Hebrew*, Vol. 117
1926 'Israel Abrahams', *Transactions of the Jewish Historical Society of England*, Vol. 11
'Whose the Fault?', *The American Hebrew*, Vol. 118
1927 'Israel Abrahams and Liberal Judaism', in *Jewish Studies in Memory of Israel Abrahams*, New York: Jewish Institute of Religion
'Religion and Learning in Jewish Studies', in *Jewish Studies in Memory of Israel Abrahams*, New York: Jewish Institute of Religion
'Some Reflections of the Rabbinic Religion in its Relation to the Old Testament and the New Testament', *The Quest*
The Survival of Israel', in *The Legacy of Israel*, eds., E.R. Bevan and C. Singer, London: Oxford University Press
1929 'The Attempted Conversion of the Jews', *Holborn Review*, Vol. 21
4th Ezra – a Study in the Development of Universalism, London: Allen & Unwin
The Originality of Jesus', *HJ*, Vol. 28
1930 'The Achievement of the Old Testament', *Holborn Review*, Vol. 21
'Jewish Conceptions of Christianity', *HJ*, Vol. 28
'Many Pathways, One Goal', London: LJS
Rabbinic Literature and Gospel Teachings, London: Macmillan
1931 'The Importance of Reform Judaism and its Difficulties' (an address to the American Hebrew Congregation), Philadelphia: CCAR
'Religion and Politics', *PFJP*
1932 'Why Jews have no Missionaries', in *Jewish Views on Jewish Missions*, London: JRU
'Dr Robert Eisler on the Beginnings of Christianity', *HJ*, Vol. 30
The Old Testament and the Modern Jew', *HJ*, Vol. 30
'A Plea for Better Theologians', *The American Hebrew*, Vol. 131
1934 'Jewish Conceptions of Immortality', in *In Spirit and In Truth*, ed. George A.

Yates, London: Hodder and Stoughton
'Jewish Emancipation and the English Jew', *HJ*, Vol. 32
'In Memoriam – Lionel Jacob 1858-1934', London: LJS
1935 'Gesetz und Freiheit', *Minhat Torah* (Frankfurt)
'What a Jew thinks about Jesus', *HJ*, Vol. 33
'Why the Jewish Religious Union can be, and justifiably is, neutral towards Zionism' (with M.L. Perlzweig), *PFJP*
1936 'On the Use of the Word Jewish', *Contemporary Review*, Vol. 149
'The Question of Authority in Liberal Judaism', *PFJP*
A Short Devotional Introduction to the Hebrew Bible, London: Macmillan
1938 'The Day of Atonement', *PFJP*
'The Old Testament and Judaism', in *Record and Revelation*, ed. H. Wheeler-Robinson, London: Oxford University Press
A Rabbinic Anthology (with Herbert Loewe), London: Macmillan
1964 *What is Judaism?* (with Lucien Wolf), New York: Living Books Inc. A collection of some of his writings collated by Lucien Wolf

2. UNPUBLISHED SERMONS, ADDRESSES AND LECTURES

LJS archives unless stated.

1898 'Some Thoughts on Friendship', James Parkes Library, University of Southampton
1905 'Truth' (Box 93)
'You are my Witnesses' (Box 95)
1906 'A Personal Sermon' (Box 35)
1908 'Day of Atonement' (Box 94)
'The Jewish Religious Union and its Cause' (Box 95)
1913 'If I strive not for my own salvation who shall strive for me? And if not now, when?' (Box 35)
1915 'Day of Atonement' (Box 94)
'He was wounded for our transgressions; he was bruised for our iniquities' (Box 95)
'The lives of the great and good men are the best sermons' (Box 35)
'New Year Address' (Box 94)
'The Rich and Poor meet together; the Lord is the Maker of them all' (Box 94)
1916 'Ancient Jewish and Greek Encouragement and Consolation in Sorrow and Calamity' (Box 95)
'Day of Atonement' (Box 94)
'On keeping young and growing old', James Parkes Library, University of Southampton
1917 'Day of Atonement' (Box 94)
'You shall be unto me a kingdom of priests and a holy nation' (Box 35)
1918 'Day of Atonement' (Box 94)
'Judaism and the World' (Box 94)
'The morning cometh but also the night' (Box 94)
'The Proclamation and the Declaration' (Box 94)
1919 'The Authorised and Revised Versions of the Hebrew Bible' (Box 93)
'The best is yet to be' (Box 35)

'Day of Atonement' (Box 94)
'The Outlook for Judaism' (Box 95)
1920 'An Address to the Liberal Jewish Synagogue at the Consecration of a memorial to those members who fell in the War' (Box 97)
'Emanuel' (Box 94)
'The Mission of Israel' (Box 35)
'New Year Address' (Box 94)
'Sin and Death' (Box 95)
'Who is so blind as my servant or deaf as the messenger that I send?' (Box 35)
1921 'Belief in God' (Box 35)
'Day of Atonement' (Box 95)
'If the Lord be God, follow Him; but if Baal, follow him' (Box 95)
'The Old Testament' (Box 35)
'The Positive Elements of Liberal Judaism' (Box 35)
'The 73rd Psalm' (Box 35)
1922 'Day of Atonement' (Box 95)
'Solidarity' (Box 93)
1923 'Assimilation' (Box 35)
'Liberal Judaism in England' (Box 95)
'You are my Witnesses' (Box 95)
1924 'Day of Atonement' (Box 95)
'Our Religion and other Religions' (Box 35)
'Prospects of Liberal Judaism' (Box 35)
1925 'Anti-Semitism' (Box 93)
'Day of Atonement' (Box 95)
'Ye are the fewest of all peoples' (Box 35)
1926 'Liberal Judaism' (Box 94)
1927 'Day of Atonement' (Box 95)
'The Jewish Approach to God' (Box 95)
'The Maccabeans War Memorial' (Box 94)
'Pharisaism – a permanent danger in religion?', London Society for the Study of Religion (LSSR)
'Some problems connected with the conception of God' (Box 93)
1928 'An Address at Taunton School' (Box 94)
'Day of Atonement' (Box 95)
'The Importance of Liberal Judaism to the religious life of the individual' (Box 95)
'Judaism and Truth' (Box 35)
'The Originality of Jesus', LSSR
'Passover' (Box 97)
'Unitarianism and Judaism' (Box 93)
1929 'New Year Address' (Box 94)
1930 'An Address to the Liverpool Liberal Jewish Synagogue' (Box 93)
'An Address of Welcome to the World Union of Progressive Judaism's conference in London' (Box 94)
'A Few Rabbinic Ideals' (Box 95)
'The Law' (Box 95)
'New Year Address' (Box 94)
'The Ten Commandments and the Sabbath' (Box 94)

BIBLIOGRAPHY

1931 'Lady Battersea' (Box 97)
     'College Opportunities' (Box 94)
     'The Froebel Society' (Box 94)
     'Liberal Judaism and the Old Testament' (Box 94)
     'Shabat T'Shuvah' (Box 93)
     'A Welcome and a Farewell' (Box 94)
     'What does Revelation mean to me?', LSSR
     'What of the night?' (Box 35)
1932 'Day of Atonement and its Purpose' (Box 93)
     'Liberal Judaism' (Box 94)
1933 'Armistice Day' (Box 93)
     'Day of Atonement' (Box 94)
1934 'A Rabbinic Paradox' (Box 93)
1935 'Day of Atonement' (Box 35)
     'A Diehard's Confession', LSSR
     'God and Man' (Box 35)
     'The Shema' (Box 35)
1936 'Day of Atonement' (Box 95)
     'The Devotional Value of the Old Testament' (Box 95)
     'Some old fashioned reflections about the Jews', LSSR
1937 'The Jews' Responsibility' (Box 35)

3. UNDATED SERMONS, ADDRESSES AND LECTURES

LJS archives unless stated.

'Authority' (Box 94)
'Bible Teaching' (Box 95)
'Conventionality' (Box 93)
'The Customs of the Nations' (Box 93)
'Day of Atonement' (Box 95)
'Day of Atonement' (Box 95)
'Day of Atonement' (Box 35)
'Day of Atonement' (Box 94)
'4th Ezra' (Box 93)
'Ezra and his Work' (Box 93)
'An Explanation of Liberal Judaism' (Box 93)
'Faith and Evil' (Box 93)
'Future Life' (Box 93)
'Hard is the Good' (Box 93)
'Is Goodness Real?' (Box 35)
'Jewish Nationalism and Liberal Judaism' (Box 94)
'A Jewish view of Christendom' (Box 94)
'Jewish Nationalism' (Box 95)
'Law and Freedom' (Box 93)
'Let a man speak Truth in his Heart' (Box 94)
'Liberal Judaism (Box 35)
'Modern Judaism' (Box 35)
'Moses' Wish' (Box 35)
'The New Therapeutics' (Box 35)

'Non-Resistance' (Box 35)
'Paul the Apostle' (Box 93)
'A Popular Introduction to the Book of Job', James Parkes Library, University of Southampton
'The Prophetic Writings' (Box 35)
'Proselytism' (Box 95)
'Rabbinic Stories' (Box 93)
'The Reality of God' (Box 94)
'The Relation between Liberal Christians and Jews' (Box 95)
'Revelation and World Religion' (Box 95)
'Some Introductory Remarks on the Book of Psalms', James Parkes Library, University of Southampton
'Stay me with raisins, comfort me with apples: for I am sick of love' (Box 93)
'So teach us to number our days that we may get a heart of wisdom' (Box 95)
'What Jews believe today' (Box 94)
'A Word about Nationalism' (Box 95)

B. WORKS ABOUT CLAUDE MONTEFIORE

P. Abrahams, 'Claude Goldsmid Montefiore', *Synagogue Review*, 36, no. 5, London: Reform Synagogues of Great Britain (1965)

J. Agus, 'Claude Montefiore and Liberal Judaism', *Conservative Judaism*, Vol. 13 (1959)

S. Atlas, 'Some Notes on Claude Montefiore's Conception of Rabbinic Judaism', London (publisher unknown) (1954)

N. Bentwich, 'Claude Montefiore and his tutor in Rabbinics: founders of Liberal and Conservative Judaism', University of Southampton (1966)

M. Bowler, 'C.G. Montefiore and his Quest', *Judaism*, Vol. 30, (1981)

L. Cohen, *Some Recollections of Claude Goldsmid Montefiore*, London, Faber & Faber (1940)

L. Edgar, 'Claude Montefiore's thought and the present religious situation', London: Liberal Jewish Synagogue (1966)

B.L.Q. Enriques, 'C.G. Montefiore – Some Personal Recollections', *Synagogue Review*, 32, no. 10, London: The Association of Synagogues in Great Britain (1958)

—, 'Sermon preached at the service of Commemoration in Gratitude for Claude Goldsmid Montefiore, President of the College 1915–34', University of Southampton (1938)

Festgabe Für Claude Montefiore, Berlin: Philoverlag (1928)

W. Jacob, 'Claude Montefiore's Reappraisal of Christianity', *Judaism*, Vol. 19 (1970)

L. Jacobs, 'Montefiore and Loewe on the Rabbis', London: Liberal Jewish Synagogue (1962)

Liberal Jewish Monthly Memorial Number (dedicated to Claude Montefiore), London: Liberal Jewish Synagogue (1938)

H.M. Lily, 'Claude Goldsmid Montefiore: His Life', *The Link*, Vol. 29, London: Froebel Educational Institute (1938)

I. Mattuck, 'Our Debt to Claude Montefiore', London: Liberal Jewish Synagogue (1938)

BIBLIOGRAPHY

W. R. Matthews, 'Claude Montefiore: the man and his thought', University of Southampton (1956)

L. Montagu, 'Notes on the life and work of Claude Montefiore', London: Liberal Jewish Synagogue, 1938

H. Montefiore, 'Sir Moses Montefiore and his Great Nephew', University of Southampton (1979)

J. D. Rayner, 'C. G. Montefiore – his Religious Teaching', *The Synagogue Review*, 32, no. 10, London: The Association of Synagogues in Great Britain (1958)

F. C. Schwartz, 'Claude Montefiore on Law and Tradition', *Jewish Quarterly Review* (New Series), Vol. 55 (1964–5)

C. Singer, 'Memories of a Montefiore', *Jewish Chronicle*, no. 4650, London (1958)

Speculum Religionis (presented by members of the staff of) University of Southampton, Oxford: The Clarendon Press (1929)

W. D. Thomas, 'The Hebrew Bible since Claude Montefiore', London: Liberal Jewish Synagogue (1958)

A. J. Wolf, 'The Dilemma of Claude Montefiore', *Conservative Judaism*, Vol. 13 (1959)

—, 'Claude Montefiore', *La Question d'Israel*, nos. 68 and 69 (1939)